Military Investigations in Armed Conflict

An allegation is made that a war crime was committed by a soldier during a conflict. Who should investigate the allegation? How should they investigate? This book explores a topic of critical importance in legal and policy discussions surrounding the accountability of military operations in armed conflict, and problematises some presumptions that are often made about the topic. The work provides the international legal framework necessary to address these questions and establishes the precise standards of independence and impartiality as applicable to investigations in armed conflict. It questions the assumption that the standards of independence and impartiality of investigations should be measured in the same way that we measure these standards for judges, courts, and tribunals. It also explores the ways in which military institutions and culture, as well as the context of armed conflict, may impact on the effectiveness of investigations or the perception of justice by those affected. By demonstrating the precise ways in which military investigations can contribute to or hinder the effectiveness of investigations, the book clarifies States' responsibilities with regard to their accountability efforts for serious violations of international law in armed conflict. The work will be a valuable resource for academics, researchers, and policy-makers working in the areas of international humanitarian law, international human rights law, as well as political science and military ethics.

Claire Simmons is a Senior Lecturer in the Department of Defence & International Affairs at the Royal Military Academy Sandhurst, and Fellow of the Essex Armed Conflict and Crisis Hub, part of the Human Rights Centre at the University of Essex (UK).

Routledge Research in the Law of Armed Conflict

Available titles in this series include:

The Concept of Military Objectives in International Law and Targeting Practice
Agnieszka Jachec-Neale

Cosmopolitan Ethics and Law on Autonomous Weapons in Modern Warfare
Ozlem Ulgen

A Guide to International Disarmament Law
Stuart Casey-Maslen and Tobias Vestner

Protection of Civilians and Individual Accountability
Obligations and Responsibilities of Military Commanders in United Nations Peacekeeping Operations
Lenneke Sprik

Africa and International Criminal Justice
Radical Evils and the International Criminal Court
Fred Aja Agwu

Occupation and Control in International Humanitarian Law
Natia Kalandarishvili-Mueller

Stabilization and Human Security in UN Peace Operations
Alexander Gilder

Atrocity Crimes and International Law
Responsibility to Protect, Intercession, and Non-Forceful Responses
Stacey Henderson

Military Investigations in Armed Conflict
Independence and Impartiality under International Law
Claire Simmons

Military Investigations in Armed Conflict

Independence and Impartiality under International Law

Claire Simmons

Routledge
Taylor & Francis Group
LONDON AND NEW YORK

First published 2024
by Routledge
4 Park Square, Milton Park, Abingdon, Oxon OX14 4RN

and by Routledge
605 Third Avenue, New York, NY 10158

Routledge is an imprint of the Taylor & Francis Group, an informa business

British Library Cataloguing-in-Publication Data
A catalogue record for this book is available from the British Library

Library of Congress Cataloging-in-Publication Data
Names: Simmons, Claire, author.
Title: Military investigations in armed conflict: independence and impartiality under international law / Claire Simmons.
Description: Abingdon, Oxon [UK]; New York, NY: Routledge, 2024. | Series: Routledge research in the law of armed conflict | Includes bibliographical references and index. |
Identifiers: LCCN 2023047833 (print) | LCCN 2023047834 (ebook) | ISBN 9781032415673 (hardback) | ISBN 9781032418889 (paperback) | ISBN 9781003360223 (ebook)
Subjects: LCSH: War (International law) | War crimes (International law) | Criminal investigation (International law) | Courts-martial and courts of inquiry. | Military interrogation. | Fairness.
Classification: LCC KZ6385 .S59 2024 (print) | LCC KZ6385 (ebook) | DDC 341.6/9--dc23/eng/20231012
LC record available at https://lccn.loc.gov/2023047833
LC ebook record available at https://lccn.loc.gov/2023047834

ISBN: 9781032415673 (hbk)
ISBN: 9781032418889 (pbk)
ISBN: 9781003360223 (ebk)

DOI: 10.4324/9781003360223

Typeset in Galliard
by Deanta Global Publishing Services, Chennai, India

To Noam and Françoise, and all those who have taught me there is room for hope, justice, and humanity in war.

Contents

Acknowledgements

My deepest thanks to those without whom this book couldn't have been written: Professor Noam Lubell, Professor Françoise Hampson, Dr Katya Alkhateeb, and Dr Delia Sánchez del Angel. Noam and Françoise, your guidance and mentoring throughout and beyond the PhD have shaped my professional and personal self and helped carve these ideas into a book. Thank you both for being incredible role models, and never accepting a bad argument. Katya and Delia, your friendship and zoom coffees over the years kept me going. Thank you all for inspiring and challenging me to achieve something worth writing.

Thank you also to Dr Gus Waschefort and Professor Yuval Shany for your insights on the original research and encouraging me to turn it into a book. My thanks are also owed to many of the participants of the Investigations Guidelines project who inspired me to explore this topic in the first place, and especially to Jelena Pejic.

Thank you to those who have supported me throughout, including Luis, Jenny, Carla, Cristóbal, Tlacua, the SC village people, and the Simmons crew.

And thank you to Alison Kirk and colleagues at Routledge, and the peer reviewers, for believing in the book and encouraging me along the way.

1 Introduction

Introduction

I have had the honour of teaching students from a wide diversity of backgrounds and of many different nationalities. When teaching the topic of investigations in armed conflict, this gives me the opportunity to get particularly interesting responses to a set of questions I like to ask.

> First scenario. If you were back in your home country and a medical doctor was accused of wrongdoing, would you trust a board of medical practitioners to investigate the situation?
>
> Second scenario. A police member is accused of wrongdoing. Would you trust a police investigative body to investigate?
>
> Third scenario. A member of the military in your home country is accused of wrongdoing. Would you trust a military body to investigate?

As often happens with student participation, some students are reluctant to commit and assume it is somehow a trick question while others would like answers to some follow-up questions before casting their vote. "Is the wrongdoing a death? Are the medical doctors from the same hospital or team as the person they are investigating?"

The results of this very non-scientific survey often go along the following lines: many (but by no means all) would trust medical doctors to investigate a medical incident and few (but some do) trust the police or military to investigate incidents by their own forces. I find it an interesting activity both because it is questioning their perception of justice and because it highlights to me, and to each other as a diverse class, that the country of origin very much matters in the assertion of this perception. Some students have spoken to me later privately, wanting to add personal experiences to justify their responses, in particular those who have negative perceptions of these bodies. Some of them have experienced night-raids of military personnel going through offices where they worked or have seen police shoot their fellow citizens with impunity.

DOI: 10.4324/9781003360223-1

Others have had to contend with medical institutions keeping their family members on expensive treatments to gather insurance money.

These reflections also serve to introduce the topic of military investigations on the battlefield. As a teacher of international humanitarian law (IHL – also known as the laws of armed conflict, or laws of war), I am emphasising that laws and concepts of justice should and do matter in armed conflict, despite the many challenges. Such as in the following cases:

> On 4th July 1991, members of the Peruvian military carried out an operation in the Andean community of Santa Bárbara that led to the forced disappearances of fifteen civilians. These community members were later found to have been tortured and killed, their bodies dumped and mutilated in an abandoned mine.[1]
>
> On 13th December 1998, during the armed conflict between the Colombian government and the FARC, a cluster bomb was dropped by the Colombian air force in the urban area surrounding the village of Santo Domingo, in the Arauca department. This resulted in the death of 17 civilians including 6 children, and the injury of 27 further civilians.[2]
>
> On the night of 16–17th June 2007 during the battle of Chora in Uruzgan province, Afghanistan, the NATO-led International Security Assistance Force (ISAF), including the Netherlands armed forces, destroyed a residential complex. 18 persons died, with several others wounded.[3]
>
> On 4th September 2009, in another ISAF operation, a German colonel ordered an airstrike on two fuel tankers thought to have been hijacked and surrounded by insurgents. The strike killed 91 civilians and injured 11.[4]
>
> On 21st July 2012, Safari Kateatea Amos, a Colonel of the armed forces of the Democratic Republic of Congo, led his troops to the villages of Karimba and Musinziro in South Kivo, where the civilian villagers were killed, tortured, raped, and their property destroyed.[5]

1 "Santa Bárbara Community," *CEJIL*, available at: https://cejil.org/en/case/santa-barbara-community/.

2 Galvis, L., & Kovalik, D., "Santo Domingo Massacre in Colombia: A Testimony," *International Labor Rights Forum* (10 October 2005), available at: https://laborrights.org/in-the-news/santo-domingo-massacre-colombia-testimony.

3 Zwanenburg, M., "Dutch Judgment on IHL Compliance in Chora District, Afghanistan," *Articles of War*, Lieber Institute (19 December 2022).

4 ECtHR, *Hanan v Germany*, App. No. 4871/16, Judgment of 16 February 2021, paras 9–25.

5 "DRC: Seven Years after the Crimes, Lieutenant-Colonel Safari Kateatea Amos Finally Condemned," *Trial International* (9 December 2019), available at: https://trialinternational.org/latest-post/drc-seven-years-after-the-crimes-justice-has-cornered-lieutenant-colonel-safari-kateatea-amos/.

> In 2021, the French counterterrorism force operating in Mali carried out an airstrike outside the town of Bounti, reportedly killing 19 civilians and three armed men.[6]

All of these cases involve allegations that a State's military committed violations of international law in conflict situations. Most were investigated, and many involved military investigators in different stages. Readers may know the outcomes of some or all of the above cases, especially if they eventually made it to domestic or international courts, but the outcomes were by no means predictable in all of the cases and show stark differences in the investigative procedures.

Peru's military never investigated the enforced disappearances, and the Santa Bárbara community had to go to the Inter-American Court of Human Rights to obtain recognition of the violations they suffered.[7] Colombia's military found no reason to continue an investigation into the airstrike on Santo Domingo, although the Colombian civilian Prosecutor's office (specifically, the Human Rights Unit) disagreed, and conducted its own investigation, eventually finding individuals criminally liable and the Colombian State responsible for what has come to be known as the Santo Domingo Massacre.[8] Both ISAF incidents in Afghanistan were investigated by a range of actors, including German and Dutch military police under the authority of their civilian public prosecutors.[9] In a rare act of self-accountability under IHL, the Netherlands Supreme Court found the State responsible for violations of this body of law.[10] The Congolese military is working alongside a network of international players to investigate and prosecute international crimes committed by its own armed forces as well as other actors during the ongoing conflicts in the country.[11] In December 2019, a military court in South Kivu province convicted Safari Kateatea Amos of crimes against humanity, and he was sentenced to five years in prison (changed to ten years on appeal in 2022).[12] As far as we know, France has not investigated the incident in Mali, although a UN

6 MacLean, R., "A wedding, an airstrike, and outrage at the French military," *New York Times* (30 March 2021).

7 IACtHR, *Comunidad Campesina de Santa Bárbara v Peru*, Ser. C No. 299, Judgment of 1 September 2015 (Preliminary Objections, Merits, Reparations and Costs).

8 *Santo Domingo Massacre v Colombia*, Ser. C No. 259, Judgment of 14 November 2014 (Preliminary Objections, Merits, and Reparations), paras 154–173.

9 *Hanan v Germany* (n. 4); Zwanenburg (n. 3).

10 Zwanenburg (n. 3).

11 As reported by *Trial International.* See "DRC: Three Militiamen Convicted in Kalehe," *Trial International* (7 September 2020), available at: https://trialinternational.org/latest-post/drc-three-militiamen-convicted-in-kalehe/. See also UN Team of Experts on Rule of Law and Sexual Violence in Conflict, available at: www.un.org/sexualviolenceinconflict/our-work/team-of-experts/.

12 *Trial international* (n. 5).

investigation carried out by MINUSMA suggested France was responsible for the wrongful civilian deaths.[13]

What factors led to these investigations and their outcomes? What was the role of the military in the likelihood of achieving accountability or impunity for these violations of international law in armed conflict? This book deconstructs and addresses some of the complexities behind these questions by focusing on one specific context, namely, the independence and impartiality of military institutions investigating alleged serious violations of international humanitarian law committed by their own members. Can a military institution really be expected to carry out an independent and impartial investigation when it is one of its own personnel who is under scrutiny, or do such situations necessarily violate these principles and foster impunity?

The problem with "militaryness"

The question is of real and increasing relevance in practice. Accounting for the lawfulness of actions during military operations can be a challenge in situations of armed conflict yet is crucial to the implementation of IHL. The role of investigations as key to accountability under international law has gained further attention in recent decades, evidenced through their increasing scrutiny in treaty interpretation, and attention by international bodies including the UN. But the importance of investigations is also made clear through the observable tendency by affected individuals, civil society, and the international community to call for an investigation following an act in armed conflict which has serious consequences, whether by the actors involved, and/or international monitoring bodies. During the outbreak of hostilities in Nagorno-Karabakh in 2020, Amnesty International called for "an independent investigation to identify the perpetrators of war crimes allegedly committed by Azerbaijani and Armenian forces during recent fighting."[14] Also in 2020, the UK's Afghanistan Independent Human Rights Commission called on the UK government to investigate alleged war crimes in Afghanistan.[15] In 2021, Iranians in Stockholm called on the UN to investigate the role of Ebrahim Raisi in the 1988 massacre in Iran.[16] From the outset of the Russian invasion of Ukraine

13 UN News, "UN Investigation Concludes French Military Airstrike Killed Mali Civilians" (30 March 2021), available at: https://news.un.org/en/story/2021/03/1088722.

14 "Amnesty International Calls for Investigation into Alleged War Crimes in Nagorno-Karabakh," *EuroNews* (10 December 2020), available at: www.euronews.com/2020/12/10/amnesty-international-calls-for-investigation-into-alleged-war-crimes-in-nagorno-karabakh.

15 Callinan, R., "Calls for UK to investigate possible war crimes in Afghanistan," *The Guardian* (20 November 2020), available at: www.theguardian.com/australia-news/2020/nov/20/calls-for-uk-to-investigate-possible-war-crimes-afghanistan-australian-report.

16 "Stockholm Rally: Iranians Call on the UN to Investigate the Role of Ebrahim Raisi in 1988 Massacre in Iran," *EU Reporter* (25 August 2021), available at: www.eureporter.co/world/iran/2021/08/25/stockholm-rally-iranians-call-on-the-un-to-investigate-the-role-of-ebrahim-raisi-in-1988-massacre-in-iran/.

in 2022, Ukrainian president Volodymyr Zelensky and others have called for Russia to be investigated for war crimes.[17]

These examples show that investigations are not only important in theory because of their potential utility in implementing legal obligations; they are also perceived as important by the affected communities who are seeking justice. The cases above involve civil society, the international community, or government actors calling for investigations, albeit *who* is being called upon to investigate is not always made clear (for example, whether it should be domestic, international, State, or UN bodies).

Investigations can also be a means, if credible, of establishing that no violation occurred and that State actions were carried out lawfully. This is also central for accountability, especially as the legality of events can be challenged a long time after the events occurred. Effective investigations can be key to protect the rights of those involved in the military operations, as well as the potential victims of military operations.

Given that investigations hold such an important role for accountability in armed conflict, it is unsurprising that the way in which such investigations are carried out is receiving increasing attention. Yet as the law and practice of investigations in armed conflict gain clarity, there are certain key areas which are emerging as particularly contentious. One of these areas is the alleged inability of military justice systems to effectively carry out investigations and trials into serious violations of international law, a perspective which is becoming well established within certain regions and human rights institutions.

It is suggested that what is at play when a military is accused of "investigating itself" may be understood under the lens of independence and impartiality, although other factors are also relevant, as will be seen across the book. The lack of independence and impartiality of military justice institutions appears to be the implicit, if not always explicit, criticism towards military investigations. In Nigeria, Amnesty International criticised investigations into alleged war crimes "led by the military and carried out by internal investigation teams set up by the military."[18] In the UK, Liberty has repeatedly called for "all serious offences" to be investigated by civilian, not military, police.[19] In Israel, the fact that the same authority (the Military Advocate General) provides both legal counsel and decides whether to open investigations has led civil society to claim this dual role creates inherent conflicts of interest and undermines the

17 Lonas, L., "Ukraine's Zelensky Calls for War Crimes Investigation over Russian Attack," *The Hill* (3 January 2022), available at: https://thehill.com/policy/international/596245-ukraines-zelensky-calls-for-war-crimes-investigation-over-russian-attack/.

18 Amnesty International, "Stars on Their Shoulders, Blood on Their Hands: War Crimes Committed by the Nigerian Military" (2015), p. 11.

19 Norton, E., "Military Justice, Second-Rate Justice: Criminal Justice, Complaints and Human Rights Myths in the Armed Forces," *Liberty* (January 2019), p. 48.

effectiveness and legitimacy of investigations.[20] These examples are all drawn from different systems and all merit their own in-depth consideration, but this also serves to show the diversity of what can be meant by a "military" investigation.

In order to address this topic, it is therefore necessary to contend with the matter of whether "military justice" is an oxymoron in itself. As is often cited in works on military justice, a citation attributed to Georges Clemenceau suggests that "Military justice is to justice what military music is to music," supposedly implying that military justice and military music are not real versions of either justice or music.[21] The blanket statement that the military nature of an institution will mean it is *ipso facto* unable to effectively investigate certain violations appears to suggest there is something inherent in "militaryness" that will necessarily preclude justice.

This argument, usually considered in the context of human rights violations, raises various concerns, many of which will be deconstructed throughout the book. Most problematic, in my opinion, is the blanket dismissal of the extremely diverse military systems which exist across the world. Having considered the different contexts in which the use of military justice has indeed led to widespread injustice, I find it more useful to focus on the specific factors which lead to impunity rather than the abstract concept of "militaryness." There are, as will be seen, unique characteristics of military institutions and lifestyle which may impact on the way in which justice might be sought. There is also no denying that military justice systems are increasingly strange beasts in contemporary domestic legal systems. Where military criminal justice systems exist, they are often the only part of society which have their own criminal justice systems. Other parts of society, such as religious institutions, which used to have a separate criminal system, have been abolished in many States.[22]

But relating the nature of the institution to an inability to carry out justice can have graver consequences beyond the scope of jurisdiction. First, such an assumption appears to suggest that the "civilian" is always better than the "military." Yet flawed investigations are not unique to military personnel – being "non-military" does not exempt an individual from being corrupt, and

20 B'Tselem, "Whitewash Protocol: The So-Called Investigation of 'Operation Protective Edge'" (2016), p. 3; Yesh Dish, "Investigating themselves: Results of the military law enforcement system's examination of incidents of Palestinians killed and wounded in the Gaza Strip during 'Operation Guardian of the Walls'" (31 May 2022), available at: www.yesh-din.org/en/investigating-themselves-results-of-the-military-law-enforcement-systems-examination-of-incidents-of-palestinians-killed-and-wounded-in-the-gaza-strip-during-operation-guardian-of/.

21 Gilissen, J., "Évolution actuelle de la justice militaire," *Recueils de la Société Internationale de Droit Pénal Militaire et de Droit de la Guerre* Vol. 8 (1981), pp. 36–37.

22 Collins, P., *The Military As a Separate Society: Consequences for Discipline in the United States and Australia*, Lexington Books (2019), p. 9. This is certainly not the case in all States, especially those with State religions and legal systems based on religious codes.

issues of independence and impartiality can arise beyond military institutions. Second, starting from the premise that the military is fundamentally unable to uphold systems of justice would force us to put into question their ability to uphold many tenets of IHL – the obligation to give quarter when the enemy surrenders even in the midst of a battlefield or the obligation not to misuse protected emblems in carrying out military operations even if it would provide a military advantage.[23] These obligations are solely reliant on military personnel "doing the lawful thing," although the systems of accountability obviously matter in the likelihood of them being upheld. What is more, there are very practical reasons why people present on the ground need to be able to do the right thing. As explored throughout the book, in many situations there simply is nobody else able and/or available to investigate.

This book therefore starts from the premise that there is nothing in the "militaryness" of proceedings which makes them inherently unable to uphold the principles of independence and impartiality in investigating. Instead, it is important to provide legal and practical clarity on how a properly structured military justice system can carry out an effective investigation into serious violations of IHL. As long as armed conflicts exist, it appears, military institutions will also exist,[24] and it is important to be able to scrutinise fairly whether they are compliant with their legal obligations. If anything, such fair scrutiny only imposes additional burdens on military institutions, as it recognises that they are subject to international legal standards applicable in armed conflict. These standards require States to ensure there is an effective judicial procedure able to uphold the law even in the most difficult circumstances.

Why focus on armed conflict?

The question of independence and impartiality of military investigations, or of military justice proceedings more generally, is not contentious only in situations of armed conflict. In fact, it is perhaps mostly criticised for its use in times of peace, and one argument for the suppression of military justice altogether is that the military nowadays is often expected to operate in peacetime, and therefore that the wartime rationale for which military institutions were created cannot be claimed still to be relevant.[25] There is indeed a danger in expanding

23 Protocol Additional to the Geneva Conventions of 12 August 1949 and Relating to the Protection of Victims of International Armed Conflicts, 1125 UNTS 3 (1977) [API], Arts 40–41 and Arts 37–38.

24 Although the privatisation of military forces certainly raises questions about military justice, as does the increasing use of technology in warfare. ICRC, "The Montreux Document: On Pertinent International Legal Obligations and Good Practices for States Related to Operations of Private Military and Security Companies During Armed Conflict" (2009); Sassòli, M., "Autonomous Weapons and International Humanitarian Law: Advantages, Open Technical Questions and Legal Issues to be Clarified," *International Law Studies* Vol. 90 (2014).

25 Collins (n. 22), pp. 20 and 25. See also Chapter 6.

exceptional wartime measures to peacetime, a tool often used by authoritarian governments. Nevertheless, it is the unfortunate reality that armed conflicts (if not always "wars") do exist, and militaries of many different States do engage in them. During the research for this book, the Russian invasion of Ukraine in 2022 has exacerbated the ongoing international armed conflict in the region and threatened to involve many other States. IHL starts from the premise that if conflicts do happen, States must have a legal way of operating within them. In this sense, the criticisms of military justice proceedings that neglect or dismiss situations of armed conflict or the associated difficulties and circumstances are ignoring an important reality that needs addressing. This does not mean that the case for abolition of military justice systems in times of peace may not be made. It does, however, mean that we need to have answers as to how justice systems may or may not lawfully operate in situations of conflict.

Another practical element which is not always considered is the fact that militaries often engage in extraterritorial operations, whether or not in situations of armed conflict. In an increasingly globalised world, extraterritorial military operations appear unlikely to become less prevalent, although what may change is the purely "military" nature of those involved.[26] Both of these reasons are considered to matter very much in assessing the question of *who* can investigate. Strikingly, in at least one State, the abolition of military criminal courts in peacetime has led to partial backtracking a few years later (through a specialist criminal court), due to the need for specialised jurisdiction in such cases.[27] This example points to the fact that States do still consider a need for specialised jurisdiction for military matters.

With the presence of armed conflict comes the application of IHL, the body of international law in which the obligations surrounding investigations are least developed. It is clear that the drafters of IHL treaties did envisage a role for military institutions in the implementation of the provisions, and this may include investigations into possible violations.[28] However, it is important to consider whether the reasons for this remain relevant today in light of the evolution of international law, and some of these issues are addressed throughout this book. The lack of interpretative bodies or adjudicatory courts specifically tailored to IHL means that treaty and customary law may be less easy to interpret consistently and authoritatively. The existing authorities on the interpretation of IHL include documents produced by the International Committee of the Red Cross (ICRC),[29] as well as the UN, including those produced by

26 See above, n. 24.

27 See the example of France described in Chapter 6.

28 Simmons, C., "The Scope of Military Jurisdiction for Violations of International Humanitarian Law," *Israel Law Review* Vol. 54 No. 1 (2021), p. 3.

29 E.g., Henckaerts, J.-M., & Doswald-Beck, L., *Customary International Humanitarian Law*, ICRC (2006) [ICRC Customary Study]; Pictet, J., *The Geneva Conventions of 12 August 1949: Commentary*, ICRC (1960) [Pictet Commentary]; Sandoz, Y., Swinarski, C., & Zimmermann, B., *Commentary to the Additional Protocols of 8 June 1977 to the Geneva Conven-*

special rapporteurs, the General Assembly, and soft law documents.[30] State practice and academic scholarship complement the evolving understanding of how obligations must be implemented under this body of law,[31] and it is to the academic literature which this book contributes.

What is an Investigation?

It may also be questioned why the focus is solely on the investigative stage of proceedings, when the independence and impartiality of military courts is as controversial. The simple answer is that I believe the investigation stage has been neglected in critical analysis of military proceedings. Works which very eloquently and convincingly criticise military justice systems often leave me with the question, "but what about the investigation stage?" Documents addressing the adequacy of military justice systems do not always consider investigations as separate from the trial stage, and it hence may sometimes

tions of 12 August 1949, Martinus Nijhoff Publishers (1987) [ICRC Commentary to API]; Henckaerts, J.-M. et al., *Updated Commentary on the First Geneva Convention*, ICRC (2016) [ICRC Updated Commentary to GCI]; , ICRC, *Updated Commentary on the Second Geneva Convention* (2017); ICRC, *Updated Commentary to Third Geneva Convention* (2020) [ICRC Updated Commentary to GCIII].

30 See, e.g., UN OHCHR, Basic Principles and Guidelines on the Right to a Remedy and Reparation for Victims of Gross Violations of International Human Rights Law and Serious Violations of International Humanitarian Law, A/RES/60/147 (2005); UN, Report of the Special Rapporteur on Extrajudicial, Summary or Arbitrary Executions, Philip Alston: Civil and Political Rights, Including the Questions of Disappearances and Summary Executions, E/CN4/2006/53 (8 March 2006); UN, Report of the Committee of Independent Experts in International Humanitarian and Human Rights Laws to Monitor and Assess Any Domestic, Legal or Other Proceedings Undertaken by Both the Government of Israel and the Palestinian Side, in the Light of General Assembly Resolution 254/64, including the Independence, Effectiveness, Genuineness of These Investigations and Their Conformity with International Standards, A/HRC/15/50 (23 September 2010) [Tomuschat Report]; UN OHCHCR, Revision of the UN Manual on the Effective Prevention and Investigation of Extra-Legal, Arbitrary and Summary Executions (2016) [Minnesota Protocol]; UN Human Rights Committee, General Comment No. 36 on Article 6 of the International Covenant on Civil and Political Rights, on the Right to Life (30 October 2018), CCPR/C/GC/36, paras 27–29.

31 See, e.g., Schmitt, M. N., "Investigating Violations of International Law in Armed Conflict," *Harvard National Security Journal* Vol. 2 (2011); updated in Radin, S., & Schmitt, M. N., "Investigations Under International Humanitarian Law," *Routledge Handbook of the Law of Armed Conflict*, Routledge (2016); Cohen, A., & Shany, Y., "Beyond the Grave Breaches Regime: The Duty to Investigate Alleged Violations of International Law Governing Armed Conflicts," *Yearbook of International Humanitarian Law* Vol. 14 (2011); Margalit, A., *Investigating Civilian Casualties in Time of Armed Conflict and Belligerent Occupation: Manoeuvring Between Leal Regimes and Paradigms For the Use of Force*, Brill (2018); Hampson, F., "An Investigation of Alleged Violations of The Law of Armed Conflict," *Israel Yearbook on Human Rights* Vol. 46 (2016), p. 8; Second Report of the Public Commission to Examine the Maritime Incident of 31 May 2010: Israel's Mechanisms for Examining and Investigating Complaints and Claims of Violations of the Laws of Armed Conflict According to International Law (Israel, February 2013) [Second Turkel Report].

be assumed that the applicable standards are the same. As will be made clear in Chapter 4, and other parts of the book, this assumption is not true. If the standards applicable to investigations are unclear, they cannot be effectively scrutinised. Although there remains much to be clarified on the topic of military courts, this focus on the investigation stage was therefore seen as important to begin with.

The precise standards under international law of how an investigation should be carried out are developing through practice as well as domestic and international jurisprudence, but it is indubitable that there remains much to be clarified on various aspects of how investigations are to be carried out under IHL. Prior to research for this book, I was involved in the drafting of the Guidelines on Investigating Violations of International Humanitarian Law, which aim to clarify the legal obligations of States and give practical guidance on investigating violations of this body of law.[32] It was clear during the development of the Guidelines that the question, "What is an investigation?" was not going to be easy to answer, as it is a term used to describe a myriad of different processes, from asking a few questions of one's subordinates to international inquiries that can take years and vast resources. The scope of what may be understood to constitute an investigation is therefore extremely broad. Insofar as this book is interested in investigative proceedings the purpose of which is to suppress or repress violations of IHL, such activities include both criminal and non-criminal (or administrative) investigations, and these may have many different names in domestic settings.[33] It is impossible to generalise, at such a broad level, the different stages of an investigation or the actors involved, as this will vary in each system. For the purpose of this book, I am using the term in line with the Guidelines, to denote "activity which has the purpose of establishing the facts surrounding an incident in order to allow for a subsequent determination of individual and/or State responsibility for a possible violation of international humanitarian law."[34] Which stages this applies to in each system will need to be made on a case-by-case basis.

Finally, the research also implicitly focuses on the responsibilities of States with regard to violations committed by members of their own armed forces, partly because the most direct obligations for a duty to investigate under IHL are regarding violations committed by a State's own armed forces. Clarity on this subject may help clarify responsibilities in other areas, such as those regarding non-state actors, civilian personnel working for the armed forces, members

32 Lubell, N., Pejic, J., & Simmons, C., "Guidelines on Investigating Violations of International Humanitarian Law: Law, Policy, and Good Practice," Geneva Academy/ICRC (2019).

33 "Guidelines on Investigating Violations of International Humanitarian Law" (n. 32), paras 53–60. See further, Chapter 3.

34 "Guidelines on Investigating Violations of International Humanitarian Law" (n. 32), para. 53.

of other armed forces, armed groups, or private military corporations.[35] At the time of writing, Ukraine is investigating Russian forces for alleged war crimes committed within its territory, obviously raising questions of independence and impartiality of these investigations into possible violations committed by "enemy" forces. It is suggested that the concepts of independence and impartiality of investigations as laid out in this book will be a useful starting point to address these situations.

Book outline

This book is divided into eight chapters, considering how military justice systems fit into international concepts of justice, the effectiveness of investigations under international law, including their independence and impartiality, and challenges to such investigations. Chapter 2 explores questions related to the legitimacy of military justice and tracing the principal lines of development which have influenced changes in the constitution of military justice systems over time. It looks at the historical rationale for the development of military jurisdiction across different systems and considers the general trends which emerged in the setting up of the first military forces and their accompanying justice systems. It also explores what factors have influenced the expansion and limitations of military jurisdiction over time (including the development of IHL and international human rights law). It sees that domestic differences play a key role in the scope of military jurisdiction but that applicable international standards will still guide certain aspects of the way in which they are used.

Chapter 3 explores the legal source and scope of the duty to investigate violations of IHL, and uses this legal background to argue that, above all, investigations into violations of IHL must be effective. It also finds that the requirement that investigations be independent and impartial is not clear *per se* in international law. Rather, the interpretation of adequate independence and impartiality standards must be made according to the overall standard of an effective investigation. Chapter 4 looks at the understanding of independence and impartiality of investigations with relation to this effectiveness. As the terms "independence and impartiality" are traditionally held to refer to the standards applicable to courts, judges, and tribunals, the chapter considers whether and how this discourse applies to investigations. The chapter suggests that while these principles may inform those applicable to investigations, the difference in purpose of the two paradigms necessarily affects their implementation. Nevertheless, a further element related to the perception of justice both at a domestic and international level can mean that further independence may on occasion be required.

35 See, e.g., Liivoja, R., "Trying Civilian Contractors in Military Courts: A Necessary Evil?" in Duxbury, A., & Groves, M., *Military Justice in the Modern Age*, Cambridge University Press (2016).

Chapter 5 focuses on the specific factors related to the context of military institutions which may affect the standards of independence and impartiality of investigations. It addresses unique military contexts such as investigators operating within a hierarchy and chain of command, and the implications of the concept of command responsibility on impartiality. It also examines the more intangible factors related to military life which may be seen as hindering independence and impartiality, especially the concept of loyalty and its effect on the administration of justice. While problematising the scope of presumed toxic loyalties in some cases, the chapter also highlights the role of appearances in a military context, and how this may affect perceptions of justice. Chapter 6, on the other hand, explores the theoretical and practical obstacles to independence and impartiality of investigations which are unique, or particularly aggravated, in situations of armed conflict. The presence and location of armed conflict may affect who is able to investigate in both practice and law. Furthermore, the very nature of armed conflict may be based upon issues of State legitimacy, or hostility towards another State, thus raising interesting concerns in relation to the role of the need for *perceived* independence and impartiality. The chapter addresses these challenges through the lens of reasonableness in fulfilling an international obligation, which should guide the way in which the standards of independence and impartiality are implemented for investigations in armed conflict.

Finally, Chapter 7 considers what effectiveness means in the context of a failure to investigate, patterns of violations, and systematic impunity. It addresses the broader contextual issues which may affect the effectiveness of investigations into violations of IHL, as well as the complex role of a failure to investigate in the commission of these violations. It considers the role of domestic and international oversight and safeguarding mechanisms in addressing the concerns relating to independence and impartiality in the context of systematic impunity.

Chapter 8 concludes the book by bringing together the different elements to be taken into account in assessing the independence and impartiality of military investigations into violations of IHL, as elucidated in previous chapters. The role and limits of military justice in implementing IHL are laid out in an attempt to highlight the importance of military investigations into violations in some circumstances. The need to understand independence and impartiality according to an investigation's effectiveness will also affect how the standards are implemented. Some obstacles, and ways of overcoming them, are explained. Finally, a general outline of the standards of independence and impartiality of military investigations into violations of IHL is suggested that takes into account the conclusions established throughout the book.

Conclusion

This book starts from the premise that there is nothing in the "militaryness" of proceedings which makes them inherently unable to uphold the principles of independence and impartiality in investigating. As odd, exceptional, or undesirable as military justice systems may be, for the purposes of understanding whether or not they can contribute towards combating impunity for violations of IHL, the key question is whether a given military justice system is an effective system of justice subject to the rule of law, or whether it is a tool of abuse used, for example, by an oppressive regime. Rather than suggesting a blanket dismissal of all military justice systems, it is considered more important to understand the unique elements in military institutions that may affect their independence and impartiality, as well as aggravating elements present in armed conflicts that may affect matters of justice. The book also suggests that the principle of effectiveness means that any investigating body must be competent and able to carry out an investigation in any situation in which violations occur. In situations of armed conflict, and in extraterritorial operations, this body may well be the military. Given this, the research aims to establish which factors should guide the establishment of adequate standards of independence and impartiality for military investigations under international law.

As an IHL scholar, I have had to come to terms with the fact that what may be lawful under IHL may not sit comfortably with what I find morally acceptable. A new type of discomfort arose during the research for this book, namely the feeling that some of my arguments would be seen as seeking to "defend the military" or justify the atrocities committed by some members of armed forces. As stated by an author for a report in the Brereton Inquiry into abuses committed by the Australian Defence Force in Afghanistan, "it is easy to muddle up seeking to understand why war crimes are committed with an attempt to excuse them."[36] I have been keenly aware of this muddle throughout my research, and I hope I have developed further sensitivities to "both sides": to both the victims of violations and their families who have suffered greatly through abuse by military members, and also to members of armed forces who often find themselves in situations which a civilian living in times of peace may struggle to fully comprehend.

It is not to be doubted that certain military investigations have not only been flawed but actively served to promote impunity for atrocities committed by military personnel. There are many good reasons to question the ability of individuals to carry out independent and impartial investigations into actions by individuals they hold many ties to. Yet we also need to go much further in understanding the details of the proper and improper use of military institutions in investigating violations of international law. If we expect to hold States and their militaries to account, scrutiny needs to be based on legal reasoning, and criticisms need to be fully informed of all the circumstances, practical and legal. It is hoped that this book goes some way to provide tools for such a fair scrutiny.

36 Whetham, D., "Special Operations Command: Leadership and Ethics Review," Annex A to Chapter 3.03, Inspector-General of the Australian Defence Force Afghanistan Inquiry Report (2020) [Brereton Report], p. 528.

2 The legitimacy of military justice

Introduction

Anyone following contemporary global news will be familiar with problematic uses of military justice systems. States such as Pakistan, Egypt, Myanmar, and Tunisia continue to use military courts to oppress political dissent, despite international condemnation of the practice. Peru, Mexico, and Colombia have been brought to the Inter-American Court for Human Rights many times for gross failures to investigate and prosecute soldiers in their military justice systems. In Europe, the UK, Turkey, and the Netherlands have all been found to have insufficient fair trial safeguards in their military courts by the European Court of Human Rights. The use of military tribunals by the USA in Guantánamo Bay has drawn international condemnation. History also holds many such examples: the trial of Captain Alfred Dreyfus in French courts martial in the nineteenth century remains emblematic of a miscarriage of justice and antisemitism; military dictatorships in the twentieth century widely used military courts to suppress political opposition in Brazil, Chile, Spain, and the USSR, among many others. For anyone who is familiar with or has been directly affected by these cases, the legitimacy of military justice systems may well appear non-existent.

But history also tells us of the use of military tribunals following the Second World War to prosecute war crimes committed by Nazi and Japanese perpetrators, setting the foundations for international criminal law and the prosecution of individuals directly for international crimes. More recently, a Swiss military court prosecuted a Rwandan former mayor for his role in committing war crimes during the Rwandan genocide.[1] In the Democratic Republic of the Congo (DRC), military tribunals have prosecuted war criminals for their role in mass crimes across the country.[2]

1 See the trial of Fulgence Niyonteze in Switzerland described in Kastenberg, J. E.,"Universal Jurisdiction and the Concept of a Fair Trial: Prosecutor v Fulgence Niyonteze; A Swiss Military Tribunal Cases Study," *University of Miami International & Comparative Law Review* Vol. 12 No. 1 (2004).

2 See, e.g., "DRC: Three Militiamen Convicted in Kalehe," *Trial International* (7 September 2020), available at: https://trialinternational.org/latest-post/drc-three-militiamen-convicted-in-kalehe/.

DOI: 10.4324/9781003360223-2

The examples given do not absolve the use of military justice systems in all contexts – the passage of time and evolution of international and domestic legal standards have affected and will continue to affect and improve the manner in which justice is dispensed, including in times of war. It is undeniable that the restriction of the use of military justice systems in certain circumstances is a positive trend that has served to improve the rights of many. But it is also undeniable that not everyone everywhere (or in every time) has had the same experience of "military justice," or the same perception of its legitimacy.

Before engaging in the substantive legal questions regarding military investigations, there is therefore a need to explore a point of contention in contemporary discourse on military justice, namely, the legitimacy of military jurisdiction over violations of international law, or in some spheres the very legitimacy of military justice systems as such. A variety of historical events have triggered progressive criticisms of military justice systems, in particular as to their jurisdictional scope (over what offences or over whom should military courts have jurisdiction?), and with regard to the individual treatment, and eventually rights, afforded to those under their jurisdiction.

This chapter briefly examines the history of military justice and traces the principal lines of development which have influenced changes in the constitution of military justice systems today. This attempt to understand the rationale behind the existence of military justice is done in order to address some of the contemporary criticisms of military justice systems calling for a partial or total abolition of such systems on the basis that they are archaic, unjust, or no longer needed.

A brief historical overview of military justice

There has been a gradual yet increasing scrutiny of military justice systems, from matters of almost purely commander and military interest to matters of domestic legislation, and only relatively recently as a matter of interest under international law. There are stark differences in the way military justice systems are structured domestically, shaped in part by the unique history of each State, yet certain trends can be discerned across the globe as to the purpose and rationale of contemporary military justice. Examining such trends, despite their differences, is deemed useful insofar as all military justice systems are today expected to respect certain common standards of international law.

The historical study of military justice reveals most of all an initial emphasis on commander-centred discipline, but also an increasing need to legislate as militaries and their accompanying justice systems became more sophisticated, and as public conceptions of "justice" evolved. What becomes clear from this brief overview is that military justice was not

> branched out of the ordinary justice system and [...] perverted into near-unrecognisable form by zealous military commanders. On the contrary, formalised processes of military justice developed as a counterbalance

or a limitation on the initially unconstrained disciplinary power of the military commander.[3]

Basis of military justice: discipline

The development of military jurisdiction in different States across the globe and over time did not start with concerns of justice, but was rather focused on military efficiency and necessity, and above all on the maintenance of discipline. Discipline is perhaps the oldest yet arguably most important argument for the existence of some sort of military justice.[4] It is also a concept which is of central importance in contemporary debates on military justice, something that will be returned to across this chapter. The need to maintain strict discipline within an institution whose members are required to make life-and-death decisions upon an order's notice is a well-commented-on theme running throughout the academic discussion of military justice.[5]

The enforcement of discipline in very early military institutions appears to have remained rather *ad hoc*, and reliant upon the whim of the commander, for example during the Roman Empire when "the military man was submitted to the will of his chief, of his commander."[6] Indeed, the commander who gave orders was also the one expected to sit in judgment of breaches of these orders.[7] In Europe, the creation of standing armies, principally in the Middle Ages, saw the creation of written legislation to regulate laws and punishments applicable to these armies,[8] yet in general matters of enforcement of justice remained in the hands of the commander.[9] Early European military justice was most likely "a rather summary thing" due to the "little ceremony attendant

3 Liivoja, R., *Criminal Jurisdiction Over Armed Forces Abroad*, Cambridge University Press (2017), p. 175.

4 See, e.g., from the fifth century BC, Sun Tzu, *The Art of War* (Lionel Giles trans., 1910), Chapter 9, para. 43.

5 McCarthy, A., "Erosion of the Rule of Law as a Basis for Command Responsibility Under International Humanitarian Law," *Chicago Journal of International Law* Vol. 18 No. 2 (2018); Gilissen, J., "Évolution actuelle de la justice militaire," *Recueils de la Société Internationale de Droit Pénal Militaire et de Droit de la Guerre* Vol. 8 (1981), p. 40; Gleeson, P., "Subject Matter Jurisdiction of Military Courts: Remarks by Mr Patrick Gleeson," Expert Consultation on the Administration of Justice through Military Tribunals (2014), p. 3, available at www.ohchr.org/sites/default/files/Documents/Issues/AdministrationJustice/Consultation2014/Patrick-Gleeson.docx; Gibson, M., "Military Justice in Operational Settings, Peacekeeping Missions and Situations of Transitional Justice" in Duxbury, A., & Groves, M., *Military Justice in the Modern Age*, Cambridge University Press (2016), p. 383.

6 Gilissen (n. 5), p. 48.

7 Denton, D. H., "The Australian Military Justice System: History, Organisation and Disciplinary Structure," *Victoria University Law & Justice Journal* Vol. 6 No. 1 (2016), pp. 26–27.

8 Winthrop, W., *Military Law and Precedents* (2nd ed.), Washington Governmental Printing Office (1920), p. 18.

9 Gilissen (n. 5), p. 48.

upon the event of [any] trial or hearing; concern for the rights of the individual [being] of little or no moment; and punishment follow[ing] the judgment in rapid 'one–two' order."[10] There would also have been very little review of summary justice by superior authorities.[11] Whereas future developments in military justice were to reduce the arbitrariness of proceedings, the need to maintain discipline has remained throughout the evolution of military justice institutions.

The "justice" part

As domestic legal institutions and militaries grew more sophisticated, so did the relationship between the law, judicial systems, and these militaries. The maintenance of discipline within the unique context of military institutions led to the need to legislate over specialised offences which did not exist in civilian jurisdiction. In the historical conduct of military operations, it became clear that certain behaviours or actions which did not amount to offences in civilian life most certainly posed a threat *inter alia* to the maintenance of discipline in armed forces and to the general understanding of justice.[12] But, perhaps more importantly, evolving understandings of justice led to a need to provide further procedural guarantees and fairer treatment to those subject to military discipline.

The commander-centred disciplinary systems which made up early forms of military justice presented over time various problems, not least with the perceived arbitrariness and summariness of proceedings. Changes were gradually made to military justice systems in different States, principally in response to events which brought widespread public attention to these military institutions. In France, for example, a change in judicial theory tending towards granting more rights to the accused combined with events such as the Dreyfus Affair brought military justice to the forefront of public attention.[13] This eventually led to reforms of the French Code of Military Justice in 1921 in order to "consolidate the requirements of discipline, without which there is no army, with the requirements of law, without which there is no justice."[14] Furthermore, the two world wars were catalysts to substantive changes to the form of military justice in many States. In the USA, criticisms levelled against practices during the First World War led to substantive reforms improving procedural

10 Rollman, R. O., "Of Crimes, Courts-Martial and Punishment: A Short History of Military Justice," *US Air Force JAG Law Review* Vol. 11 No. 2 (1969), p. 214.

11 Rollman (n. 10), p. 214.

12 Pariselle, J., "La Justice militaire française à la lumière de son histoire," *Military Law and Law of War Review* Vol. 19 (1980), p. 308.

13 Breurec, F., "Regards sur une évolution de la justice militaire en France," *Military Law and Law of War Review* Vol. 8 (1981), p. 333.

14 Pariselle (n. 12), p. 302, citing Hugueney, P., "Traités théorique et pratique de droit pénal et de procédure pénale militaire," *Recueil Sirey* (1933), p. 22 [my translation].

guarantees of courts martial, "all of which evidenced concern for the rights of the individual."[15] Similarly, in the UK, the general population, which had suddenly become very personally aware of the military justice system during the Second World War, "lost little time when the business of fighting was done, in making their views heard both through the press and in Parliament."[16]

It was, however, the codification of international human rights law (IHRL) following the Second World War that had the most notable influence on military justice systems worldwide.[17] The recognition of individual rights of soldiers as beneficiaries of human rights has led to important protections.[18] This is particularly evident in the jurisprudence of the European Court of Human Rights, in which cases addressing the need to provide adequate fair trial rights have triggered the reform of various European military justice systems. The development of individual rights has also led to an increased focus on the rights of victims of violations, which has had implications on the scrutiny of military justice by all regional human rights courts, as well as international human rights bodies.[19]

In the aftermath of the Second World War, military justice was used in an innovative way at the international level to prosecute crimes based on the idea that "a war crime is a violation of the laws and customs of war."[20] The UN War Crimes Commission was set up in 1942, and, following the end of the war, over two thousand military tribunal hearings were conducted at the domestic and international levels with the creation of the International Military Tribunal for Germany, and the International Military Tribunal for the Far East, among others.[21] Although these tribunals are not free from criticism, both for how they were set up and for their adjudications,[22] it is not to be doubted that the use of such military tribunals was a significant advance in the fight against impunity for atrocities committed in armed conflict.

The Second World War also had an impact on the structure of military justice systems, not least through the substantive international law which was codified

15 Rollman (n. 10), p. 219.

16 Stuart-Smith, J., "Without Partiality, Favour or Affection: An Account of the History and Present Functions of the Judge Advocate at a British Court Martial," *Military Law and Law of War Review* Vol. 2 No. 2 (1963), p. 233.

17 Gilissen (n. 5), p. 66.

18 Rowe, P., *The Impact of Human Rights Law on Armed Forces*, Cambridge University Press (2006); White, N., *Military Justice: The Rights and Duties of Soldiers and Governments*, Edward Elgar Publishing (2022), pp. 267–310.

19 Simmons, C., "The Scope of Military Jurisdiction for Violations of International Humanitarian Law," *Israel Law Review* Vol. 54 No. 1 (2021), pp. 17–21.

20 United Nations War Crimes Commission, *The History of the United Nations War Crimes Commission and the Development of the Laws of War* (1948), p. 171.

21 Henckaerts, J.-M. et al., *Updated Commentary on the First Geneva Convention*, ICRC (2016) [ICRC Updated Commentary to GCI], Commentary to Art. 49, para. 2829.

22 Sepinwall, A. J., "Failure to Punish: Command Responsibility in Domestic and International Law," *Michigan Journal of International Law* Vol. 30 No. 2 (2008), p. 262.

and developed in the following years, including the four Geneva Conventions of 1949 and subsequent Additional Protocols, the implementation of which required certain changes in military justice systems. Public scrutiny and experiences in both world wars affected the military justice systems in the UK, the USA, and in France, whereas in Germany, Austria, and Japan, all military bodies were banned in peace time, including any system of military justice.[23] This remains the case today: Japan has no standing army, and although Germany and Austria maintain an army with an advanced disciplinary system, there is no military jurisdiction over criminal offences in peacetime.[24] In other countries, there has been a general trend of "civilianisation" of military justice systems, namely, the further involvement of civilian judicial bodies in the military justice system, such as the use of civilian judges in military tribunals.[25]

While many States continue to use military justice systems to fulfil their obligation to suppress and repress violations of international humanitarian law (IHL),[26] in many contexts there is no reason why criminal offences (including war crimes) cannot be tried in the civilian justice systems. There are, indeed, domestic systems in which "serious" offences (such as war crimes) are under the jurisdiction of civilian justice systems.[27] In contrast to this, there are systems where all violations of IHL, including war crimes, are solely under military jurisdiction,[28] and a number of countries in which either civilian or military jurisdiction may apply, often depending upon decisions of the attorney general or equivalent authority.[29] It is also the case that the investigation may not always be carried out by the same body as that which may eventually take a case to court.[30]

23 Gilissen (n. 5), p. 43.

24 Gilissen (n. 5), p. 39; International Society for Military Law and the Law of War, "Comparative Study on Military Jurisdiction in the World," carried out in 2001 and 2011 (2011) [2011 ISMLLW Recueil], pp. 69–73; "Second Report of the Public Commission to Examine the Maritime Incident of 31 May 2010: Israel's Mechanisms for Examining and Investigating Complaints and Claims of Violations of the Laws of Armed Conflict According to International Law" (Israel, February 2013) [Second Turkel Report], Annex, pp. 801–864. However, see Chapters 4 and 6 on the use of military investigations (as opposed to trials) in Germany.

25 Gilissen (n. 5), p. 46; Liivoja, R., "Trying Civilian Contractors in Military Courts: A Necessary Evil?" in Duxbury & Groves (n. 5); Dahl, A. W., "Military Justice and Self-Interest in Accountability" in Bergsmo, M., & Song T., *Military Self-Interest in Accountability for Core International Crimes*, Torkel Opsahl Academic EPublisher (1st ed.) (2016).

26 See the ICRC National Implementation Database which collects information on domestic legislation on IHL obligations: https://ihl-databases.icrc.org/ihl-nat.

27 Kenya, Colombia, Belgium, Czech Republic, France, Germany, Greece. See responses to 2001 ISMLLW Recueil (n. 24).

28 Switzerland, Democratic Republic of the Congo, Tunisia, Bulgaria. See responses to 2001 ISMLLW Recueil (n. 24); Kastenberg (n. 1).

29 UK, Australia, New Zealand, Cameroon, Canada, USA, Singapore, Ireland, Netherlands. See responses to 2011 ISMLLW Recueil (n. 24) and Annex to the Second Turkel Report (n. 24).

30 This will be returned to in Chapters 4 and 6.

The case is arguably different for some violations of IHL that do not require criminal judicial proceedings. Such violations can have particularly serious consequences even though there is no indication of criminal liability, for example with a failure to take precautions in attack resulting in accidental loss of civilian life.[31] In dealing with violations that have solely a disciplinary component, military institutions may have a broad range of regulations and associated punishments which do not have equivalents in civilian life and are often solely within the remit of an individual's commander.[32] The civilian justice system would be inadequate and ineffective in most such cases, because their disciplinary nature often requires them being imposed by a superior officer (for example, the individual's commander). Other incidents may constitute violations of IHL yet may not be attributable to any individual fault but rather due to a systemic problem within the military. Internal systems of military investigation and review can be crucial in effectively investigating such incidents and ensuring they are not repeated.[33] The latter example does not mandate exclusive military jurisdiction, and in some particularly serious cases civilian systems of inquiry are used. Nevertheless, military systems of review can be an effective first recourse for addressing administrative violations of IHL. Some of these issues will be further explored in subsequent chapters.

Military justice systems have had to come to terms with domestic and international developments protecting the rights of those involved in judicial proceedings. These developments have led to a move away from early commander-centric systems of administration of justice by military authorities and must be taken into account alongside the other legal and practical considerations in the choice and structure of civilian or military jurisdiction for the effective implementation of IHL. The increased recognition of rights, including international human rights, of individuals subject to military proceedings has had a substantive impact on both the structure and the scope of military jurisdiction, and there is little doubt that these reforms have overall contributed to a better administration of justice. Military justice systems have had to adapt over time in response to domestic and international pressure along developing normative standards.

Is it possible to compare military justice systems?

As military justice becomes increasingly scrutinised at the international level, especially as it is considered under the lenses of IHRL and IHL, it is worth

31 See Chapter 3 on the scope of serious and non-serious violations of IHL.

32 Lubell, N., Pejic, J., & Simmons, C., "Guidelines on Investigating Violations of International Humanitarian Law: Law, Policy, and Good Practice," Geneva Academy/ICRC (2019), para. 164; Rowe (n. 18), p. 64.

33 "Guidelines on Investigating Violations of International Humanitarian Law" (n. 32), Guideline 13; Goldrick, J., "A Strategic Commander's Perspective" in Lovell, D. W., *Investigating Operational Incidents in a Military Context*, Brill (2015), pp. 23–27.

questioning to what extent it is possible to compare domestic military justice systems, and what factors must be borne in mind when doing so. Any scrutiny of compliance of a domestic system with international norms will need to look at national specificities, and few common denominators are to be found across the systems.[34] "Comparative cherry-picking" of standards across systems can have counter-productive effects if they do not adequately take into account national and regional specificities.[35] However, this does not mean that parallels and trends cannot be drawn, especially in light of the increasing internationalisation of standards applicable to systems which affect individual rights. This section explores the ways in which military justice systems may be compared, looking at their evolution and how the applicable standards have changed over time. Nevertheless it also recognises limitations and invites further consideration of comparative analysis of historical and contemporary systems of military justice.

Defining military justice

One difficulty in comparing systems of military justice is the lack of uniform definition for the term. Critics of military justice often have one specific type of system or one specific region in mind when discussing "military justice." As will be explored in this chapter, this has been a particular criticism of the drafters of the draft Decaux principles on the administration of justice by military tribunals.[36] A definition of the term "military" may itself be difficult to pinpoint in a cross-cutting manner at the international level.

Domestically, at least in peacetime, it will usually be clear enough who constitutes a "military person," usually understood as a member of the armed forces.[37] Elements such as the wearing of uniform, the possession of rank, and perhaps the right to use weapons are often also associated to military personnel. However, the arrangements of what constitutes the "armed forces" will differ depending on each State, with some States having, for example, "gendarmerie," or other forms of militarised police forces, which may be considered part of the armed forces or not.[38] Belgium, for example, ceased to

34 Andreu-Guzmán, F., *Military Jurisdiction and International Law: Military Courts and Gross Human Rights Violations* Vol. 1, International Commission of Jurists (2003), p. 154.

35 Madden, M., "Comparative Cherry-Picking in a Military Justice Context: The Misplaced Quest to Give Universally Expansive Meaning to International Human Rights," *George Washington International Law Review* Vol. 46 No. 713.

36 Decaux, E., "Issue of the Administration of Justice Through Military Tribunals: Report Submitted by the Special Rapporteur of the Sub-Commission on the Promotion and Protection of Human Rights, Emmanuel Decaux," E/CN.4/2006/58 (2006) [Draft Decaux Principles].

37 White (n. 18), p. 3.

38 See, e.g., practice relating to Rule 4 of Henckaerts, J.-M., & Doswald-Beck, L., *Customary International Humanitarian Law*, ICRC (2006). Upon ratification, Belgium stated that the national gendarmerie were members of the armed forces for the purposes of Article 43 Additional Protocol I [API] in situations of armed conflict but put an end to this connection in 1991.

consider its gendarmerie as part of the armed forces in 1991, and merged it with the civilian police forces in 2000. France, on the other hand, considers its gendarmerie to be members of the armed forces (at least with relation to armed conflicts), even though the gendarmerie heavily rely on the Ministry of Interior rather than Ministry of Defence.[39] In Colombia, the National Police are considered part of the domestic "public forces" and share a disciplinary and criminal code with military institutions.[40] Despite being constitutionally "civilian," their apparent militarisation has led to public and legal protest.[41]

This ambiguity is even more complicated when looking at what may constitute a "military justice" procedure. It is clear that military justice systems are not homogeneous across different States and legal systems.[42] For courts, it appears that the military nature of a proceeding is usually determined by the nature of the personnel who conduct the procedure rather than the subject matter. One military personnel sitting on a court alongside civilians will usually be sufficient to consider it military in nature, whereas a court staffed entirely by civilians, yet which deals exclusively with military matters, will usually be considered a civilian court. However, this is not necessarily the case for investigations. As will be explored throughout this book, there are supposedly civilian proceedings (under civilian jurisdiction and courts) that nevertheless rely on military personnel for parts of the investigation, for example evidence-gathering or technical expertise. This is of particular relevance insofar as this book is addressing only the investigation stage of justice proceedings.

In France, for example, the civilian judges and magistrates of the *Tribunal de Grande Instance de Paris* are trained in military matters (not rendering them any less civilian). Yet military personnel can have a role in criminal proceedings which will ultimately be brought before civilian courts, as military provosts (police) on the scene of possible criminal incidents have the initial responsibilities of gathering evidence which will later be brought to civilian

39 Code de justice militaire L211; Code de justice militaire, Vol. 4, *Des prévôtés et des tribunaux prévôtaux L411-1*; 2011 ISMLLW Recueil (n. 24), pp. 259–261; "Instruction No. 30619/DEF/SGA/DAJ/DAPM/EDP relative aux poursuites pénales à l'encontre des membres des forces armées" (23 September 2015), para. 2.4 available at: www.police-nationale.net/gendarmerie/.

40 Colombia, "Ley No. 1407 de 2010, por la cual se expide el Código Penal Militar," Arts 1–5.

41 See, e.g., Pardo, D., "Policía en Colombia: por qué es militar y no civil (y qué tiene que ver con las demandas de las recientes protestas)," BBC Mundo (10 September 2020), available at: www.bbc.com/mundo/noticias-america-latina-54112641. The military or civilian nature of a police member according to IHL during the Colombian armed conflict was considered by the Special Jurisdiction for Peace (JEP) in an amnesty case: JEP, "Sentencia TP-SA-AM 168 de 2020, En el asunto de Luis Alberto Guzmán Díaz" (18 June 2020), paras 19.7.1–19.7.10.

42 Rowe, P., "How Well Do International Human Rights Bodies Understand Military Courts?" in Duxbury & Groves (n. 5), p. 16; Liivoja, R., "Military Justice" in Dubber, M. D., and Hörnle, T., *The Oxford Handbook of Criminal Law*, Oxford University Press (2014), p. 326.

judicial authorities.[43] Although they are military personnel, they are part of the *gendarmerie nationale* belonging to the Ministry of Interior, and act under the authority of the civilian Public Prosecutor. They are independent of the chain of command in carrying out their investigative duties.[44] Similar structural arrangements exist in other continental European States, such as the Netherlands and Germany.

For the purposes of this book, the term "military" and "military justice" are therefore deliberately kept very broad. Military justice systems are understood to encompass a variety of proceedings used to enforce laws and regulations within the armed forces, from informal disciplinary proceedings to criminal judicial proceedings. Usually, they are understood to be partly or entirely carried out by military personnel. In practice, they will vary considerably in their institutional structure and their relationship to the operational branches of the armed forces.[45] The fact that a narrow definition of "military justice" cannot be established serves to emphasise the arguments, laid out in the following chapters, that what matters more than the nature of the body is its structure and the likelihood of accountability. Although specificities of military institutions and culture are relevant, as will be explored in Chapter 5, it is suggested that whether a body is "military" or not is only secondary to whether it is one which is capable of carrying out justice. This matters all the more in light of the fact that naming a procedure "civilian" rather than military will do little to solve structural problems should they exist.

The common/civil law divide: A useful problematic divide

Agreeing upon the meaning of the term "military justice" therefore means encompassing a broad range of different types of proceedings. Within these, other groupings are often made between systems which hold more or less comparable similarities. The different approaches to military justice in the world often focus on the differences between the common law and civil law (or Roman law) traditions,[46] although these are not the only existing legal traditions, nor are they homogeneous within themselves. The main differences which can be seen between the common and civil law systems are that, traditionally, common law systems would convene military tribunals on a case-by-

43 See also the example of Germany as explored in ECtHR, *Hanan v Germany*, App. No. 4871/16, Judgment of 16 February 2021, paras 179–181.

44 Code de justice militaire L211; Code de justice militaire Vol. 4 (n. 39); 2011 ISMLLW Recueil (n. 24), pp. 259–261; "Instruction No. 30619/DEF/SGA/DAJ/DAPM/EDP relative aux poursuites pénales à l'encontre des membres des forces armées" (23 September 2015), para. 2.4.

45 Simmons (n. 19), p. 3.

46 Denton (n. 7), pp. 26–27. Despite being frequently named "civil law systems" by anglophone scholars, the latter of these systems, *inter alia*, those of continental Europe, commonly refer to their own as "Romanist" systems.

case basis, whereas civil law systems usually had standing (military) courts.[47] There are further common patterns which will be elucidated in this chapter, although it is also the case that the differences between the two traditions are decreasing.

The civil/common law approach, and the focus on the "usual suspects" of global North/Western (Euro-centric) history can be useful insofar as it traces the roots of European colonial powers. Using this divide and focus can be useful to a certain degree in understanding certain patterns and trends which have occurred over time and is necessary to understand some of the debates occurring today at the international level. Colonisation – and decolonisation – had a great impact on the militaries and military justice systems of affected countries around the world. In new States created following decolonisation in the Americas, Africa, and Asia, the organisation of military justice was generally inspired by that of the former colonial power,[48] often due to the common languages used and the possibility of using these codes as models for new national legislation.[49] States from former British colonies almost unanimously adopted in the 1960s and 70s an "Army Act" very similar to that of the UK in 1955,[50] although a contemporary comparison of these Acts will usually find important differences as systems have evolved separately. In former French colonies, the French Code of Military Justice similarly served as a blueprint for new military justice legislation.[51] In Spanish colonies, militaries developed the "*fuero militar*," privileging military jurisdiction over many matters.[52] Understanding the bases and common patterns of the colonial influences in the military justice systems therefore gives a (limited) understanding of the military justice systems in these States.

Nevertheless, it is important to recognise the limitations of the common/civil law approach. This colonial influence on military justice was not true everywhere, as in some cases they clashed with more local or traditional influences such as in South Korea,[53] or where newly formed States were too small to have a substantive standing army, but rather established "a disciplinary regime halfway between military discipline and the discipline of large civilian bodies."[54] It neglects important military traditions in parts of the world such as East Asia and the Middle East, or other legal traditions such as Islamic law or indigenous laws that have also shaped military institutions.[55] It is also uncritical of the

47 Denton (n. 7), pp. 26–27.
48 Gilissen (n. 5), p. 47.
49 Gilissen (n. 5), p. 65.
50 Gilissen (n. 5), p. 47.
51 Gilissen (n. 5), p. 47.
52 Kyle, B., & Reiter, A., *Military Courts, Civil–Military Relations, and the Legal Battle for Democracy: The Politics of Military Justice*, Routledge (2021), p. 26.
53 Gilissen (n. 5), p. 47.
54 Gilissen (n. 5), p. 38.
55 Gálvez Montero briefly addresses the impact of indigenous laws in shaping the Peruvian military justice system. Gálvez Montero, J. F., *La Justicia Militar en la Historia del Perú*,

narrative which traces back the roots of a singular civilisation to early Greeks and Romans, which neglects the complexity of historical development and influences.[56] Finally, it perpetuates a colonial approach to international law, which is thankfully being increasingly challenged. I am afraid to somewhat perpetuate some of these flaws, as unfortunately, due to my own subject-area and language limitations, the limited scope of this chapter and book, and the paucity of literature on the subject, I am not able here to do justice to the actual diversity of global military justice institutions or the historical influences which have shaped them. I hope more diverse research on this topic may come later.

"Disciplinary" versus "criminal" in the common and civil law systems

The debate at the international level concerning the adequacy of military jurisdiction over violations of international law is compounded in part by the difficulties in translating concepts which have defined meanings within a domestic system, not least to do with the domestic legal differences between common law and civil law countries. The concept of military jurisdiction, namely the scope of what and whom should be submitted to judicial proceedings run by military personnel, is today substantially different in common and civil law legal traditions despite both being founded on concerns of discipline and the need for specialised judicial measures in a military context.

In common law countries the concept of discipline was broadened and integrated into a growing military judicial system that evolved as a parallel (but not exceptional) system of justice to the ordinary civilian judicial systems. Military justice systems have jurisdiction over all "military offences" (also known as "service offences"), which are understood in most common law systems to encompass all breaches of the military laws to which military personnel are subject, including criminal and non-criminal (administrative) offences.[57] "Disciplinary offences" are any offences in breach of military discipline, regardless of whether or not they also include criminal elements – "criminal" and "disciplinary" are not mutually exclusive in the common law understanding of the term.

In civil law countries, on the other hand, the concept of discipline seems to have been perceived as a necessary way to enforce laws and regulations in the military context where the civilian system could not. For matters of justice,

---

Fuero Militar Policial (2017). See also Watts, S., & Martin, C., "Nation-Building in Afghanistan: Lessons Identified in Military Justice Reform" *Army Law* 1 (2006); Bassiouni, C., *The Sharīʿa and Islamic Criminal Justice in Time of War and Peace*, Cambridge University Press (2014).

56 Liivoja (2017) (n. 3), p. 175; Andreu-Guzmán (n. 34), p. 153.

57 Gibson, M., "International Human Rights Law and the Administration of Justice Through Military Tribunals: Preserving Utility While Precluding Impunity," *Journal of International Law and International Relations* Vol. 4 No. 1 (2008), p. 39; "Guidelines on Investigating Violations of International Humanitarian Law" (n. 32), para. 57.

especially criminal justice, the civilian system was to be preferred when possible. In this sense, military justice systems may be understood as more "exceptional." Unlike common law systems, most civil law systems clearly distinguish between criminal offences and non-criminal (disciplinary) offences. In France, for example, the latter is purely dealt with by the military hierarchy.[58] Criminal military offences ("*infractions militaires*"), on the other hand, were until 2012 dealt with by the Army Tribunal of Paris (composed of both civilian and military personnel).[59] After its dissolution, its competence was transferred to specialised chambers in the Tribunal de Grande Instance de Paris, which is made up entirely of civilian personnel who nonetheless have particular expertise in military affairs.[60] In this sense, "military offences" are dealt with by civilian specialised courts in the French system, but do not cover "disciplinary" (non-criminal) offences. The same offence can be dealt with in both jurisdictions for different reasons (e.g., if a criminal offence has implications on military discipline).[61]

To compound the difficulties in understanding the disciplinary/criminal divide, the concept of "discipline" as used in IHL can usually be understood as cross-cutting both criminal and non-criminal violations.[62] The disciplinary authority of a commander is explicit under the notion of command responsibility for the actions of their subordinates, as commanders have an explicit duty to suppress all violations of IHL.[63] Cases adjudicated under international criminal law on the concept of command responsibility have turned on the very fact that a commander has not instilled discipline, or may have lost disciplinary power, over their troops.[64] Despite this clear and obvious link between discipline and criminal repression in the context of command responsibility, "discipline" is also used in some of the commentaries to the Geneva Conventions in contrast to "criminal" offences.[65] The concept is therefore used in IHL texts

58 2011 ISMLLW Recueil (n. 24), p. 249.

59 France, Loi no. 2011-1862 du 13 décembre 2011 relative à la répartition des contentieux et à l'allègement de certaines procédures juridictionnelle.

60 France, Code de justice militaire, Art. 111-1 (modifié par Loi no. 2011-1862 du 13 décembre 2011).

61 2011 ISMLLW Recueil (n. 24), pp. 248 and 261.

62 Simmons (n. 19), pp. 8–13.

63 Protocol Additional to the Geneva Conventions of 12 August 1949 and relating to the Protection of Victims of International Armed Conflicts, 1125 UNTS 3 (1977) [API], Art. 87.

64 McCarthy (n. 5); United States Military Commission, *Trial of General Tomoyuki Yamashita*, Manila (8 October–7 December 1945) and the Supreme Court of the United States (4 February 1946), as recorded in United Nations War Crimes Commission, *Law Reports of Trials of War Criminals* Vol. 4 (1948), pp. 1–96; International Criminal Tribunal for the Former Yugoslavia (ICTY), *Prosecutor v Enver Hadžihasanović & Amir Kubura*, IT-01-47-A, Appeals Chamber Judgment of 22 April 2008, para. 1777; International Criminal Tribunal for Rwanda (ICTR), *Prosecutor v Bagilishema*, ICTR-95-1A-T, Trial Chamber I, Judgment of 7 June 2001, para. 50.

65 Pictet, J., *The Geneva Conventions of 12 August 1949: Commentary*, ICRC (1960), Commentary to Article 49, p. 368 and Commentary to Article 1, para. 2841: "Penal sanctions,

both to refer to responsibilities with regard to the repression of war crimes and to refer to responsibilities which exclude criminal matters.

Comparing standards of fair trial and due process

Finally, it is useful to consider the slight differences in the way in which the human rights concept of "fair trial" is interpreted in different systems, as this serves in part to clarify the current apparent contrast in the regional human rights approach to military jurisdiction, which will be explored below.

To understand this contrast, it is important to note that the term "fair trial" is interpreted slightly differently in different contexts. The International Covenant on Civil and Political Rights (ICCPR) and European Court of Human Rights (ECtHR) refer to the concept of "fair trial" as a catch-all term for human rights applicable to the judicial procedures, often (but not exclusively) in criminal court cases. On the other hand, it has become common for the Inter-American Court of Human Rights (IACtHR) to refer to the concept of *debido proceso* (due process) while referring to Articles 1, 8, and 25 jointly, and is the preferred catch-all term when referring to similar issues as considered by the term "fair trial" in Anglophone texts.[66] The implications of this slight difference for our purposes are twofold. First, that the concept of "fair trial" before the EctHR and ICCPR focus solely on the rights of the accused to a fair trial (and not the alleged victim),[67] while the concept of due process before the IACtHR relates to procedural rights of suspects and accused involved in a criminal or civil trial, but also to victims of human rights violations. The second implication is the applicability of these rights to the investigation stage, as opposed to only the court and trial process. This second point will be elaborated further in Chapter 4.

This difference in approach, in which we see the IACtHR including the rights of victims as a fundamental part of a fair judicial process may in part be linked to the tradition of *amparo* in Hispanic jurisdictions, where there is a focus on the rights of victims to remedy as part of a judicial procedure.[68] The different levels of involvement of victims in judicial procedures is evident

as opposed to disciplinary ones, will be issued by judicial institutions, be they military or civilian."

66 Corte Interamericana de Derechos Humanos (CIADH), *Cuadernillo de Jurisprudencia de la Corte Interamericana de Derechos Humanos* No. 12, *Debido Proceso* (2017); IACtHR, *Bámaca Velásquez v Guatemala*, Ser. C No. 70, Judgment of 25 November 2000 (Merits), para. 197.

67 Zappalà, S., "The Rights of Victims *v.* the Rights of the Accused," *Journal of International Criminal Justice* Vol. 8 (2014), p. 149.

68 Of course, not all States party to the ACHR are of Hispanic tradition, yet the prevalence of cases concerning such states before the IACtHR is undeniable. Weissbrodt, D., *The Right to a Fair Trial: Articles 8, 10 and 11 of the Universal Declaration of Human Rights,* Martinus Nijhoff Publishers (2001), p. 29.

in comparing common and civil law systems.[69] The result is that the Inter-American system of human rights has addressed the rights of victims from the perspective of a broad right to due process, while the European Court of Human Rights has focused on the procedural obligations stemming from other substantive rights (see Chapter 3).

This has had interesting implications on the evolution of the regional jurisprudence related to military jurisdiction. The IACtHR, in finding that military jurisdiction is not appropriate for cases involving civilians, extended this fact to both the accused or the victim being a civilian. In the *Castillo Petruzzi* case, which dealt with a civilian (the accused) being tried by military jurisdiction, the Court stated that military jurisdiction was inappropriate *inter alia* because, "in the instant case," the military courts "did not meet the requirements implicit in the guarantees of independence and impartiality that Article 8(1) of the American Convention recognises as essentials of due process of law."[70] This case was subsequently cited in finding military jurisdiction inappropriate for cases in which the *victim* was a civilian.[71] It is important to note that there were fundamental flaws with the military justice proceedings in question beyond the matter of jurisdiction,[72] but the cases illustrate well the unique approach to due process taken by the Inter-American Court of Human Rights. Before the European Court of Human Rights, on the other hand, the interaction between a military judicial procedure and a victim involved in such procedures (not a suspect) has focused on the way in which the ineffectiveness of such systems has inhibited the provision of substantive rights, such as the right to life.[73] Rather than restricting the scope of military jurisdiction for situations in which the victim is a civilian, this has had the effect of leading to reforms in the way States structure domestically their military justice systems. This is not to say the regional courts are fundamentally at odds with each other in the

69 Zappalà (n. 66); Wilson, L. A., "The Rights of Victims vs the Rights of the Accused: Striking a Balance between the Rights of Victims and Accused Persons in the International Criminal Justice Setting," *University of Western Australia Law Review* Vol. 38 No. 2 (2015), p. 159.

70 IACtHR, *Castillo Petruzzi et al v Peru*, Ser. C No. 59, Judgment of 30 May 1999 (Merits, Reparations, and Costs), para. 132.

71 IACtHR, *Las Palmeras v Colombia*, Ser. C No. 67, Judgment of 4 February 2000 (Merits), paras 52–53. See also cases surrounding Article 13 of the Mexican Constitution of 1917, e.g., *Ortega v Mexico*, Ser C. No. 215, Judgment of 30 August 2010 (Preliminary Objections, Merits, Reparations, and Costs).

72 In *Castillo Petruzzi* (n. 70), there were structural flaws with the military justice system, *inter alia*, that military judges remained subordinate to the operational chain of command and were not composed of legal professionals (para. 125(e)). In *Las Palmeras* (n. 71), there were significant concerns about the independence and impartiality of the investigators (para. 53), in addition to the fact that the initial phases of the investigations were fundamentally flawed, including in the tampering, concealing, and destruction of evidence (para. 57).

73 ECtHR, *Al-Skeini v UK*, App. No. 55721/07, Judgment of 7 July 2011; *Jaloud v The Netherlands*, App. No. 47708-08, Judgment of 20 November 2014.

interpretation of human rights guarantees,[74] something which will be returned to in subsequent chapters, but it does highlight their differences in approach.

This section has explored some of the general trends across common and civil law States and considered to what extent the systems may be compared under international legal standards. Military jurisdiction in civil law countries is often restricted to non-criminal disciplinary offences, at least in peacetime. Military expertise is nonetheless found for both types of offences, through specialisation of civilian judges, and the involvement of military investigative personnel. Military jurisdiction in common law systems, on the other hand, covers all criminal and non-criminal offences committed by members of the armed forces.

Nevertheless, domestic systems of military justice vary immensely from State to State, and one must be cautious in trying to apply lessons learned from one system to another without fully understanding the reasons regarding the set up of each system. In the following section, the above will usefully inform an exploration of how international law has impacted on the scope of military jurisdiction internationally. Importantly, it will be seen that in Latin America the use of military systems as tools of oppression by authoritarian governments has dramatically influenced the perception of the adequate scope of military jurisdiction.

The scope of military jurisdiction over serious violations of IHL and IHRL

One of the most important contemporary debates affecting the existence of military justice systems is the question of their jurisdictional scope: over whom and over what should the military have jurisdiction? There are other questions that should also be asked alongside these, including when and where should the military have jurisdiction (peace/war, territory/extraterritorial), and what factors should be used to answer these questions (rights of military personnel, rights of victims, requirements of discipline, security requirements, the existence (or lack) of adequate civilian systems, or a more abstract sense of "justice"). Some of these questions will be explored in further detail in subsequent chapters. Nevertheless, it is useful to address at this stage one specific criticism directed towards military jurisdiction, namely, the criticism claiming that military justice systems should never have jurisdiction over serious violations of IHRL (and, by implication, some serious violations of IHL).

This criticism is often tied into what can be called the "military nexus" debate, namely, that military justice systems, where they exist, should only

74 See, e.g., the similar approach on jurisdiction: ECtHR, *Mustafa Tunç and Fecire Tunç v Turkey*, App. No. 24014/05, Judgment 14 April 2015, paras 223–234; IACtHR, *Favela Novela Brasilia v Brazil*, Ser. C. No. 345, Judgment of 16 February 2017 (Preliminary Objections, Merits, Reparations, and Costs), paras 186–191.

have jurisdiction over offences of a purely military nature committed by military personnel in active service in relation to this service (and where there is no civilian equivalent offence). The argument may be continued as saying that insofar as violations of IHRL can never be considered to be in connection to military service, they cannot come under the jurisdiction of military justice systems.

The main sources and elements of this debate are laid out below, and some misunderstandings and generalisations are drawn out. I suggest there are multiple aspects of this debate which are often left unclarified: whether jurisdiction means all stages of a judicial process, including the very preliminary investigation stages; the definition of a "purely military" offence; and the confusing manner in which IHRL and IHL are often included into the debate. Importantly, the common law/civil law differences are also crucial to understanding the debate, and how to address it.

Basis of the "military nexus" criticism

The debate on military nexus, at the global level, at least, finds one of its sources in the report by the Special Rapporteur of the United Nations Sub-Commission on the Promotion and Protection of Human Rights, Louis Joinet, in 2001, followed by an updated report in 2006 by Emmanuel Decaux, which constitute the Draft Principles on the Administration of Justice by Military Tribunals.[75] The status of these Draft Principles is unclear: they are still considered "draft" and have not been directly endorsed by the General Assembly or any other UN body, and are unlikely to constitute soft law in their current state. Nevertheless, they are increasingly cited by international and regional bodies, despite their unfinished status.[76] This may be in part due to the unfortunate lack of any other authoritative commentary directly addressing the topic of military justice at an international level.

Principle 8 of the Draft Principles states that "the jurisdiction of military courts should be limited to offences of a strictly military nature committed by

75 "Issue of the administration of justice through military tribunals Report submitted by Mr. Louis Joinet pursuant to Sub-Commission decision 2001/103," E/CN.4/Sub.2/2002/4 (2002); Draft Decaux Principles.

76 The Draft Principles have been cited by UN Special Rapporteurs, the three regional human rights courts, NGOs, and international organisations. See, e.g., "Report of the Special Rapporteur on the Independence of Judges and Lawyers, Gabriela Knaul," A/68/285 (2013), para. 18; Council of Europe, "Human Rights of Members of the Armed Forces: Recommendation CM/Rec (2010) 4 of the Committee of Ministers and Explanatory Memorandum" (2010), p. 44; ECtHR, *Ergin v Turkey*, App. No. 47533/99, Judgment of 4 May 2006, para. 24; Human Rights Watch, "Promoting Impunity: The Israeli Military's Failure to Investigate Wrongdoing," *Human Rights Watch* Vol. 17, No. 7(E) (2005), p. 28. A workshop held at Yale Law School in 2018 examined how some of the provisions could be updated. Decaux Principles Workshop, "The Yale Draft," Yale Law School (2018), available at: www.court-martial-ucmj.com/files/2018/06/The-Yale-Draft.pdf.

military personnel. Military courts may try persons treated as military personnel for infractions strictly related to their military status."[77] The Commentary to this Principle goes on to explain its reasoning that military jurisdiction

> should remain exceptional and apply only to the requirements of military service. This concept constitutes the "nexus" of military justice, particularly as regards field operations, when the territorial court cannot exercise its jurisdiction. Only such a functional necessity can justify the limited but irreducible existence of military justice.[78]

The basis for this Principle is clearly tied to the historical trends regarding the development of military justice in civil law States.

The commentary to the following Principle goes on to explore this "military nexus" argument further in a more problematic way. Principle 9 states that

> the jurisdiction of military courts should be set aside in favour of the jurisdiction of the ordinary courts to conduct inquiries into serious human rights violations such as extrajudicial executions, enforced disappearances and torture, and to prosecute and try persons accused of such crimes.[79]

The Commentary to this Principle explains that

> Contrary to the functional concept of the jurisdiction of military tribunals, there is today a growing tendency to consider that persons accused of serious human rights violations cannot be tried by military tribunals insofar as such acts would, by their very nature, not fall within the scope of the duties performed by such persons. Moreover, the military authorities might be tempted to cover up such cases by questioning the appropriateness of prosecutions, tending to file cases with no action taken or manipulating "guilty pleas" to victims' detriment.[80]

There are various problems with the Draft Principle and its commentary, not least in the restricted understanding of the "functional concept" of military jurisdiction, the generalisation of the "growing tendency" to restrict military jurisdiction, and the lack of explanation as to how a "serious human rights violation" may be excluded from a jurisdictional scope. Nuances of the claim that military authorities are more likely to promote impunity than civilian authorities are explored further in Chapters 5 and 7, and for now this claim is set aside as too sweeping to be considered useful.

77 Draft Decaux Principles (n. 36), Principle 8.
78 Draft Decaux Principles (n. 36), Commentary, para. 29.
79 Draft Decaux Principles (n. 36), Principle 9.
80 Draft Decaux Principles (n. 36) Commentary, para. 32.

The "functional concept" of military jurisdiction

It has been pointed out that much of the criticism of the scope of military jurisdiction has stemmed from the Latin American experience, namely, from the observation of mass atrocities committed by military personnel during dictatorships and/or armed conflict in Latin America in the twentieth century.[81] While this is undoubtedly true, it is arguably not only the *atrocities* of this region that have led to the criticism and development of the stringent military nexus argument. The civil law tradition which predominates in most of these States also has a role to play. Crucially, Draft Principle 8 and its commentary, and the accompanying military nexus argument, is very much rooted in the civil law tradition and rationale for military jurisdiction.

Various Latin American States, such as Colombia and Mexico, have a constitutional clause limiting military jurisdiction to specific offences of a purely military nature related to their military service (the "functional concept").[82] This has been the subject of various cases before the IACtHR and has greatly influenced the Court's approach to military justice. Although initial cases dealing with flawed military justice procedures commented on the explicit due process issues related to that system, there has been an arguably unfortunate focus in more recent cases on an inherent "militaryness" as problematic to fair trial guarantees.[83] As all such analyses were based in States with similar (civil law) constitutional provisions, this has led to a regional trend by the Inter-American System of Human Rights, and to an apparent favouring of the abolition of military jurisdiction.[84]

However, from the perspective of a common law tradition, the military nexus debate arguing for a functional jurisdiction makes little sense of the rationale for military jurisdiction.[85] Gibson has commented on the problem of the military nexus argument being conflated with the issue of whether an offence falls "within the scope of duties" of a military person. He remarks that

81 Gibson (2008) (n. 57), p. 38; Schmid, E., "A Few Comments on a Comment: The UNHRC GC32 on Art. 14 ICCPR on the Question of Civilians Tried by Military Courts," *International Journal of Human Rights* Vol. 14 No. 7 (2010), p. 1061.

82 Constitución Política de Colombia 1991, Actualizada con los Actos Legislativos a 2016, Art. 22, modificado por el Acto Legislativo 01 de 2015; Art. 13 de la Constitución Política Mexicana.

83 IACtHR, *Castillo Petruzzi et al. v Peru* (n. 70), para. 132; IACtHR, *La Rochela Massacre v Colombia*, Ser. C No. 163, Judgment of 11 May 2007 (Merits, Reparations, and Costs), para. 200.

84 IACtHR, *Palamara-Iribarne v Chile*, Ser. C. No. 135, Judgment of 22 November 2005 (Merits, Reparations, and Costs), para. 132. IACtHR, *Palamara-Iribarne v Chile* (Merits, Reparations, and Costs) (22 November 2005), Concurrent opinion of Judge García-Ramírez, para. 12.

85 There is a caveat to this statement, insofar as the "military nexus" has been used in common law States to justify the restriction of military jurisdiction at certain times, but it is not the predominant legal justification for the scope of military jurisdiction. See Canadian Supreme Court, *R. v Stillman*, 2019 SCC 40, Judgment of 26 July 2019, paras 89–90.

> the fallacy of this assertion in this context is apparent: neither is the commission of such "ordinary" crimes as murder, rape, fraud or theft properly within the scope of military duties. They are crimes and breaches of discipline. That is why they are offences under military and criminal law, just as participation in extrajudicial executions, enforced disappearances and torture would be.[86]

As seen above, in common law systems, offences being "disciplinary" or "military" are not put in opposition to them being criminal or serious, because they are tied to the status of the perpetrator, and practical matters related to the constitution of judicial systems, rather than the nature of the offence.

Broadening a regional trend to the international level raises a couple of concerns: first, while these conclusions may be correct for the region, these cases have been (perhaps mistakenly) cited in IHRL documents claiming they should also be applicable broadly under international law; second, such jurisprudence may preclude common law States (which do exist, albeit as a minority, within the Inter-American System) from being in compliance with their regional human rights obligations, as the jurisprudential conclusions of the IACtHR was not developed with common law jurisdictions in mind. Chapter 6 will explore some of the jurisdictional difficulties related to armed conflict which can particularly affect common law States. It is suggested that the "military nexus" debate is therefore too region-specific-focused and should not be generalised at the international level when commenting on the appropriateness of military justice systems *in general* under international law. Rather, if any trends are to be extrapolated from the experiences of Latin American States as to when military jurisdiction should be restricted, these would benefit from being focused on the specific procedural flaws of the military systems, and from considering the broader context of impunity. The rest of this book explores such elements.

This is not to say that the debate does not have value, or that common law systems cannot change. One impact of international law on domestic systems is the convergence to a certain degree of certain legal principles, and a less marked difference between different legal traditions.[87] For example, and as will be seen in Chapter 4, the UK has recently taken an approach to the concept of separation of powers which is more closely related to the US and continental Europe approach than was previously the case. Nevertheless, the debate on the appropriate scope of military jurisdiction must be appropriately framed if it is to have a serious impact on combating impunity.

86 Gibson (2008) (n. 57), p. 39.
87 Denton (n. 7), pp. 26–27.

Jurisdiction over serious violations of IHRL and IHL

As a final point of reflection on the draft Decaux principles, it is worth considering the possibility of excluding serious human rights violations from the scope of military jurisdiction, and the implications this may have on jurisdiction over serious violations of IHL. The examples given in Draft Principle 8 of serious human rights violations would also simultaneously be serious violations of IHL (if committed in an armed conflict), namely "extrajudicial executions, enforced disappearances and torture." Military commanders do have a responsibility under IHL to act to repress such offences, and international law in general does not prohibit the use of military jurisdiction to investigate and prosecute such offences. As will be seen in Chapter 3, what is much clearer than *who* should investigate and prosecute, is that such serious violations of international law must be *effectively* investigated and prosecuted.

In order to gain a more general understanding of when military jurisdiction should be legitimately restricted, i.e., when they may not effectively investigate, it is therefore important to understand the real problems behind some of the atrocities committed by military systems and redirect the debate to a clear understanding of the sources of impunity. It has been rightfully pointed out that the issues being considered in the draft Decaux principles are not issues of "military nexus" but issues to do with systematic impunity.[88] The issue appears to be "whether military courts in a given state are 'real' courts possessed of sufficient integrity, independence and impartiality to try such grave offences. [...] If they are not, then there is a broader systemic problem with the particular military justice system which goes to its ability to properly try any sort of grave offence, not just these particular ones."[89] If a system is unable to effectively adjudicate over IHRL violations, it may be necessary to question its ability to effectively carry out any sort of justice. Therefore, one must consider which types of systemic problems are possible or likely to arise in a military context, and one must understand whether and how they can be overcome. This is also important because if the issue in a military justice system is the lack of integrity, independence, and impartiality, there is no reason to suggest as a blanket statement that the civilian justice system is any less flawed, especially in armed conflict. Chapter 7 will explore the topic of systematic impunity in more detail.

The question at the domestic level then remains as to who may most effectively investigate serious violations of IHL (which may also be serious violations of IHRL), which is understood to be an issue of independence and impartiality. The rest of this book attempts to answer this question. It will consider how some domestic systems do use military jurisdiction over a wide scope of violations, but often have specific provisions for "serious" violations to increase independence and impartiality. Furthermore, a case will be made

88 Gibson (2008) (n. 57), pp. 39–40.
89 Gibson (2008) (n. 57), pp. 39–40.

that in the context of systematic impunity leading to pattern of violations and a repeated failure to investigate, the increased likelihood of impunity may justify enhanced safeguards of independence and impartiality.

Conclusion

Although the creation of early military justice systems was based on the need to maintain discipline for reasons of military efficiency, its evolution over time demonstrates that many factors have come to influence the constitution of modern military justice systems. Military justice systems have had to align themselves with evolving understandings of justice, including through the development of international law. As suspects and victims have gained recognition as rights-holders, procedural guarantees and protections were needed to maintain military justice systems as legitimate "justice" institutions. Where such systems did not adapt and change to the evolving standards, domestic, regional, or international bodies have condemned them as archaic remnants of history.

Military jurisdiction has almost always been subject to restrictions, including those based on what may be considered a "military offence." Nevertheless, the different understandings of jurisdictional scope have affected the constitution of military justice in common and civil law countries. This difference has become important in the debate on the scope of military jurisdiction under international law, especially through the dissemination of the draft Decaux principles.

In engaging this debate, it is important to separate the "militaryness" of such systems from their procedural flaws. Although the historical rationale for military jurisdiction has evolved, it has not, in my view, been made completely redundant. As long as military operations exist, and while armed conflicts continue to be fought by military personnel, there will necessarily be an element of military justice present alongside this. This is because the fundamental tenet of discipline is necessary to the lawful conduct of armed conflict, at least while individual human soldiers are still the principal constituents of military forces. This does not mean that all types of offences and all personnel involved in judicial proceedings concerning the military must be encompassed in "military jurisdiction." Rather, as will be made clear in subsequent chapters, what matters is that these judicial proceedings be effective in combating impunity.

3 The obligation to investigate effectively under international law

Introduction

On 23 January 1991, during an armed operation in the locality of Las Palmeras in Putumayo, Colombia, members of the National Police (part of the Colombian armed forces) opened fire from a helicopter, wounding a six-year-old boy on his way to school, and subsequently executed six civilian bystanders. The officers implicated tampered with, concealed, and destroyed evidence, including dressing some of the victims in military clothing to make them appear as "subversives" in a supposed armed clash, and threatened and intimidated relatives and witnesses.[1] An initial five-day investigation carried out by their superior cleared the five participants of all wrongdoing.[2] A subsequent investigation opened by the military criminal justice system lasted for seven years without ever identifying, prosecuting, or convicting any of the responsible parties.[3]

On 6 December 1991, during the Croatian war of independence, several hundred shells were fired by the Yugoslav's People's Army (JNA) on the old city centre of Dubrovnik, killing 19 people, injuring 60, and destroying buildings which were part of a UNESCO world heritage site, provoking international condemnation. The forces involved were under the immediate command of Admiral Jokić, who gave unqualified assurances to his superiors that he would carry out a "thorough investigation" and deal with the perpetrators. His investigation, which consisted of "a few written statements and reports," led to no further criminal or administrative action. The Captain who had commanded the attack was promoted.[4]

1 IACtHR, *Las Palmeras v Colombia*, Ser. C No. 67, Judgment of 4 February 2000 (Merits), para. 2.
2 IACtHR, *Las Palmeras v Colombia*, Ser. C No. 67, Judgment of 4 February 2000 (Merits), para. 49.
3 IACtHR, *Las Palmeras v Colombia*, Ser. C No. 67, Judgment of 4 February 2000 (Merits), para. 53.
4 ICTY, *Prosecutor v Pavle Strugar*, IT-01-42-T, Trial Chamber II, Judgment of 31 January 2005, paras 173–174, 436.

DOI: 10.4324/9781003360223-3

Examples of such ineffective investigations are unfortunately easy to find,[5] and are often carried out in such a way so as to attempt to cover up possible violations, or to do "damage control." They can, however, also be the source of some of the biggest public scandals and subsequent (expensive and time-consuming) inquiries into historical events.

But how should an investigation into possible violations be carried out under international law? Where does the duty come from and what standards apply? Although a duty to investigate is rarely explicitly mentioned in international law treaties, such a duty has been inferred in different ways through State practice, adjudication, and other authoritative interpretation of treaty law. Investigations have been found to be central for the general implementation of treaties in relation to "serious" violations of these bodies of law. They have also been found as an important part of the duty to provide effective remedy or reparation for serious violations of international law. This chapter provides an overview of the developments related to a duty to investigate a possible violation of international human rights law (IHRL), international criminal law (ICL), and general laws of State responsibility, to elucidate the sources of the obligation and the legal framework applicable to investigations under international humanitarian law (IHL). It establishes that investigations carried out in fulfilment of State responsibility with relation to serious violations under these bodies of law must be carried out "effectively." By paying attention to the reasoning given by interpretative bodies for the development of the duty from various sources, it is possible to develop a cross-cutting explanation of what is meant by an "effective" investigation, and why it is a necessary element of the duty to investigate. This, in turn, enables an assessment of how military investigations may, or may not, comply with the applicable international legal standards.

While much literature on the duty to investigate arising under these bodies of law has focused on specific provisions stemming from treaty law (e.g., on the duty to investigate right to life violations),[6] this chapter takes a broader approach to a State's responsibility with regard to its obligations for all serious violations of IHL and IHRL. It considers investigative duties arising under

5 See further examples in Sepinwall, A. J., "Failure to Punish: Command Responsibility in Domestic and International Law," *Michigan Journal of International Law* Vol. 30 No. 2 (2008).

6 See, e.g., Leach, P., Murray, R., & Sandoval, C., "The Duty to Investigate Right to Life Violations Across Three Regional Systems: Harmonisation or Fragmentation of IHRL?" in Buckley, C. M., Donald, A., & Leach, P., *Towards Convergence in IHRL: Approaches of Regional and International Systems*, Brill (2017); Chevalier-Watts, J., "Effective Investigations under Article 2 of the ECHR: Securing the Right to Life or an Onerous Burden on a State?" *European Journal of International Law* Vol. 21 No. 3 (2010); Margalit, A., *Investigating Civilian Casualties in Time of Armed Conflict and Belligerent Occupation: Manoeuvring between Legal Regimes and Paradigms for the Use of Force*, Brill (2018); Quénivet, N., "The Obligation to Investigate after a Potential Breach of Article 2 ECHR in an Extra-Territorial Context: Mission Impossible for the Armed Forces?" *Netherlands Quarterly of Human Rights* Vol. 20 No. 1 (2019).

any provision of international law under these bodies of law, and the fact that such investigations may be criminal or non-criminal in nature. Such a broad approach is necessary in order to elucidate more general principles on *when* and *how* investigations should be carried out, beyond the context of specific treaty provisions or rights. This matters in the context of IHL where the lack of interpretative bodies means specific standards have not been developed, and where the concept of "rights" cannot be transposed as it exists under IHRL. A cross-cutting concept of an effective investigation is therefore useful to provide some clarity as to the interplay of the bodies of law when it may be unclear which standards should take precedence. If, under international law, the obligation for a State is to carry out an "effective" investigation into a possible serious violation of various bodies of law, then the goal of achieving this effectiveness should dictate the way in which such an investigation should be carried out. Specifically, it is hoped that a coherent cross-cutting concept of effectiveness can clarify the practical steps to be taken where uncertainty remains as to how the duty to investigate must be applied under IHL in which the standards are the least developed. This will be an indispensable premise to the development of the rest of the book regarding the applicable standards of independence and impartiality to investigations.

A Duty to Investigate Under IHL

Despite the lack of explicit treaty provisions to this effect, it is clear today that States have an obligation to investigate certain violations of IHL. The source of this duty to investigate has been explored elsewhere,[7] but there is value in re-tracing briefly the main legal sources and the role of other bodies of law in establishing this obligation, insofar as this will also inform the standards applicable, including those of independence and impartiality. First, however, a comment must be made on the approach taken throughout this research on the interplay of different bodies of international law.

A Comment on the Interplay of Bodies of International Law

In part due to the lack of specialised interpretative bodies, and limited literature on the topic under IHL, a lot of this research uses other bodies of

7 Lubell, N., Pejic, J., & Simmons, C., *Guidelines on Investigating Violations of International Humanitarian Law: Law, Policy, and Good Practice*, Geneva Academy/ICRC (2019); "Second Report of the Public Commission to Examine the Maritime Incident of 31 May 2010: Israel's Mechanisms for Examining and Investigating Complaints and Claims of Violations of the Laws of Armed Conflict According to International Law" (Israel, February 2013) [Second Turkel Report]. For an overview of the evolution of the duty to investigate under IHRL and IHL, see Simmons, C., "Investigations in Armed Conflict" in Kolb, R., Gaggioli, G., & Kilibarda, P., *Research Handbook on Human Rights and Humanitarian Law: Further Reflections and Perspectives*, Edward Elgar Publishing (2022).

law to understand legal concepts and practical applications of how a duty to investigate may operate under IHL, especially IHRL and ICL. It is not the purpose of this chapter to re-open or address the scope of arguments on the interplay of bodies of law, which has comprehensively been done elsewhere.[8] However, it is relevant to explain the extensive use of IHRL to address the duty to investigate, as well as the standards of independence and impartiality in the following chapter.

In general, this book takes the approach that IHRL and IHL are complementary bodies of law which may usefully inform each other on the application and interpretation of treaty provisions.[9] The "filling the gaps" function of the complementary approach enables looking at IHRL to understand what existing obligations under IHL may look like.[10] As will be seen below, IHRL bodies have had the opportunity to interpret in detail how the duty to "ensure" respect with treaty provisions implies a duty to investigate violations of such treaties. This, alongside other developments in public international law, enables a coherent interpretation of existing IHL obligations as implying a duty to investigate. Furthermore, it provides useful information on the content of the duty to investigate violations of IHL, once such a duty has been established. Insofar as the obligation to investigate may be a procedural or "secondary" obligation found under "primary" rules of IHL, it is IHRL "which can provide us with an understanding of the elements required to determine whether a specific procedure meets the necessary standard."[11] This has been done, for example, in interpreting the content of fair trial rights,[12] or the content of the obligation of humane treatment and the prohibition of torture and cruel, inhuman, or degrading treatment,[13] which both exist as primary obligations under IHL. Furthermore, "investigative measures taken in response [to war crimes] are not an integral part of the military operation and are not necessarily

8 See, e.g., Prud'homme, N., "*Lex Specialis:* Oversimplifying a More Complex and Multifaceted Relationship?" *Israel Law Review* Vol. 40 No. 2 (2007), p. 362; Gowlland-Debbas, V., & Gaggioli, G., "The Relationship Between International Human Rights and Humanitarian Law: An Overview" in Kolb, R., & Gaggioli, G., *Research Handbook on Human Rights and Humanitarian Law*, Edward Elgar Publishing (2013); Droege, C., "The Interplay between International Humanitarian Law and International Human Rights Law in Situations of Armed Conflict," *Israel Law Review* Vol. 40 No. 2 (2007), p. 310; Lubell, N., & Prud'homme, N., "Impact of Human Rights Law" in Liivoja, R., & McCormack, T., *Routledge Handbook of the Law of Armed Conflict*, Routledge (2016). For a succinct explanation with regard to investigations, see Margalit (2018) (n. 6), pp. 77–80.

9 Prud'homme (n. 8); UN Human Rights Committee, "General Comment No. 36 on Article 6 of the International Covenant on Civil and Political Rights, on the Right to Life" (30 October 2018), CCPR/C/GC/, para. 64.

10 Lubell & Prud'homme (n. 8); Margalit (2018) (n. 6), p. 79.

11 Lubell & Prud'homme (n. 8), p. 113.

12 Lubell & Prud'homme (n. 8), p. 113.

13 Henckaerts, J.-M., & Doswald-Beck, L., *Customary International Humanitarian Law*, ICRC (2006) [ICRC Customary Study], Rules 87, 90, 100.

performed by those involved in combat."[14] Their removal from the context of military operations arguably justifies further resort to standards developed under law enforcement paradigms, using the same judicial procedures, just as in the case of fair trial provisions. In this way, exploring the standards of independence and impartiality as developed under IHRL usefully informs the standards applicable under IHL, as long as the contextual framework of reasonableness is maintained.

The use of ICL in relation to IHL is slightly different, although analogous to the interplay with IHRL in some contexts. First, it is worth pointing out that ICL and IHL are separate bodies of public international law. ICL covers international crimes beyond those found under IHL and is not restricted to situations of armed conflict. IHL, in turn, does not solely focus on individual criminal responsibility, but primarily deals with State responsibility. Nevertheless, there is a definite overlap. ICL evolved from a need to confirm the customary international law surrounding the individual criminal prosecution of the most serious violations of international law, including IHL.[15] As opposed to the previous emphasis on State responsibility for such violations, ICL focused on the obligation to investigate, prosecute, and punish individual perpetrators.[16] ICL therefore focuses on one aspect of the enforcement of IHL, namely, "the punishment of individuals as war criminals,"[17] although with its own body of international law it has been framed beyond IHL.[18] The role of specialised ICL courts and tribunals (which do not exist for IHL) have been instrumental in developing the scope and content of a duty to investigate war crimes. In this way, the jurisprudence of ICL courts also aids in "filling the gaps" of parallel existing obligations under IHL. This is, however, recognising that not all elements of IHL will be adequately covered by provisions developed under ICL. The implementation of IHL is broader than the prosecution of war crimes. It is also a body of law which deals with State responsibility to implement treaty provisions, and this book considers what this means for investigation obligations.

Finally, an encompassing approach of how the duty to investigate applies under different branches of public international law may be further justified by the fact that IHL is rarely to be interpreted as an isolated body of law. The same incident occurring in armed conflict can affect a State's responsibility under IHRL, ICL, and IHL simultaneously. It is therefore important to understand the obligations arising under the different bodies of law which may

14 Margalit (2018) (n. 6), p. 68.

15 Fleck, D., *The Handbook of International Humanitarian Law*, Oxford University Press (2nd ed.) (2008), pp. 678–686.

16 Fleck (n. 15), pp. 678–686. There is room to say that this emphasis may well have reversed in contemporary discourse of international law.

17 Fleck (n. 15), p. 685.

18 ICL also extends to the acts of genocide and crimes against humanity which do not require an armed conflict nexus.

all be applicable. In all contexts, it is clear that the specificities of each relevant body of law must be taken into account.[19] It has been my intention to avoid cherry-picking from different bodies of law; instead, I have sought to develop a comprehensive picture of how existing obligations under IHL may usefully and legitimately be informed by other developments under international law. The practical elements of the harmonisation of these bodies of law are also worth pointing out, insofar as IHRL and IHL require a contextual approach to what is reasonable within the context.[20]

Ensuring the Implementation of Treaty Provisions

There is not one source of a duty to investigate under international law, but rather chronological developments from interpretative bodies have found duties to investigate for different reasons which has created a network of different sources.

Very generally, an implicit obligation to investigate certain alleged violations of treaty provisions can be found under general rules of State responsibility insofar as a State must comply with its international treaty obligations under the general legal principle of *pacta sunt servanda*.[21] This primary rule of State responsibility is considered customary international law,[22] and is also necessary to the common sense of the concept of obligations. Compliance can take on many different forms, such as passing domestic legislation to enforce international treaties, and ensuring structural guarantees to prevent violations.[23] It is not limited to criminalisation measures but includes broader effective implementation measures of treaty provisions. This obligation of compliance with treaty obligations is often phrased in IHRL treaties as "ensuring" human rights, and under IHL as "respecting and ensuring respect" with IHL provisions.

The extensive jurisprudence of international human rights bodies is key to understanding the evolution of an implied duty to investigate as part of the implementation of treaty obligations. There are a few legal texts which explicitly mention investigations,[24] but in general the principal focus on inves-

19 As an example, see Chapter 6 on reasonableness under IHL versus other bodies of law.

20 *Guidelines on Investigating Violations of International Humanitarian Law* (n. 7), para. 34.

21 Vienna Convention on the Law of Treaties, 1155 UNTS 331 (1980), Art. 26; International Law Commission, *Articles on Responsibility of States for Internationally Wrongful Acts* (2001) [Articles on State Responsibility], Art. 1.

22 Sassòli, M., "State Responsibility for Violations of International Humanitarian Law," *International Review of the Red Cross* Vol. 84 No. 846 (2002), pp. 401–402.

23 UN Human Rights Committee, "General Comment No. 31: The Nature of the General Legal Obligation Imposed on State Parties to the Covenant" (29 March 2004), CCPR/C/Rev.1/Add.13 [General Comment No. 31], para. 7; Sassòli, M., "The Implementation of International Humanitarian Law: Current and Inherent Challenges," *Yearbook of International Humanitarian Law* Vol. 10 (2007), p. 46.

24 Convention against Torture and Other Cruel, Inhuman or Degrading Treatment or Punishment, 1465 UNTS 85 (1984), Art. 6; International Convention for the Protection of

tigative obligations under IHRL has been in relation to the development of an implicit "procedural" duty to investigate, as found under certain provisions of the International Covenant on Civil and Political Rights (ICCPR) and the three regional human rights treaties. The reasoning in all of these cases relates to a logical inference: in order to uphold its obligations under a human rights convention, a State may need to investigate allegations of serious violations of said convention. Failing to do so would void the meaning of the rights, as their implementation would be ineffective.

Initial emphasis was made on passing domestic legislation to criminalise human rights violations, which subsequently led to the logical step that violations of such legislation needed to be criminally investigated.[25] Yet the implementation of human rights obligations cannot be restricted to criminalisation and criminal investigations into their violations. Insofar as human rights obligations are obligations on States, it is States, not individuals, who have responsibility for their implementation and who therefore also must be held accountable for their violation. For example, finding and fixing structural flaws in the way in which human rights are implemented is one element of State accountability which necessarily goes beyond the criminal responsibility of the individuals which make up State agents. This move away from the focus on criminalisation in investigations has been made clear in interpretation by the Human Rights Committee,[26] but most notably through the case law of regional human rights bodies. All three regional human rights bodies have considered a duty to investigate as arising from the general obligation under Article 1 of the respective treaties to ensure that the rights within the treaties are upheld.[27] Other international human rights bodies have also extensively

All Persons from Enforced Disappearance, 2716 UNTS 3 (2006), Art. 12; Inter-American Convention to Prevent and Punish Torture, Organization of American States Treaty Series 67 (1985), Art. 8; Inter-American Convention on the Forced Disappearance of Persons (1994), Art. VI; Principles on the Effective Prevention and Investigation of Extra-Legal, Arbitrary and Summary Executions, UN ECOSOC Res. 1989/65 (1989), para. 9; United Nations Basic Principles on the Use of Force and Firearms by Law Enforcement Officials, UNGA Res. 45/166 (1990); UN OHCHR, Basic Principles and Guidelines on the Right to a Remedy and Reparation for Victims of Gross Violations of International Human Rights Law and Serious Violations of International Humanitarian Law, A/RES/60/147 (2005) [Basic Principles on the Right to Remedy], para. 22; UN OHCHCR, Revision of the UN Manual on the Effective Prevention and Investigation of Extra-Legal, Arbitrary and Summary Executions (2016) [Minnesota Protocol].

25 UN Human Rights Committee, "General Comment No. 20: Article 7 (Prohibition of Torture, or Other Cruel, Inhuman or Degrading Treatment or Punishment)" (10 March 1992), para. 1; General Comment No. 31 (n. 23), paras 15, 18; see also General Comment No. 36 (n. 9), paras 27–29.

26 General Comment No. 31 (n. 23), paras 15 and 18; General Comment No. 36 (n. 9), paras 27–29.

27 IACtHR, *Velásquez Rodríguez v Honduras*, Ser. C No. 4, Judgment of 29 July 1988 (Merits), para. 167; ECtHR, *McCann and Others v UK*, App. No. 18984/91, Judgment of 17 September 1995, para. 161; African Charter on Human and Peoples' Rights (ACHPR), *Commission*

addressed States' investigative obligations.[28] Exploring how these systems derived and developed this duty, it becomes evident that it goes beyond investigations into individual criminal responsibility. An investigation under the obligation to "ensure" human rights must take into account a much broader context including the State's responsibility.

A Procedural Duty Under IHL

A similar procedural duty to investigate certain violations to ensure the implementation of treaty provisions may be inferred under IHL. The obligation for States to criminally repress war crimes is found in the grave breaches provisions of the Geneva Conventions of 1949 and Additional Protocol I, which require State Parties to provide "effective penal sanctions" for grave breaches, and to "search for" and "bring [...] before its own courts" perpetrators of such crimes.[29] Whereas the texts of the Conventions mention grave breaches, it is clear that customary international law today extends this obligation to war crimes, including those committed in non-international armed conflicts.[30] This has certain implications for the obligation to investigate: in order to bring an alleged perpetrator before a court, a State must first carry out a criminal investigation, for reasons of fair trial of the accused and general principles of

---

Nationale des Droits de l'Homme et des Libertés v Chad, App. 74/92, Decision on Merits (11 October 1995), para. 20; Leach, Murray, & Sandoval (n. 6), p. 34.

28 See, e.g., "Report of the Special Rapporteur on Extrajudicial, Summary or Arbitrary Executions, Philip Alston: Civil and Political Rights, Including the Questions of Disappearances and Summary Executions" (8 March 2006), E/CN4/2006/53; "Study on Targeted Killings by the Special Rapporteur on Extrajudicial, Summary or Arbitrary Executions, Philip Alston," A/HRC/14/24/Add.6 (28 May 2010); "Report of the Committee of Independent Experts in International Humanitarian and Human Rights Laws to Monitor and Assess Any Domestic, Legal or Other Proceedings Undertaken by Both the Government of Israel and the Palestinian Side, in the Light of General Assembly Resolution 254/64, Including the Independence, Effectiveness, Genuineness of These Investigations and Their Conformity with International Standards, A/HRC/15/50 (23 September 2010) [Tomuschat Report]; "Report of the Special Rapporteur on Extrajudicial, Summary or Arbitrary Executions, Philip Alston: Promotion and Protection of All Human Rights, Civil, Political, Economic, Social and Cultural Rights, Including the Right to Development," A/HRC/8/3 (2 May 2008).

29 Geneva Convention I for the Amelioration of the Condition of the Wounded and Sick in Armed Forces in the Field, 75 UNTS 31 (1949) [GCI], Art. 49; Geneva Convention II for the Amelioration of the Condition of Wounded, Sick and Shipwrecked Members of Armed Forces at Sea, 75 UNTS 85 (1949) [GCII], Art. 50; Geneva Convention III Relative to the Treatment of Prisoners of War, 75 UNTS 135 (1949) [GCIII], Art. 129; Geneva Convention IV Relative to the Protection of Civilian Persons in Time of War, 75 UNTS 287 (1949) [GCIV], Art. 146; Protocol I Additional to the Geneva Conventions of 12 August 1949 and Relating to the Protection of Victims of International Armed Conflicts, 1125 UNTS 3 (1977) [API], Art. 85.

30 ICRC Customary Study (n. 13), Rule 158; Rome Statute of the International Criminal Court, 2187 UNTS 3 (1998) [ICC Statute], Art. 8(a); Dinstein, Y., *The Conduct of Hostilities Under the Law of International Armed Conflict*, Cambridge University Press (2016), pp. 298–300.

justice. It is commonly accepted in all modern judicial systems that the finding of criminal guilt must be set at a very high threshold (for example, beyond reasonable doubt), and based on the best possible gathering of facts. An investigation may also be needed even in the case of extradition.[31] The customary international obligation of *aut dedere aut judicare* for international crimes (which goes beyond IHL) is now understood to include the State obligation to investigate such crimes.[32]

Despite commanders holding individual responsibilities to investigate, it is not the case that the State obligation to investigate war crimes is transferred to military commanders. Indeed, the ultimate responsibility for the repression of war crimes under IHL still lies with the State. Rather, it is the case that the responsibility to investigate war crimes on States implies that the domestic investigative mechanisms, including the way in which commanders' responsibilities are implemented in domestic legislation and practice, must be effective. A commander's responsibility to act in an appropriate manner with regard to the actions of their subordinates can only be framed within this context.[33]

Although the repression of war crimes has been the focus of accountability for violations of IHL since the Second World War, as with human rights violations, the obligations under this body of law go beyond the criminalisation of the provisions. Similarly to the developments in relation to States' duties to "ensure" human rights, the duty to "ensure respect" with the provisions of IHL as required by Common Article 1 to the four Geneva Conventions of 1949 has been interpreted as requiring proactive measures of implementation and prevention such as investigations.[34] For the repression of war crimes, this requires a criminal investigation, as explored above. Yet the repression of war crimes may arguably also require broader contextual measures to be implemented for the more general prevention and repression, such as investigating any possible contextual factors or systemic issues which may be causing the violations, such as poor training or organisational culture.

Furthermore, not all violations of IHL constitute war crimes, but they all do nonetheless require suppression under international law. IHL treaties mandate

31 International Law Commission, "The Obligation to Extradite or Prosecute (*aut dedere aut judicare*)," *Yearbook of the International Law Commission* (2014), vol. II, para. 17.

32 ICJ, "Questions Relating to the Obligation to Prosecute or Extradite (Belgium v Senegal)," Judgment of 20 July 2012, para. 85; Kreß, C., "Reflection on the *Iudicare* Limb of the Grave Breaches Regime," *Journal of International Criminal Justice* Vol. 7 (2009), p. 801; International Law Commission, "The Obligation to Extradite or Prosecute (*aut dedere aut judicare*)," *Yearbook of the International Law Commission* (2014), vol. II (Part Two).

33 See Chapter 5 on the current international legal framework surrounding a commander's responsibility to investigate.

34 Hampson, F., "An Investigation of Alleged Violations of The Law of Armed Conflict," *Israel Yearbook on Human Rights* Vol. 46 (2016), p. 12; Pictet, J., "The Geneva Conventions of 12 August 1949: Commentary," ICRC (1960) [Pictet Commentary], Commentary to Art. 1 GCI, p. 26; ICRC, "Updated Commentary to First Geneva Convention" (2016) [ICRC, Updated Commentary to GCI], Commentary to Art. 1, paras 121 and 124.

the "suppression" of all other breaches other than grave breaches.[35] The term "suppress" is also found in relation to the duty of commanders to suppress and report all breaches of the Conventions and Additional Protocol I.[36] Unlike the obligation to search for and bring to trial, the concepts of "ensuring respect" and "suppressing" do not automatically implicitly require criminal investigations, or any investigation at all. Rather, what action is required to implement each provision, or suppress a violation, may differ in each case. The scope of such broader non-criminal implementation activities under a State's IHL obligations may include investigations into systemic issues which may have caused or contributed towards violations (whether war crimes or not).[37] This is similar to the procedural requirements under IHRL, for example under the right to life, requiring the investigation into the planning and other contextual elements which may have led to a death.[38]

Investigations as Effective Remedies

There is a separate yet related source for the duty to investigate as part of the obligation to provide effective remedy or reparation for violations of international law,[39] under the secondary rules of State responsibility. The duty to investigate as part of an effective remedy has been developed in detail under IHRL, and it is argued below that there is room to extend some of this rationale to effective remedies for violations of IHL. It is also suggested that investigations, as part of an effective remedy, are not always completely separate from the general implementation obligations of treaties (e.g., the obligation to ensure respect). The concept of providing effective remedies in itself is often seen as part of the general implementation of substantive treaty provisions. Nevertheless, there is value in considering the separate obligations arising under the principle of remedial action.

It is a general principle of international law that a State responsible for an internationally wrongful act must provide reparation.[40] Insofar as States are

35 See references above, n. 29.

36 API (n. 29), Art. 87; Cohen, A., & Shany, Y., "Beyond the Grave Breaches Regime: The Duty to Investigate Alleged Violations of International Law Governing Armed Conflicts," *Yearbook of International Humanitarian Law* Vol. 14 (2011), p. 44; Hampson (n. 34), p. 12.

37 Hampson (n. 34), p. 16.

38 Hampson (n. 34), p. 6; ECtHR, *McCann and Others v UK* (n. 27).

39 The concept of a "remedy" for a violation of international law is usually understood as a broader category of actions than "reparation," the latter having specific implications for actions consequential to an internationally wrongful act. However, the terms are sometimes used interchangeably, and may differ depending on the language used. Shelton, D., *Remedies in International Human Rights Law*, Oxford University Press (3rd ed.) (2015), pp. 16–17; Evans, C., *The Right to Reparation in International Law for Victims of Armed Conflict*, Cambridge University Press (2012), p. 13.

40 Gillard, E.-C., "Reparations for Violations of International Humanitarian Law," *International Review of the Red Cross* Vol. 85 No. 851 (2003), pp. 530–531; Permanent Court of

bound by "primary" obligations arising under treaty and/or customary international law, a breach of such an obligation entails certain "secondary" rules as consequences for these breaches.[41] These secondary rules of State responsibility are codified in the ILC Articles on Responsibility of States for Internationally Wrongful Acts (Articles on State Responsibility),[42] and include the prevention of violations, their cessation where they occur, as well as providing guarantees of non-repetition and reparation after they occur.[43] Reparations under international law are usually understood to include restitution, compensation, and/or just satisfaction.[44] The guarantees of non-repetition, although a separate obligation, may also be part of reparation.[45] The obligation to provide reparation only arises after a breach has been committed, although provisions can also serve as a preventive measure for future violations.[46]

The general obligation under international law to provide reparation for an internationally wrongful act as a secondary rule of State responsibility has taken on a very specific meaning under IHRL. In fact, the obligation to provide an effective remedy has been codified in some human rights treaties and is therefore arguably also a primary rule in such cases.[47] In this way, they are obligations additional to the positive provision of other human rights and entail their own separate responsibility. The right to a remedy is, however, distinct from other human rights insofar as it necessarily arises only *after* a violation has occurred. Investigations may serve multiple remedial actions. They are often understood as being part of the satisfaction element of a right to remedy, as a form of reparation for the non-material harms which cannot be addressed by restitution or compensation.[48] The elements of satisfaction are amongst other things understood to include the "verification of facts and full public disclosure of the truth,"[49] to which an investigation can obviously contribute. This also ties into the role of investigations within the broader concept of the victims' and their families' right to truth.[50] Nevertheless, investigations can also serve

International Justice, *Factory at Chorzow (Claim for Indemnity) case (Germany v Poland)*, (*Merits*), PCIJ Ser. A No. 17 (1928), p. 29.

41 Sassòli (2002) (n. 22), pp. 401–402.

42 Articles on State Responsibility (n. 21), Arts 28–33.

43 Sassòli (2002) (n. 22), pp. 401–402; Shelton (n. 39), p. 94.

44 Shelton (n. 39), p. 94; Articles on State Responsibility (n. 21), Art. 34.

45 Articles on State Responsibility (n. 21), Commentary to Article 37, para. 5.

46 Articles on State Responsibility (n. 21), Commentary to Article 30, para. 11.

47 International Covenant on Civil and Political Rights (1966) 999 UNTS 171 [ICCPR], Art. 2; American Convention on Human Rights, "Pact of San Jose" (1969) [ACHR], Art. 25; European Convention for the Protection of Human Rights and Fundamental Freedoms (1950) ETS 5 [ECHR], Art. 13.

48 Evans (n. 39), p. 45; Hoss, C., "Satisfaction," *Oxford Public International Law* (April 2011), para. 3.

49 Basic Principles on the Right to Remedy (n. 24), para. 22(b).

50 IACtHR, *Bámaca Velásquez v Guatemala*, Ser. C No. 70, Judgment of 25 November 2000 (Merits), para. 201; Evans (n. 39), p. 51; Szoke-Burke, S., "Searching for the Right to Truth:

important purposes for other elements of reparations. For example, whether a remedy is needed or not, and what the content of this remedy should be, may not be made clear until an investigation is carried out.[51] Furthermore, the need to guarantee non-repetition may require an investigation into the causes of a violation in order to understand why it occurred and set up the necessary preventive measures to ensure it does not happen again.[52] It can also fulfil other purposes, for example, bringing perpetrators to justice. All three regional human rights bodies have recommended or ordered investigations as reparation or remedy once they have themselves established human rights violations.[53] The Human Rights Committee has also emphasised the role of investigations in providing effective remedy in country procedures.[54]

Unlike IHRL, what constitutes adequate reparation for violations of IHL is not clear under international law.[55] The development of the role of investigations in remedial action for human rights violations has informed the development of the "UN Basic Principles on the Right to a Remedy and Reparation for Victims of Gross Violations of IHRL and Serious Violations of IHL," a soft law document endorsed by the UN General Assembly.[56] While these principles are widely used, their legal bases for covering violations of IHL (as opposed only to violations of IHRL) is not always clear.

Looking at IHL violations from the angle of the secondary rules of State responsibility, it is suggested that investigations can have a role in the provision

---

The Impact of International Human Rights Law on National Transitional Justice Policies," *Berkeley Journal of International Law* (2015), pp. 532–535; Ferrer Mac-Gregor, E., "The Right to Truth as an Autonomous Right Under the Inter-American Human Rights System," *Mexican Law Review* Vol. 9 (2016), pp. 122–126.

51 Mowbray, A., *Cases, Materials, and Commentary on the European Convention on Human Rights*, Oxford University Press (3rd ed.) (2012), p. 807; ECtHR, *Ilhan v Turkey*, App. No. 22277/93, Judgment of 27 June 2000, para. 103.

52 Shelton (n. 39), p. 94.

53 IACtHR: *Case of the "White Van" (Paniagua-Morales et al.) v Guatemala*, Ser C No 37, Judgment of 8 March 1998 (Merits), para. 178; Ibáñez Rivas, J. M., "Artículo 25. Protección Judicial" in Steiner, C., & Uribe, P., Convención Americana sobre Derechos Humanos: Comentario, Konrad Adenauer Stiftung (2014), p. 632; ECtHR: *Aslakhanova and Others v Russia*, Apps. Nos. 2944/06 and 8300/07, 50184/07, 332/08, 42509/10, Judgment of 18 December 2012, para. 221; ACHPR, *Malawi Africa Association, Amnesty International, Ms Sarr Diop, Union interafricaine des droits de l'Homme and RADDHO, Collectif des veuves et ayants-droits, Association mauritanienne des droits de l'Homme v Mauritania*, App. No. 54/91, 61/91, 96/93, 98/93, 164/97, 196/97, 210/98l, Decision on Merits (11 May 2000), Recommendation 1; Leach, Murray & Sandoval (n. 6), pp. 59 and 63.

54 HRC, *Rodríguez v Uruguay*, Communication No. 322/1988 (9 August 1994), para. 14; *Jegatheeswara v Sri Lanka*, Communication No. 950/2000 (31 July 2003), paras 9.5, 6.2, 11; *El Hassy v Libya*, Communication No. 1422/2005 (24 October 2007); *Sharma v Nepal*, Communication No. 1469/2006 (28 October 2008). Evans (n. 39), p. 49.

55 Gillard (n. 40), pp. 530–531; Zegveld, L., "Remedies for Victims of Violations of International Humanitarian Law," *International Review of the Red Cross* Vol. 85 No. 851 (2003), p. 500.

56 Basic Principles on the Right to Remedy (n. 24).

of reparation for violations. The section above established that investigation and prosecution already constitute obligations under certain primary rules of State responsibility for IHL. It was also seen that in IHRL, investigations have been considered as constituting part of adequate reparation for human rights violations. It has been suggested that "human rights law can complement [IHL] when it comes to secondary rules, meaning the remedy available to victims of [an IHL] violation, since the question of remedy is not sufficiently regulated by [IHL]."[57] It is therefore possible that investigating violations of IHL could constitute a reasonable measure which should be expected of States as part of their international obligations for internationally wrongful acts. This is not only because they serve to implement the primary obligations (as in the case of war crimes, and some other non-criminal violations of IHL as elucidated above), but also because investigations can be crucial for the cessation and non-repetition of violations. In cases in which a violation is found, and the question of reparation is therefore relevant, a State may have a responsibility not only to carry out an investigation, but also to provide information on the investigation carried out and whether or not a violation was found to have occurred, as well as information on whether perpetrators were punished and systemic errors fixed. This is in line with the Articles on State Responsibility, which mention the acknowledgement of a violation as part of adequate satisfaction for a violation,[58] but also in line with the Basic Principles on Right to a Remedy's articulation of the concept of "satisfaction," which "should include [...] verification of the facts and full and public disclosure of the truth to the extent that such disclosure does not cause further harm or threaten the safety and interests of the victim."[59] The law and practice on reparations for violations of IHL remain to be clarified, but it is suggested that investigations, with a particular focus on transparency as part of effectiveness, may at least contribute towards a realistic and adequate form of remedy in the case of some violations of IHL.

The general State responsibility to ensure the implementation of treaty obligations may therefore be understood under IHRL and IHL to entail a duty to investigate. Such a duty is clearly not restricted to criminal investigations but must take into account the broader measures which are necessary to the effective implementation of treaty obligations. A duty to investigate may also arise under the obligation to provide effective remedy for internationally wrongful acts in certain circumstances. Such an obligation, although fundamentally linked to the general implementation of treaty provisions, nevertheless is important in itself. Investigations as remedies may have to go beyond

57 Margalit, A., "Did LOAC Take the Lead? Reassessing Israel's Targeted Killing of Salah Shehadeh and the Subsequent Calls for Criminal Accountability," *Journal of Conflict and Security Law* Vol. 17 No. 1 (2012), p. 171.

58 Articles on State Responsibility (n. 21), Art. 37(2); Gillard (n. 40), pp. 531–532.

59 Basic Principles on the Right to Remedy (n. 24), para. 22.

establishing whether or not a violation occurred and, if relevant, punishing perpetrators. Remedial investigations may require more transparency in order to clarify the truth surrounding the violations and may need to focus more on broader guarantees of non-repetition.

A Duty to Investigate Serious Violations

A duty to investigate violations under IHRL and IHL can therefore be found as a consequence of the State responsibility to implement treaty and customary obligations, as well as to provide effective remedy for treaty violations. Although this has not been explicitly addressed in the case law, it is suggested that there is not, however, a duty to investigate "all" alleged violations under these bodies of law. Looking at the rationale of the duty to investigate, and the jurisprudence of interpretative bodies under IHRL, it may be inferred that there is a duty to effectively investigate "serious" violations of IHRL and IHL, as laid out in this section.

Despite its prevalent use, there is no single agreed definition of the term "serious" in relation to violations of IHL, or other bodies of international law.[60] The term "serious" violations of IHL is most commonly understood as referring to war crimes, as understood in the obligation to bring criminal prosecutions for "grave breaches and other serious violations of IHL."[61] The concept of a crime in itself is used in domestic law to refer to particularly serious offences committed by an individual. All war crimes (and grave breaches as a smaller subset of war crimes) are considered as serious violations of IHL. Nevertheless, it is suggested that certain other violations of IHL and IHRL also hold an element of seriousness, not necessarily tied to the individual (criminal) liability of the perpetrator involved, for example a failure to take feasible precautions in attack leading to "serious collateral damage."[62] As IHL and IHRL are bodies of law which deal with State responsibility, it seems relevant to also consider as serious other unlawful acts, not tied to individual criminal liability, that result in serious consequences.

For the purposes of this research, serious violations of IHL are considered to be those which may give rise to "serious harm." The harm is understood to be serious either because it affects bodily integrity of victims of the violations, or because of its scale (if it is part of a pattern). As seen above, the need to ensure respect with IHL, and provide effective remedy, may be understood to create a State responsibility to investigate such violations. It is suggested

60 Siatitsa, I.-M., "'A Serious Violation of International Human Rights Law': An Attempt to Clarify a Crucial Provision of the Arms Trade Treaty," *European Journal of Human Rights* Vol. 5 (2015).

61 See references above, n 24.

62 Margalit, A., "The Duty to Investigate Civilian Casualties During Armed Conflict and Its Implementation in Practice," *Yearbook of International Humanitarian Law* Vol. 15 (2012), pp. 158–160.

that particular procedural attention needs to be paid to the investigations carried out into these serious violations, including to their independence and impartiality.

Although there is still an obligation on States (and commanders) to suppress non-serious violations of IHL, the procedural requirements for such suppression are arguably much more flexible and less complex and may lie almost entirely within the discretion of the State in question. Therefore, while the duty to suppress "non-serious" violations may also be implemented by carrying out investigations in some circumstances, in general there is more flexibility for the suppression of such violations, as long as they are effectively suppressed.

Violations Affecting Physical Integrity

Under IHRL, a duty to investigate is clearest with relation to violations affecting physical integrity. In general, the duty to investigate before regional bodies has been found in relation to violations of the right to life, the prohibition of torture and inhuman or degrading treatment, the prohibition of enforced disappearances, and other human rights violations related to the above rights and prohibitions. This is clearest through the jurisprudence of the European Court of Human Rights (ECtHR), which has examined the procedural duty to investigate only under specific provisions and declined to find such a duty in others. It has used the same argument first laid out in the *McCann* case to read an implied procedural obligation to investigate arguable claims of violations into other cases of a possible violation of the right to life,[63] the prohibition of torture and inhuman/degrading treatment,[64] and the right to liberty and security in cases of unacknowledged detention.[65] It has also found a specific investigative duty under the prohibition of slavery in situations of potential

63 These are: to cases where it is uncertain that deaths were by State agents (*Ergi v Turkey*, App. No. 66/1997/850/1057, Judgment of 28 July 1998, para. 85), in cases where the victim was last seen in custody of the State even if it is not sure that they were unlawfully killed (*Cyprus v Turkey*, App. No. Application No. 25781/94, Judgment of 10 May 2001, para. 131), any death in custody (*Paul & Audrey Edwards v UK*, App. No. 46477/99, Judgment of 14 March 2002, para. 74), deaths in hospitals or medical facilities deaths in suspicions circumstances even without the involvement of State agents (*Calvelli & Ciglio v Italy*, App. No. 32967/96, Judgment of 17 January 2002, para. 49), and deaths caused in the context of "dangerous activities" under the responsibility of public authorities (*Oneryildiz v Turkey*, App. No. 48939/99, Judgment of 30 November 2004, para. 93). Mowbray, A., "Duties of Investigation under the ECHR," *International and Comparative Law Quarterly* Vol. 51 No. 2 (2002), p. 438; Chevalier-Watts (n. 6), p. 705.

64 ECtHR, *Assenov and Others v Bulgaria*, App. No. 90/1997/874/1086, Judgment of 28 October 1998, para. 102; Mowbray (2002) (n. 63), p. 444; *Sakir v Greece*, App. No. 48475/09, Judgment of 24 March 2016, para. 61.

65 ECtHR, *Kurt v Turkey*, App. No. 15/1997/799/1002, Judgment of 25 May 1998, para. 124; Mowbray (2002) (n. 63), p. 446; *Cyprus v Turkey* (2001) (n. 60), paras 143 and 150.

trafficking.[66] The obligation to carry out investigations as a procedural obligation stemming from other Articles of the European Convention on Human Rights has been invoked by claimants in cases involving others' rights, by analogy to the right to life or prohibition of torture in particular. The ECtHR has on occasion found such an obligation in relation to the right to family and private life,[67] freedom of expression,[68] and non-discrimination,[69] but only ever in conjunction with the above-mentioned rights and never on their own.

The African Commission has considered the obligation of a State to investigate under the right to life[70] and the prohibition of slavery, torture, cruel, inhuman, or degrading punishment and treatment.[71] The Inter-American Court of Human Rights (IACtHR), on the other hand, early on suggested that an investigative obligation existed for the violation of *any* right under the ACHR.[72] To date, the IACtHR has found an explicit duty to investigate in relation to the right to life, right against torture and inhuman or degrading treatment, right to liberty, and other rights when tied into the above-mentioned ones.[73] However, it has not addressed the duty to investigate in all of its case law, in particular for what may be considered "non-serious" human rights violations in the meaning of the term being used in this book. Although this remains to be explicitly stated, it appears consistent with its overall practice that the IACtHR does indeed understand a duty to investigate only in cases of serious human rights violations.

A similar consideration for the duty to investigate arises under IHL, as the reasoning given above for elucidating a duty to investigate does not necessarily mandate investigative action in all cases. The obligation is clearest for violations constituting war crimes, as a criminal investigation would be necessary in every such case. On the other hand, the broader obligation to suppress *all* violations of IHL only requires an investigation where this is necessary for the

66 ECtHR, *Rantsev v Cyprus & Russia*, App. No. 25965/04, Judgment of 7 January 2010, para. 288; Mowbray (2012) (n. 51), p. 242.

67 ECtHR, *R. B. v Hungary*, App. No. 64602/12, Judgment of 12 April 2016, para. 81.

68 ECtHR, *Özgür Gündem v Turkey*, App. No. 23144/93, Judgment of 16 March 2000.

69 ECtHR, *Bekos and Koutropoulos v Greece*, App. No. 15250/02, Judgment of 13 December 2005, paras 69–75; *Petropoulou-Tsakiris v Greece*, App. No. 44803/04, Judgment of 6 December 2007, para. 66.

70 ACHPR, *Association Amnesty International, Comité Loosli Bachelard and Lawyers Committee for Human Rights, Association of Members of the Episcopal Conference of East Africa v Sudan*, App. No. 48/90, 50/91, 52/91, 89/93, Decision on Merits (15 November 1999), para. 51; *Sudan Human Rights Organisation & Centre on Housing Rights and Evictions v Republic of Sudan*, App. No. 279/03, 296/05, Decision on Merits (27 May 2009), para. 147.

71 *Association of Members of the Episcopal Conference of East Africa v Sudan*, App. No. 48/90, 50/91, 52/91, 89/93, Decision on Merits (15 November 1999), para. 56.

72 IACtHR, *Velásquez Rodríguez v Honduras* (n. 27), para. 166.

73 Ibáñez Rivas (n. 53), pp. 643–652; IACtHR, *El Amparo v Venezuela*, Ser. C No. 28, Judgment of 14 September 1996 (Reparations and Costs), para. 61; *Case of the Street Children (Villagrán Morales et al.) v Guatemala*, Ser. C No. 77, Judgment of 26 May 2001 (Reparations and Costs), para. 100.

effective suppression of the violation. If the violation affects bodily integrity (e.g., resulting in serious injury or death) of a protected person, there is arguably a heightened legal obligation to learn from mistakes in order to prevent such incidents in the future. This is of course recognising that not all actions in armed conflict that affect the bodily integrity of protected persons constitute violations, as they can be a result of lawful acts of war. It is not suggested that there is a duty to investigate all such cases.[74] This is in contrast to the situation under IHRL, under which the focus of rights-holders as opposed to duty-bearers will often mean that serious harm to individuals will mean a violation of their rights may have committed and must be investigated. Yet, in the context of possible violations (for example, a failure to take precautions in attack), the duty to investigate arises under international obligations of treaty implementation and provision of remedial action. The practice of investigating accidental deaths or serious harm arising from internationally wrongful acts may be found beyond situations of armed conflict,[75] and, as seen above, investigations in such contexts may serve to contribute to remedial action for such violations.[76] In light of the gravity of the consequences, even without the presence of a war crime, it is suggested that there is therefore a duty to investigate violations of IHL which lead to serious injury or death of protected persons.

Finally, the interplay of both bodies of law also provides a strong argument to investigate violations of IHL which affect physical integrity. Insofar as both bodies of law can be simultaneously applicable, and insofar as the application of one may be usefully informed by the other, a violation of IHL in which the life of an individual is at risk could also constitute a violation of the right to life under IHRL.[77] As a violation of IHRL, as well as IHL, it would therefore require an investigation according to this body of law.[78] While details on the interplay of these bodies of law are not always agreed upon,[79] this interpretation only strengthens the obligation which may be found separately under IHL.

Violations Which Are Part of a Pattern

The need to learn from mistakes leads us to another context in which violations need to be investigated. It would appear that violations which may be part of a pattern would require an investigation, regardless of whether or not

74 Margalit (2018) (n. 6), p. 42.

75 Articles on State Responsibility (n. 21), Commentary para. 106; Margalit (2018) (n. 6), p. 34.

76 Margalit (2018) (n. 6), p. 34.

77 General Comment No. 36 (n. 9), para. 64; ICJ, "Legality of the Threat or Use of Nuclear Weapons," Advisory Opinion of 8 July 1996, para. 25.

78 Margalit (2018) (n. 6), p. 79; General Comment No. 36 (n. 9), para. 64.

79 Whether IHRL is considered to apply alongside IHL may depend upon, for example, the interpretation of the application of IHRL extraterritorially, and under what circumstances. See, e.g., General Comment No. 36 (n. 9), para. 63; Quénivet (n. 6); Lubell & Prud'homme (n. 8), pp. 147–149.

they affect physical integrity. The rationale for such a duty may be found under the obligations to prevent violations,[80] and under general obligations of due diligence under international law.[81] An investigation may also be necessary in order to put an end to violations, and to guarantee their non-repetition as required under the secondary rules of State responsibility, as it may not be sufficient for their cessation and non-repetition that one individual is stopped and if relevant punished. Rather, an investigation into the root causes of the problem may be necessary in order to provide such guarantees.[82] IHRL bodies have found on multiple occasions that the possible patterns associated to certain violations has enhanced the importance of investigating such violations.[83]

Under IHL, there may even be a broader obligation to investigate systemic problems, regardless of whether or not they actually result in violations. This could be either because a previous incident could constitute sufficient information for a commander to "reasonably know" in subsequent operations that this may happen again;[84] or because the obligation to take constant care in military operations mandates that ongoing reviews (as types of investigations) occur in such circumstances (e.g., when unexpected results occur).[85]

It may therefore be said that there is also an obligation to investigate violations of IHL and IHRL which are part of a pattern, principally tied to the secondary obligations under State responsibility to prevent, put an end to, and guarantee non-repetition for violations. Some of this rationale will be explored further in Chapter 7, which will consider patterns of violations and systematic impunity.

Non-Serious Violations?

Finally, it is worth mentioning that some "non-serious" violations, namely (for our purposes) those that do not affect physical integrity and are not part of a pattern, may require investigating for their effective suppression. The concept

80 Hampson (n. 34), pp. 12 and 14.

81 Sassòli (2002) (n. 22), p. 411, Articles on State Responsibility (n. 21), Commentary, p. 87; Koivurova, T., "Due Diligence," *Max Planck Encyclopedia of Public International Law*, Elsevier (1992), para. 2.

82 *Guidelines on Investigating Violations of International Humanitarian Law* (n. 7), para. 16.

83 ECtHR, *Sakir v Greece* (n. 61), para. 72; ECtHR *R.B. v Hungary* (n. 67), para. 84; IACtHR, *La Rochela Massacre v Colombia*, Ser. C No. 163, Judgment of 11 May 2007 (Merits, Reparations, and Costs), para. 165; *Manuel Cepeda Vargas*, Ser. C No. 213, Judgment of 26 May 2010 (Preliminary Objections, Merits, Reparations, and Costs), para. 118.

84 "The first time something occurs, there may be no liability. That does not mean that there would continue to be no liability where the State ignored the evidence of its own experience." Hampson (n. 34), p. 9.

85 The obligation to take constant care can be understood in some ways in a proactive and reactive obligation on those involved at any stage of military operations (not just commanders) to keep an eye out for possible unexpected and undesired results of operations. See International Law Association Study Group, "The Conduct of Hostilities and International Humanitarian Law: Challenges of 21st Century Warfare," Presented at the 77th ILA Conference in Johannesburg, South Africa (2016), p. 330.

of suppression refers to the need to put an end to a violation, as well as to prevent its recurrence in the future. Some violations of IHL may be so simple or straightforward that action to redress the violation can be taken immediately, for example, by taking non-criminal disciplinary action. If the action is not a crime, the notions of fair trial do not apply and therefore an investigation is unlikely to be needed for these reasons (to protect the accused). Furthermore, if the facts about the violation are clear, then investigation into the facts will not be necessary to clarify the situation and/or identify the perpetrator. In such a situation, there is indeed an obligation to suppress the violation, but this may be effectively accomplished by ceasing the violation and punishing the perpetrator. Nevertheless, there are other contexts in which the facts surrounding why the violation happened, what exactly happened, and whether individual responsibility is at play may remain unclear. In order to "effectively" suppress any such violation, it may be necessary to gain an understanding of what happened and why, and identify possible perpetrators.[86]

It may be the case that some sort of procedure which looks like an investigation may be necessary in such contexts, such as a review or inquiry. Insofar as such a procedure may be necessary for the effective suppression of the violation, there may be a duty to investigate. Part of this may depend on the definition of an investigation. It is clear that investigative obligations under international law are broader than only criminal investigations. Yet, how broad this definition should be, and what type of activities it should encompass, is unclear. Does a commander asking a few soldiers some clarification on the events count as an investigation? Does a commander going through a mental check-list of whether or not further action is required count as an investigation? It is suggested that in such cases the flexibility of procedure may be greater than in cases of "serious" violations. Although such processes should also be subject to the concept of "effectiveness," it is unlikely that the same investigative standards (e.g., of independence and impartiality) will be necessary for effectiveness in such cases. The rest of this book will therefore not focus on such non-serious violations.

It may therefore be argued that there is a duty to investigate serious violations of IHL and IHRL, understood as violations which affect physical integrity and/or which are part of a pattern of violations. For IHRL, the rationale may be found in the jurisprudence of regional courts which have only found a duty to investigate such violations. Under IHL, beyond war crimes, the scope of investigative duties is unclear. Nevertheless, the obligation to provide remedy and other secondary obligations under the rules of State responsibility may be found to lead to a duty to investigate such serious violations. Non-serious violations also need to be effectively suppressed, but whether or not an

86 *Guidelines on Investigating Violations of International Humanitarian Law* (n. 7), paras 163 and 178.

investigation is required in the latter case will depend on how such a violation can be effectively suppressed.

A Duty to Investigate Effectively

The section above established that there are clearly obligations to investigate certain violations under international law, yet the sources of these obligations are not necessarily explicit nor are they consistently interpreted by different adjudicatory bodies. In the case of IHL, the lack of interpretative bodies makes it even harder to lay out clear standards applicable to the investigative stage. This can cause uncertainty in determining how an investigation should be carried out once the legal obligation to do so has been established. What is clear in all cases, however, is that the duty to investigate has to do with the effective implementation of primary obligations, as well as secondary obligations of effective remedy for violation of primary obligations. The concept of "effectiveness" in both these cases is a useful tool to understand the way in which investigations must be carried out in context where the precise standards may be unclear. Furthermore, the concept also helps to look at situations of interplay of different bodies of international law, as the common denominator can be crucial in understanding how to reconcile these bodies of law in a coherent manner.

In considering the effectiveness of an investigation, it will be necessary to assess whether reasonable means have been put into the investigation in light of seeking to achieve its purpose within the given context. This is because effectiveness requires employing the appropriate and reasonable means to render the investigation capable of achieving its purpose.[87] As well as the concept of effectiveness, it is therefore necessary to consider the means used, as well as the purpose, objective, or goal of an investigation in each given context.

The Concept of Effectiveness

If a State has a duty to investigate under international law (as described above), it is suggested that such an investigation must be effective. This focus on effectiveness can be found in many of the sources of the duty to investigate under both IHL and IHRL: in the obligation to provide for "effective penal sanctions" for war crimes,[88] the obligation to provide for "effective remedies,"[89] and various iterations of the explicit obligation to carry out

87 Second Turkel Report (n. 7), pp. 114–117, 129; *Guidelines on Investigating Violations of International Humanitarian Law* (n. 7), para. 32.

88 See Geneva Convention provisions (n. 29); see also Convention on the Prevention and Punishment of the Crime of Genocide, 78 UNTS 277 (1948), Art. V.

89 Shelton (n. 39), p. 94; General Comment No. 31 (n. 23), para. 15; ACHR (n. 47), Art. 25; IACtHR, *Velásquez Rodríguez v Honduras* (n. 27), para. 91; ECHR (n. 44), Art. 13; *Kurt v Turkey* (n. 65), para. 139.

"effective investigations."[90] The suggestion that a process must be effective in general refers to the need for that process to be appropriate and undertaken in good faith, with all reasonable means employed to achieve its goal.[91] For obligations under international law, this can be in part understood as part of the obligation of *pacta sunt servanda*; that States must perform their treaty obligations in "good faith."[92] To imply that an investigation need not be effective would be to undermine its very purpose, and would not discharge a State's international obligations.[93]

The term "effectiveness" has been used differently in specific contexts with relation to investigations, for example alongside the standards of independence, impartiality, thoroughness, and promptness.[94] In such an interpretation, an investigation needing to be "effective" would be just one additional standard alongside others. Nevertheless, it is suggested that it is preferable to see "effectiveness" as an umbrella term addressing the overall standards applicable to an investigation. The value in keeping it as an umbrella term rather than just one of many elements which an investigation must meet lies in its potential to be used as an overarching assessment standard, in particular when the precise standards are unclear. For example, promptness, independence, and thoroughness in investigating might look different depending on the context and the applicable body of law (see below and Chapter 6), but it is argued that the concept of effectiveness addresses a more fundamental element to the investigative process. An investigation must be sufficiently independent, impartial, thorough, prompt, and transparent to be effective.[95] Therefore, the levels of independence and impartiality required will be assessed by their contribution to the effectiveness of an investigation. This cross-cutting understanding of effectiveness will enable subsequent chapters to clarify the levels

90 ICTY, *Prosecutor v Ljube Boškoski and Johan Tarčulovski*, IT-04-82-T, Judgment of the Trial Chamber of 10 July 2008, para. 418; ECtHR, *Al-Skeini v UK*, App. No. 55721/07, Judgment of 7 July 2011, para. 166; IACtHR, *Acosta and Others v Nicaragua*, Ser. C No. 334, Judgment of 25 March 2017 (Preliminary Objections, Merits, Reparations, and Costs), para. 136; ACHPR, *Sudan Human Rights Organisation & Centre on Housing Rights and Evictions v Republic of Sudan*, App. No. 279/03-296/05, Decision on Merits (27 May 2009), para. 147; UN Human Rights Committee, "General Comment No. 20: Article 7 (Prohibition of Torture, or Other Cruel, Inhuman or Degrading Treatment or Punishment)" (10 March 1992), para. 14.

91 *Guidelines on Investigating Violations of International Humanitarian Law* (n. 7), para. 30.

92 Vienna Convention on the Law of Treaties (n. 17), Art. 26; Schmitt, M. N., "Investigating Violations of International Law in Armed Conflict," *Harvard National Security Journal* Vol. 2 (2011), p. 48; Kotzur, M., "Good Faith (bona fide)," *Max Planck Encyclopedia of Public International Law*, Elsevier (2009), para. 20.

93 Tomuschat Report (n. 28), para. 30; IACtHR, *Mapiripán Massacre v Colombia*, Series C No. 134, Judgment of 15 September 2005 (Merits, Reparations, and Costs), para. 223.

94 See, e.g., the way in which the standards are explained by the Turkel Commission, Second Turkel Report (n. 7), p. 114, and n. 193.

95 *Guidelines on Investigating Violations of International Humanitarian Law* (n. 7), para. 32.

of independence and impartiality required for investigations into violations of IHL in situations of armed conflict.

Reasonable Means

In the context of duties of investigation under international law, it has been made clear that what matters most is the *good faith efforts* put into achieving its goal, and not the goal in itself. The general principle of "good faith" under international law requires that treaties be interpreted taking into account the "reasonable expectations of all other members of the international community."[96] The concept of "reasonableness" in turn does not have a single definition, but is frequently included in international law "in order to introduce a degree of flexibility,"[97] which proves particularly important at the international legal level which must adapt to different domestic systems and legal paradigms.

For the obligation to investigate under international law, the concept of reasonableness may be understood to affect how the above-mentioned general principles of an effective investigation (independence, impartiality, thoroughness, promptness, and transparency) may be interpreted in different contexts and under different bodies of law. What is required is that States put all reasonable means into these investigative efforts with a view to achieving the identified purpose of the investigation. The concept of reasonableness in relation to situations of armed conflict and IHL will be further explored in Chapter 6. In the meantime, it is useful to elucidate how the concept of "reasonable means" for investigating may be understood broadly for effective investigations.

Under IHRL, the concept of "means not results" has been borrowed across the systems and is a helpful yet somewhat fluid one; it has been used in a variety of contexts and expanded over time. Importantly, the term was developed in part in recognition of the very difficult contexts in which human rights violations can occur, such as widespread violence or armed conflict. The ability for the regional human rights bodies to show flexibility in the interpretation of applicable human rights standards is crucial for institutions the purpose of which is to oversee the application of these rights across different legal and political systems, as well as across situations which can range from contexts of domestic peace time through to armed conflict abroad. All human rights bodies have recognised the difficulties which investigators may face,[98] and acknowledged that the means used need to be adapted to the practical situation on the ground. However, they have also highlighted that none of these

96 Kotzur (n. 92), paras 4 and 20.

97 Corten, O., "Reasonableness in International Law," *Max Planck Encyclopedia of Public International Law*, Elsevier (2013), paras 6 and 24.

98 ECtHR: *Al-Skeini v UK* (n. 90), para. 164; IACtHR: *Velásquez Rodríguez v Honduras* (n. 27), para. 177; ACHPR, *Zimbabwe Human Rights Forum v Zimbabwe*, App. No. 245/02, Decision on Merits (15 May 2006), paras 154, 175.

difficulties will ever displace the duty to investigate. In order to assess whether the investigation carried out met the standard of effectiveness as required, the courts have therefore assessed whether States put in the reasonable efforts to achieve the purpose of the investigation.[99] Whether or not the purpose is achieved (e.g., the determination of responsibility for the act) will not determine whether or not the investigation was effective.[100] The IACtHR has further emphasised this through the need for "due diligence" in investigating,[101] implying that the actions taken by the State must contribute to the overall context of effective prevention and prosecution of violations by non-State as well as State actors. The "means not results" test, which examines whether the reasonable means were put into the investigative procedure, therefore allows human rights bodies to assess the effectiveness of proceedings while taking into account the difficult circumstances which may be present in the State.

A similar concept to that of means not results is used under command responsibility in ICL to measure whether a commander carried out an effective investigation. What matters is not whether in fact the action taken by the commander achieves the objective, but whether the commander *in good faith* believes that it will.[102] Any steps taken by the commander following the commission of a possible war crime must therefore be effective insofar as they must be reasonable within the circumstances, and they must be carried out in good faith (the commander must believe they will reach the objective of bringing the perpetrators to trial). This is true when assessing both whether the commander referred the matter to the competent authority, and when assessing the investigative/punitive actions carried out by the commander themself.[103]

99 ECtHR, *Shanaghan v UK*, App. No. 37715/97, Judgment of 4 May 2001, para. 90; IACtHR, *Velásquez Rodríguez v Honduras* (n. 27), para. 177; *Baldeón-García v Peru*, Ser. C No. 147, Judgment of 6 April 2006 (Merits, Reparations, and Costs), para. 93; Leach, Murray, & Sandoval (n. 6), p. 39; Roht-Arriaza, N., "State Responsibility to Investigate and Prosecute Grave Human Rights Violations under International Law," *California Law Review* Vol. 78 No. 2 (1990), p. 471.

100 IACtHR, *Velásquez Rodríguez v Honduras* (n. 27), para. 177; ECtHR: *Brecknell v UK*, App. No. 32457/04, Judgment of 27 November 2007, para. 66.

101 IACtHR, *Serrano Cruz Sisters v El Salvador*, Ser. C No. 118, Judgment of 23 November 2004 (Preliminary Objections), para. 65; Ibáñez Rivas (n. 53), p. 629; *Acosta and Others v Nicaragua*, Ser. C No. 334, Judgment of 25 March 2017 (Preliminary Objections, Merits, Reparations, and Costs), para. 136.

102 Mettraux, G., "Breach of a Duty and Consequential Failure to Prevent or to Punish Crimes of Subordinates" in *The Law of Command Responsibility*, Oxford University Press (2009), pp. 252–253; ICTY, *Boškoski & Tarčulovski*, IT-04-82-A, Appeals Chamber Judgment of 19 May 2010, para. 234; *Prosecutor v Enver Hadžihasanović & Amir Kubura*, IT-01-47-A, Appeals Chamber Judgment of 22 April 2008, para. 154; *Prosecutor v Vujadin Popović et al*, IT-05-88-A, Appeals Chamber Judgment of 30 January 2015, para. 1938.

103 ICTY, *Prosecutor v Enver Hadžihasanović & Amir Kubura*, IT-01-47-A, Appeals Chamber Judgment of 22 April 2008, para. 154; ICTY, *Prosecutor v Ljube Boškoski and Johan Tarčulovski*, IT-04-82-T, Judgment of the Trial Chamber of 10 July 2008, para. 536; ICTY,

The matter of effectiveness may also be examined under the principle of complementarity in the Rome Statute of the International Criminal Court (ICC) – this time related to the State, and not individual commander, responsibility to effectively investigate and prosecute international crimes within their territory/jurisdiction. The obligation upon States to effectively investigate and prosecute perpetrators of violations of ICL, or extradite them, has led the ICC to examine the effectiveness (or rather, the ineffectiveness) of domestic investigations, in the principle of complementarity under the Rome Statute of the ICC. Article 17 deals with the criterion of effectiveness, namely, that the ICC will not seize jurisdiction of a case if it is being domestically investigated and prosecuted unless the State is unable or unwilling *genuinely* to carry out the proceedings.[104] The term "genuineness" is important, and arguably means the same thing as effectiveness and good faith as defined above.[105] The concept of genuineness is, however, also not a test of results: indeed, the test "cannot be based on the *outcome* of proceedings, for example from the acquittal of an obviously guilty person,"[106] as "this would undermine the accused's right to be presumed innocent at trial once before the ICC."[107] Requiring that any investigation, prosecution, and trial of a suspect of an alleged international crime result in a finding of guilt would contravene the accused's fair trial rights. Instead, "the admissibility assessment should be based on *procedural* and *institutional* factors, not the substantive outcome."[108] Thus, "in order for the ICC to challenge this outcome an assessment of all the procedural aspects that led to the outcome also seems indispensable."[109] The Court therefore looks at the way in which the proceedings are carried out, in other words what reasonable means are put into it, in order to assess genuineness.

Prosecutor v Vujadin Popović et al., IT-05-88-A, Appeals Chamber Judgment of 30 January 2015, para. 1938. See Chapter 5 for further on the role of the commander.

104 El-Zeidy, M. M., *The Principle of Complementarity in International Criminal Law*, Nijhoff (2008), p. 193; Holmes, J. T., "Complementarity: National Courts versus the ICC" in Cassese, A. et al., *The Rome Statute of the ICC: A Commentary*, Vol. 1, Oxford University Press (2002), p. 674; ICC, *Prosecutor v Muthuara et al.*, Judgment on the Appeal of the Republic of Kenya against the Decision of Pre-Trial Chamber II of 30 May 2011, entitled "Decision on the Application by the Government of Kenya Challenging the Admissibility of the Case Pursuant to Article 19(2)(b) of the Statute," ICC-01/09-02/11-274, Decision of 30 August 2011.

105 The term was adopted in the drafting of the Statute "as the least disagreeable and most objective term" despite the lack of precedent for the use of this word. Holmes, J. T., "The Principle of Complementarity" in Lee, R. S., *The International Criminal Court: The Making of the Rome Statute, Issues, Negotiations, Results*, Brill (1999), pp. 49–50; Holmes (2002) (n. 104), pp. 673–674.

106 ICC, "Informal Expert Paper: The Principle of Complementarity in Practice," ICC-OTP (2003), para. 46.

107 ICC "Informal Expert Paper" (n. 106), p. 14; El-Zeidy (n. 104), p. 174.

108 El-Zeidy (n. 104), p. 174.

109 El-Zeidy (n. 104), p. 175.

Purpose of the Investigation

Given that an investigation must be capable of achieving its purpose, it will be necessary to determine early on what this purpose should be. The purpose of an investigation will be determined by the legal source of the duty to investigate, for example whether it is an investigation into a possible violation of the right to life under IHRL, a violation of the principle of distinction under IHL, or possibly both. Identifying the source of the duty should enable clarification of the elements of the violation, levels of liability (individual and/or State responsibility), and any relevant elements of remedial action.

Human rights interpretative bodies have developed specific procedural requirements for investigations which identify the purpose of investigations into certain human rights violations,[110] which will differ depending on the specific right violated and the circumstances.[111] For example, with relation to enforced disappearances, the Human Rights Committee, ECtHR, and IACtHR have all found that an investigation must clarify the whereabouts and fate of the disappeared, determine the responsibilities, and, if relevant, punish those responsible.[112] For potentially unlawful deaths, the investigation must identify the victim, the cause of and circumstances surrounding the death, and identify potential perpetrators.[113] Investigations as an element of a reparation, on the other hand, must contain an element of victim (or relatives of the victim) participation and transparency.[114] It is also clear that investigations cannot be confined to identifying issues of individual criminal responsibility, but must also take the broader context into account in assessing a State's responsibility for its human rights obligations.[115]

Determining the purpose of investigations under IHL similarly requires looking at the specific source of the duty. In the context of the grave breaches

110 While IHRL bodies have undoubtedly influenced one another in developing these standards, the applicable international and regional law may slightly affect the precise requirements.

111 ECtHR, *Jasinskis v Latvia*, App. No. 45744/08, Judgment of 21 December 2010, para. 72; *Calvelli & Ciglio v Italy* (n. 60), para. 51; *Banks and Others v UK*, App. No. 21387/05, Judgment of 6 January 2007.

112 UN Human Rights Committee, "General Comment No. 3: Article 2 (Implementation at the National Level)" (29 July 1981), para. 38; ECtHR *Kurt v Turkey* (n. 65), para. 128; *Cyprus v Turkey* (2001) (n. 60), para. 150; IACtHR, *Ibsen Cárdenas and Ibsen Peña v Bolivia,* Ser. C No. 217, Judgment of 1 September 2010 (Merits, Reparation, and Costs), para. 215; *Trujillo-Oroza v Bolivia*, Ser. C No. 92, Judgment of 27 February 2002 (Reparations and Costs), para. 91.

113 Minnesota Protocol (n. 20), para. 25; General Comment No. 36 (n. 9), paras 28–29; *Al-Skeini v UK* (n. 90), para. 166; *Mustafa Tunç and Fecire Tunç v Turkey*, Application No. 24014/05, Judgment of 14 April 2015, para. 174; IACtHR, *Chinchilla Sandoval v Guatemala*, Ser. C No. 312, Judgment of 29 February 2016 (Preliminary Objection, Merits, Reparations, and Costs), paras 257–259; *Miguel Castro Castro Prison v Peru*, Judgment of 25 November 2006 (Merits, Reparations, and Cost), para. 383.

114 See, e.g., *Kurt v Turkey* (n. 65), para. 140.

115 Hampson (n. 34), p. 6 n. 16.

provisions, the 2016 ICRC Commentary suggests that generally States must act "in a manner compatible with the object and purpose of the provision," the object and purpose being to "prevent alleged perpetrators from going unpunished."[116] In this regard, even though there are no textual prescriptions as to the means that must be employed, it is implied that States have an obligation to employ means that will be effective in achieving this object and purpose.[117] Therefore, according to this reasoning, States parties would have certain discretion in the means employed to repress war crimes, as long as this repression is "effective." This, in turn, implies that the State's discretion is not absolute in the choice of means; if certain means are necessary to the objective of the provision (the repression of war crimes), then these means must be employed. A requirement of promptness is elucidated by the commentary as a necessary means for such effectiveness.[118] It is clear in the context of war crimes that an investigation must be carried out "with a view to establishing the facts"[119] and that it must be "capable of leading to the criminal prosecution of the perpetrators."[120]

For violations other than war crimes, the objective of each investigation would need to be determined according to the specific provision. For example, the death of a prisoner of war that does not indicate any criminal liability but may indicate systemic problems would need to establish the circumstances of the death,[121] and implement changes to prevent its recurrence. An investigation into a failure to take precautions in attack would require determining the quality and methods of information gathering, the decision-making procedures, and the circumstances surrounding the attack.[122]

Creating a full list of the investigation objectives required by treaty and customary law is beyond the scope of this chapter and would be extensive given the different international and regional obligations. Furthermore, the jurisprudence on the matter continues to evolve. Generally, it would be necessary in each case to identify the purpose of the investigation and adapt the investigative means accordingly. If an incident involves possible violations of multiple bodies of law, it would be necessary to address these in the proceedings.

116 ICRC, Updated Commentary to GCI (n. 34), paras 2866 and 2868.

117 ICRC, Updated Commentary to GCI (n. 34), para. 2868 n. 115; ICJ, "Questions Relating to the Obligation to Prosecute or Extradite (*Belgium v Senegal*)," (n. 32), paras 86 and 114.

118 ICRC, Updated Commentary to GCI (n. 34), paras 2866, 2868.

119 ICTY, *Prosecutor v Fatmir Limaj et al.*, IT-03-66-T, Trial Chamber II Judgment of 30 November 2005, para. 529, citing *Prosecutor v Pavle Strugar*, IT-01-42-T, Trial Chamber II Judgment of 31 January 2005, para. 376.

120 ICTY, *Prosecutor v Vujadin Popović et al.*, IT-05-88-A, Appeals Chamber Judgment of 30 January 2015, para. 1932; See also *Prosecutor v Sefer Halilović,* IT-01-48-A, Appeals Chamber Judgment of 16 October 2007, para. 182; *Prosecutor v Pavle Strugar* (n. 119), para. 378.

121 Pictet Commentary (n. 34), Commentary to Art. 121, GCIII, 570. See also ICRC, Updated Commentary to Third Geneva Convention (2020), paras 4657–4672.

122 Margalit (2018) (n. 6), pp. 32, 39; ICRC Commentary to API (n. 25), Art. 57, para. 1952; Cohen & Shany (n. 36), p. 47.

It is therefore suggested that the duty to investigate serious violations of international law is a duty of effectiveness. This means that a State must put all reasonable means into the investigation in order for the investigation to be capable of achieving its objective. IHRL bodies have made clear that this obligation of effectiveness is one of "means not results," focusing on the good faith efforts put into the investigation in light of the prevailing circumstances at the time. Under ICL, courts have similarly considered the "good faith" efforts of commanders in investigating, and the "genuineness" of proceedings carried out by States. It is suggested that all of these obligations, and those arising under IHL, may be understood under the overarching definition of "effectiveness," which includes this element of good faith and reasonableness. What this means in the context of armed conflict and violations of IHL will be further explored in subsequent chapters.

Conclusion

There is not one "duty to investigate" under international law. Rather, under IHL, IHRL, and ICL, specific obligations may require, explicitly or implicitly, an investigation into serious violations of these bodies of law. This chapter has explored how an obligation to effectively investigate has been inferred from the need to effectively repress criminal violations of international law, as well as from the more general obligation to implement the provisions of these bodies of law. Furthermore, the obligation to provide effective remedy and reparations for violations of international law committed by States has provided interpretive bodies the opportunity to examine the important role investigations can have in the access to such remedies, and in some cases, to the content of the remedies themselves. This chapter has also established that the duty to investigate may be understood to apply to "serious" violations of IHL and IHRL, namely those which affect physical integrity and/or form a pattern of violations.

The source of the obligation to investigate (or various sources) shapes the way in which the investigation must be carried out. This has affected the different emphasis interpretive bodies have placed on different standards an investigation must respect. Notwithstanding these differences, the above-mentioned jurisprudence demonstrates that all investigations into violations of IHRL, IHL, and ICL must be *effective*. Effectiveness in this context can be understood as an investigation's capability of achieving its objective in good faith; that is that all reasonable means are put into the investigative exercise with the view of achieving the result. Whether or not the investigation achieves the objective (for example, actually identifying the perpetrator, or actually clarifying the circumstances of the violation) is a question of results. This is the test of "means not results," or "good faith." Effectiveness will therefore require different means depending on the situation and must be adapted to the circumstances; what constitutes an effective investigation into a civilian casualty in a foreign territory with no ground control may look different to an investigation into the death of a civilian from use of force in a law enforcement operation in one's own territory. An ineffective investigation, one that is unable from the onset to achieve the desired objective, will not fulfil a State's obligations under the relevant provisions of international law.

Having established the source and general scope of a duty to investigate violations of IHL, the rest of the book can go on to consider the implications a duty to investigate effectively has on the independence and impartiality of the investigators in situations of armed conflict.

4 The independence and impartiality of investigations in relation to their effectiveness

Introduction

The lack of independence often appears to be the implicit, if not always explicit, criticism of military investigations. Human rights organisations have accused the Israeli military investigative system of being structurally ineffective in investigating allegations of violations against Palestinians,[1] UK forces of creating an environment of impunity when investigating their own troops for sexual offences,[2] and the USA of failing to address its own responsibility when investigating incidents caused by its airstrikes.[3] It is suggested that what is at play when a military is accused of "investigating itself" in these cases may be understood under the lens of independence and impartiality.

Although it may often be taken for granted that investigations need to be independent and impartial, there are various questions which merit attention regarding the application and scope of these standards. Do investigations need to be independent and impartial in the first place? If so, why? And how should such standards be measured? In light of the previous chapter's finding that investigations into serious violations of international humanitarian law (IHL) must be "effective," this chapter explores the relationship between this effectiveness and the standards of independence and impartiality which are frequently called for in the context of investigations into possible violations of IHL. It explores the basis of the assumption that investigations into violations of IHL and international human rights law (IHRL) need to be independent and impartial, and questions how such standards may apply and be measured.

1 B'Tselem, "Whitewash Protocol: The So-Called Investigation of 'Operation Protective Edge'" (2016); Amnesty International, "Stars on Their Shoulders, Blood on Their Hands: War Crimes Committed by the Nigerian Military" (2015); Yesh Din, "Alleged Investigations: The Failure of Investigations Into Offences Committed by IDF Soldiers Against Palestinians" (August 2011).

2 Norton, E., "Military Justice, Second-Rate Justice: Criminal Justice, Complaints and Human Rights Myths in the Armed Forces," Liberty (January 2019).

3 Yager, S., "Lost Innocents: The US Military's Shameful Failure to Protect Civilians," Human Rights Watch (25 January 2022), available at: www.hrw.org/news/2022/01/25/lost-innocents.

DOI: 10.4324/9781003360223-4

The independence and impartiality of investigations is yet to be fully clarified in existing scholarship. Although the topic has not been directly addressed, existing State practice, scholarship on related topics, and a growing understanding of this topic under IHRL supports an approach to coherently interpret the standards of independence and impartiality of investigations under IHL.

Defining independence and impartiality

The joint concept of "independence and impartiality" was traditionally held to refer to the standards applicable to judges, courts, and tribunals and the judicial process more generally, and it is not obvious from the outset that the same standards should apply to investigations.

The terms independence and impartiality are often used jointly with reference to standards applicable to the judiciary, and today also to investigations. This chapter, however, explores their individual meanings, which have been analysed separately by courts and scholarship. "Impartiality" is considered an internal behavioural concept, related to the lack of internal bias of an individual charged with making decisions (a person is able to behave in an impartial manner, of their own will, with regard to the matter at hand). "Independence," on the other hand, is a relational concept (a body or a person being relationally independent from another body or person), dictating that judicial persons and institutions must be free from structures of power which may pressure or influence them.[4]

Although the concepts have been examined individually, it is clear that they are fundamentally intertwined. For example, it will be seen that objective impartiality (impartiality as observable from the outside) is *inter alia* measured through safeguards of independence. Furthermore, the terms may sometimes be conflated, or used interchangeably in documents addressing standards applicable to courts or investigations. Occasionally, the term "independence" in these documents may be used as a catchall to refer to both terms, or even sometimes appear to refer to impartiality. This is perhaps because impartiality is an internal concept difficult to measure, and it is therefore often independence which is addressed as the observable form.

In general, this book takes the approach that for investigations, measures of independence are a useful and observable means to achieve impartiality. The terms are used together most of the time as an overall catchphrase addressing both standards and how they relate to one another. The terms are used separately when they are being examined individually. The concept of "implication" is also often used in documents and case law addressing investigations,

4 This distinction between the "relational" and the "behavioural" is taken, and modified, from Russell, P. H., "Toward a General Theory of Judicial Independence" in Russell, P. H., & O'Brien, D. M., *Judicial Independence in the Age of Democracy: Critical Perspectives From Around the World*, University of Virginia Press (2001), p. 6.

and refers to the involvement of someone whose individual (usually criminal) responsibility may be engaged by the incident being investigated. The matter of implication may be considered fundamentally a matter of partiality, insofar as an individual involved in a potentially unlawful act cannot be considered as lacking bias or conflict of interest with regard to that act.

Although this chapter examines some of the intricacies of the terms in order to better understand how they relate to investigations, its purpose is not necessarily to add to the literature on the standards of independence and impartiality generally, especially how they relate to judges and concepts of fair trial. Rather, existing standards are used to better understand how they relate to the effectiveness of investigations into violations of IHL, in order to provide clear recommendations of what may or may not be considered independent and impartial. It is to the literature on investigations, rather than on independence and impartiality, that this chapter contributes.

The independence and impartiality of judges, courts, and tribunals

The concepts of independence and impartiality are traditionally referred to in the context of judges, courts, or tribunals. In order to understand whether and how these concepts might apply to investigations, it is considered useful to first give a brief overview of the development of the requirements of independence and impartiality of the judiciary in political theory and international human rights law. It is often taken for granted in law that the judiciary must be independent and impartial, but clarifying why independence and impartiality contribute to common notions of justice is useful in order to understand their applicability at the investigation stage. It becomes clear that there is a fundamental connection between the impartial judge and maintenance of the rule of law by a legitimate State which means that independence and impartiality are separately and jointly necessary for judges, courts, and tribunals.

Legitimate governance and the rule of law

The importance of an independent and impartial judiciary finds its basis in the writings of political theorists on the legitimacy of governance and the rule of law which influenced the way in which modern liberal democracies structure their governments. Looking at the rationale for independence and impartiality of the judiciary, it seems that what matters the most for achieving a just outcome is impartial adjudication by a judge – that a judge is able to make decisions on the lawfulness or not of a matter based solely on relevant facts and the law, and not other irrelevant factors. This is because citizens agree in a mutual social contract to lay down some of their natural liberties, such as the right to self-adjudicate or use their own enforcement power.[5] Giving the State the monopoly on adjudication and use of force requires citizens to believe that an adjudicator will act impartially when disputes arise.[6] If individuals cannot assume that their case would be heard impartially, they would have no reason to trust in the government. If people do not trust in the government, they will resort to their own means of enforcing their rights, and therefore "the condition of war remaineth."[7]

In order to promote circumstances in which a judge is able to adjudicate impartially, both personal and institutional independence are necessary, namely protection from undue pressures on the judge as a person and the judiciary as an institution.[8] This concept of an independent and impartial judiciary stemmed from a very nation State-centric origin related to the social contract and the legitimacy of State institutions exercising power on behalf of their citizens. However, the requirements of an independent and impartial judiciary have transferred from the national to the international level (and back down to the national level) through the development of international human rights law.[9] Judicial independence and impartiality are today accepted as international standards necessary for the attainment of justice and the respect of fair trial rights of individuals.[10] Indeed, through the development of international human rights law, the focus has shifted from a general conception of justice and the legitimacy of the government by its people, to the fundamental rights belonging to individuals involved in a judicial procedure. Individuals involved in judicial proceedings now have a *right* to an independent and impartial judiciary. Furthermore, the developments of the procedural justice and notions

5 Hobbes, T., *Leviathan* (1651), edition by Tuck, R., *Cambridge Texts in the History of Political Thought* (1996), Pt I, Chap. XIV, pp. 64–66; Locke, J., *Second Treatise of Government* (1690), edition by Macpherson, C. B., Hackett (1980), Chap. VII, para. 87.

6 Hobbes (n. 5), Pt I, Chap. XV, p. 77; Locke (n. 5), Chap. IX, para. 125 and Chap. VII, para. 87.

7 Hobbes (n. 5), Pt I, Chap. XV, pp. 77–78.

8 Olbourne, B., "Independence and Impartiality: International Standards for National Judges and Courts," *The Law and Practice of International Courts and Tribunals* Vol. 2 No. 1 (2003), p. 117.

9 Shetreet, S., "Judicial Independence: New Conceptual Dimensions and Contemporary Challenges" in Shetreet, S., & Deschênes, J., *Judicial Independence: The Contemporary Debate*, Martinus Nijhoff Publishers (1985).

10 See, *inter alia*, Universal Declaration of Human Rights 217 A (III) (10 December 1948), Art. 10; International Covenant on Civil and Political Rights, 999 UNTS 171 (1966), Art. 14(1); European Convention for the Protection of Human Rights and Fundamental Freedoms, ETS 5 (1950) [ECHR], Art. 6(1); American Convention on Human Rights, "Pact of San Jose" (1969) [ACHR], Art. 8(1); African Charter on Human and Peoples' Rights ("Banjul Charter"), 21 ILM 58 (1981) [ACHPR], Art. (7); UN Human Rights Committee, "General Comment No. 32 on Article 14: Right to Equality before Courts and Tribunals and to a Fair Trial" (23 August 2007), CCPR/C/GC/32. For a discussion of the hard and soft legal standing of judicial independence in international law, see Olbourne (n. 8).

of the importance of the perception of justice have further consolidated the requirement for justice to be carried out in the procedure and not only the outcome.

Although independence in this way may originally have been set out as a tool to achieve impartiality,[11] both independence and impartiality of judges are today separately required under IHRL standards. This is key to upholding the domestic rule of law and the legitimacy of States, and to upholding the rights of individuals under international law.[12]

Impartiality

Subjective impartiality

That a judge adjudicates impartially implies that they will make judicial decisions with an "absence of bias or prejudice in favour of, or against, parties or classes of parties, as well as maintaining an open mind in considering issues that may come before [them]."[13] Impartiality therefore refers to the actual decision-making process on behalf of the judge (a behavioural concept) in making adjudicatory decisions based only on relevant facts and considerations. Inappropriate internal considerations (as opposed to external pressures, as seen below in matters affecting personal independence) that may impact on the way a judge adjudicates include consideration of how the adjudication decision will affect their career prospects; conscious or unconscious approval or disapproval of the gender, religion, race, class, or other characteristic of a party to a dispute; conscious or unconscious approval or disapproval of the religious, political, or moral implications of the outcome of the decision.[14] The actual impartial decision-making includes that judges must not harbour preconceptions about the matter put before them, and that they must not act in ways

11 Although independence is neither necessary nor sufficient to achieve impartiality. An independent judge can still act partially, and a dependent judge may still be able to make impartial decisions. Helmke, G., & Rosenbluth, F., "Regimes and the Rule of Law: Judicial Independence in Comparative Perspective," *Annual Review of Political Science* Vol. 12 No. 1 (2009), pp. 348 and 356.

12 Meron, T., "Judicial Independence and Impartiality in International Criminal Tribunals," *American Journal of International Law* Vol. 99 No. 2 (2005), p. 359.

13 Wendel, W. B., "Impartiality in Judicial Ethics: A Jurisprudential Analysis," *Notre Dame Journal of Law, Ethics & Public Policy* Vol. 22 No. 2 (2014), p. 305 n. 1.

14 Andenas, M., & Fairgrieve, D., "Judicial Independence and Accountability: National Traditions and International Standards" in Canivet, G., Andenas, M., & Fairgrieve, D., *Independence, Accountability and the Judiciary*, British Institute of International and Comparative Law (2006), pp. 23–24; Gardner Geyh, C., "The Dimensions of Judicial Impartiality," *Florida Law Review* Vol. 65 No. 2 (2014), pp. 505–506; Burbank, S. B., & Friedman B. E., "Reconsidering Judicial Independence" in Burbank, S. B., & Friedman, B. E., *Judicial Independence at the Crossroads: An Interdisciplinary Approach*, Sage Publications (2002), p. 26; Ferejohn, J., "Independent Judges, Dependent Judiciary: Explaining Judicial Independence," *South California Law Review* Vol. 72 (1999), p. 369; Russell (n. 4), p. 19.

that promote the interests of one of the parties.[15] This internal impartial state of mind has been named "subjective impartiality" by human rights bodies,[16] and it may be said to be the ultimate desired goal, that is that a judge is "subjectively free of personal prejudice or bias" in their adjudication of a case, and therefore that they give a fair judgment.

Objective impartiality

Nevertheless, such an internal behavioural process is very difficult to observe or measure, and it is generally assumed to be present unless there is proof to the contrary.[17] On the other hand, guarantees for the external perception of impartiality have been considered by human rights bodies as an additional necessary requirement "to exclude any legitimate doubt" regarding the internal behaviour.[18] This difference between the actual internal impartial decision-making of the judges and the external guarantees of appearance of impartiality has been explained as "subjective" versus "objective" impartiality.[19] The appearance of impartiality includes that the judiciary "must be, and be seen to be, independent and impartial."[20]

This perception of impartiality was central to early political theorists such as Hobbes and Locke writing on the basis of a legitimate government as built upon the premise of individuals mutually giving up their right to self-adjudicate.[21] If the public does not trust that a judicial system is impartial, they risk withdrawing their confidence in a State's ability to function as a legitimate government.[22] This legitimacy is "particularly important for a body that has to

15 HRC, *Kartunnen v Finland*, Communication No. 387/1989 (5 November 1992), para. 7.2.
16 ECtHR, *Findlay v UK*, App. No. 22107/93, Judgment of 25 February 1997, para. 73.
17 ECtHR, *Piersack v Belgium*, App. No. 8692/79, Judgment of 1 October 1982, para. 30; IACtHR, *Usón Ramírez v Venezuela*, Ser. C No. 207, Judgment of 20 November 2009 (Preliminary Objections, Merits, Reparations, and Costs), para. 117; *Atala Riffo and Daughters v Chile*, Ser. C No. 239, Judgment of 24 February 2012 (Merits, Reparations, and Costs), para. 234.
18 ECtHR, *Findlay v UK* (n. 16), para. 73.
19 UN HRC, General Comment No. 32 (n. 10), para. 21. This division between subjective and objective impartiality has been maintained by the regional human rights systems: ECtHR, *Findlay v UK* (n. 16), para. 73; IACtHR, *Palamara-Iribarne v Chile*, Ser. C. No. 135, Judgment of 22 November 2005 (Merits, Reparations, and Costs), para. 146; ACHPR, *International Pen, Constitutional Rights Project, Interights on behalf of Ken Saro-Wiwa Jr. and Civil Liberties Organisation v. Nigeria*, Apps. Nos. 137/94-139/94-154/96-161/97, Decision on Merits (31 October 1998), para. 86.
20 Human Rights Committee, *Espinoza de Polay v Peru*, Communication No. 577/1994 (6 November 1997), para. 8.8.
21 Hobbes (n. 5), Pt I, Chap. XIV, p. 64.
22 Pasquino, P., "Prolegomena to a Theory of Judicial Power: The Concept of Judicial Independence in Theory and History," *Law and Practice of International Courts and Tribunals* Vol. 2 No. 1 (2003), pp. 22–25; Shimokawa, K., "Locke's Conception of Justice" in Anstey, P. R., *The Philosophy of John Locke: New Perspectives*, Routledge (2003), pp. 66–67.

decide controversial or divisive issues" as it is "a critical determinant of compliance with unfavorable decisions."[23] Therefore, if a population does not *believe* that the judiciary is acting impartially, it may well withdraw its trust in the government as a whole. The withdrawal of popular legitimacy, as Hobbes pointed out, can in turn lead to a collapse of society.[24] It suffices to look at situations of "self-defence" armed civilian groups in countries with corrupt governments to see the practical application of this notion.[25] Without an impartial judge, citizens are likely to return to the state of war, leading Hobbes to conclude that "he therefore that is partiall in judgment [...] is the cause of Warre."[26]

The test of objective impartiality, of the perception of impartiality, was developed in detail in the case law of the European Court of Human rights (ECtHR) and picked up by other human rights bodies.[27] The objective test is related to the fact that "even appearances may be of a certain importance" in matters of justice, as "what is at stake is the confidence which the courts must inspire in the public in a democratic society."[28] Perception of lack of impartiality is therefore sufficient to violate the requirement of an independent and impartial tribunal. Human rights bodies have found that the impartiality of the tribunal "capable of appearing open to doubt" can be in violation of fair trial rights.[29] The fact that tribunals were composed of military personnel has also been found to create "the appearance, if not actual lack, of impartiality."[30] This link between military personnel and appearances will be returned to in Chapter 5.

It remains to be established whose perception is determinative in establishing the objective element of impartiality: who can be considered to hold this "objective viewpoint"? Matters of independence and impartiality are often considered under fair trial rights of the accused, yet it has been made clear that in establishing lack of objective impartiality, "the standpoint of the accused is important but not decisive."[31] Indeed, it is not only or principally

23 Brems, E., & Larysen, L., "Procedural Justice in Human Rights Adjudication: The European Court of Human Rights," *Human Rights Quarterly* Vol. 35 No. 1 (2013), p. 178.

24 Hobbes (n. 5) Pt I, Chap. XV, p. 77; Meron (n. 12), p. 359.

25 See, for example, the rise of "autodefensas" groups in Mexico: Valencia, R., "The Role of the Paramilitary in Mexican Security," *World Policy* (22 January 2014), available at: https://worldpolicy.org/2014/01/22/the-role-of-the-paramilitary-in-mexican-security/.

26 Hobbes (n. 5), Pt I, Chap. XV, p. 77.

27 ECtHR, *Piersack v Belgium* (n. 17), para. 30; IACtHR, *Herrera-Ulloa v Costa Rica*, Ser. C No. 107, Judgment of 2 July 2004 (Preliminary Objections, Merits, Reparations, and Costs), para. 170; ACHPR, *Constitutional Rights Project (In Respect of Wahab Akamu, G. Adega and Others) v Nigeria*, App. No. 60/91, Decision on Merits (22 March 1995), para. 14.

28 ECtHR, *Piersack v Belgium* (n. 17), para. 30.

29 ECtHR, *Piersack v Belgium* (n. 17), para. 31.

30 ACHPR, *Constitutional Rights Project (In Respect of Wahab Akamu, G. Adega and Others) v Nigeria* (n. 27), para. 14.

31 ECtHR, *Hauschildt v Denmark*, App. No. 10486/83, Judgment of 24 May 1989, para. 48. See also ECtHR, *Campbell & Fell v UK*, App. No. 7819/77; 7878/77, Judgment of 28 June 1984, para. 81, where the perception of inmates with regard to the partiality of a prison judicial board was found to be "probably unavoidable in a custodial setting" and "not sufficient to

the accused's point of view which is important, but rather that of the general public, and whether they are "entitled to fear that [the judge] does not offer sufficient guarantees of impartiality."[32] This is because it is the public's confidence in the courts which must be maintained through the objective test,[33] and therefore it is the perspective of the "public" that will determine whether the complainant's concerns are "objectively justified."[34] More generally under international law, it appears that what matters is that the tribunal must appear impartial "to a reasonable observer."[35] The objective test of impartiality was therefore developed to give a more tangible element to establishing whether or not a tribunal can be considered impartial, as it proactively "must offer sufficient guarantees to exclude any legitimate doubt in this respect."[36] The question to be answered in such a case may be phrased as: can a reasonable observer expect to believe that a judge is behaving impartially due to the visible relational factors? Such visible relational factors are found in guarantees of independence, as explored below.

Independence

The concept of independence can be divided into personal and institutional independence. Individual independence refers to the independence of the judge as a person,[37] whereas institutional independence refers to the independence of the judiciary as a branch of government (also known as "collective" independence).[38] This distinction is made because the pressures affecting the judiciary as a whole may be different from pressures which are targeted at or affecting judges as individuals.

Personal independence

It is generally accepted that a judge must be personally protected from financial, physical, or other threats which could lead them (consciously or not) to take into account considerations in adjudicating other than the facts at hand and the laws applicable. These factors of "personal independence" are elements

---

establish" the lack of perception, but that the test should rather be whether they were "reasonably entitled" to think that the board was dependent on the executive.

32 ECtHR, *Piersack v Belgium* (n. 17), para. 30.

33 ECtHR, *Piersack v Belgium* (n. 17), para. 30.

34 ECtHR, *Hauschildt v Denmark* (n. 31), para. 48.

35 General Comment No. 32 (n. 10), para. 21; HRC, *Kartunnen v Finland* (n. 15), para. 7.2; ICTY, *Prosecutor v Anto Furundzija*, IT-95-17/1-A, Appeals Chamber Judgment of 21 July 2000, para. 189; Meron (n. 12), p. 367.

36 ECtHR, *Findlay v UK* (n. 16), para. 73.

37 Shetreet (n. 9), p. 590.

38 Shetreet (n. 9); OHCHR/IBA, "Independence and Impartiality of Judges, Prosecutors and Lawyers" in *Human Rights in the Administration of Justice: A Manual on Human Rights for Judges, Prosecutors and Lawyers*, United Nations (2003), p. 120.

which could be seen to affect the individual judge's ability to act impartially; judges should not be placed under undue pressure and should be able to make decisions based solely on "promulgated standing laws."[39] The personal independence of a judge is secured through "judicial terms of office and tenure"[40] for the individual judge, and other factors protecting a judge's physical and employment integrity.[41] This has been emphasised by human rights bodies who have stipulated that personal independence can be affected by the manner of appointment and removal of judges, tenure, mechanisms for discipline, safeguards from inappropriate pressures and influences, and training.[42]

Institutional independence

Institutional independence is broader than personal independence, as it refers to the independence of the judiciary as a branch of government. There may be pressures that affect the institution as a whole which may be unrelated to pressures upon individuals, for example in the way the judicial branch can handle its administration, finances, decision-making processes, and jurisdictional competence.[43] Most crucially, it is understood to be institutional independence from

39 Locke (n. 5), Chap. XI, para. 136.

40 Shetreet (n. 9), p. 599.

41 OHCHR/IBA (n. 38), pp. 123–134; Russell (n. 4), pp. 18–21; "Report of the Special Rapporteur on the Independence of Judges and Lawyers," A/HRC/20/19 (7 June 2012) [Knaul Report 2012], para. 76; Shetreet (n. 9), p. 623.

42 General Comment No. 32 (n. 10), para. 19; Report of the Human Rights Committee, Fiftieth Session, A/50/40 Vol. 1, para. 288 (USA); Report of the Human Rights Committee, Fifty-First Session, A/51/40 Vol. 1, para. 202 (Zambia); Report of the Human Rights Committee, Fifty-Second Session, A/52/40 Vol. 1, para. 224 (Bolivia); Report of the Human Rights Committee, Fifty-Fifth Session, A/55/40 Vol. 1, paras 279–280 (Congo), and para. 405 (Kyrgyzstan). ECtHR, *Campbell & Fell v UK* (n. 31), para. 78. For an overview of cases using these criteria, see Power, A., "Judicial Independence and the Democratic Process: Some Case Law of the European Court of Human Rights," International Bar Association Conference (2012), pp. 5–12. IACtHR, *Constitutional Court Case (Aguirre Roca, Rey Terry and Revorado Marsano v Peru)*, Ser. C No. 71, Judgment of 31 January 2001 (Merits, Reparations, and Costs), para. 75; ACHPR, *Civil Liberties Organisation, Legal Defence Centre, Legal Defence and Assistance Project v Nigeria*, App. No. 218/98, Decision on Merits (7 May 2001), para. 27.

43 OHCHR/IBA (n. 38), pp. 120–122; Report of the Human Rights Committee, Fifty-Third Session, A/53/40 Vol. 1, para. 13 (Sudan); Report of the Human Rights Committee, Fifty-Second Session, A/52/40 Vol. 1, para. 224 (Bolivia); "Report of the Special Rapporteur on the Independence of Judges and Lawyers, Leandro Despouy," A/HRC/11/41 (2009), paras 20–43; UN Basic Principles on the Independence of the Judiciary, UN Doc A/CONF.121/22/Rev.1 (1985), para. 7; Montreal Universal Declaration on the Independence of Justice (1983) [Montreal Declaration] Art. 2.05; 2.40–2.44; International Bar Association, Code of Minimum Standards Judicial Independence (1982) [IBA Code] paras 8–10, 33–34; Beijing Statement of Principles of the Independence of the Judiciary in the LAWASIA Region (1995) [Beijing Statement], paras 33–37, 41–42.

the other branches of government.[44] Institutional independence is expressed in some constitutions through the concept of the separation of powers, although it is by no means the only way in which institutional independence may be guaranteed at a domestic level.[45] The ways in which such institutional protections are implemented to protect the judiciary from undue influence from other branches of government are as varied as their democratic legal systems.[46]

The "separation of powers" theory states that a government must be divided into three branches: the executive, the judicial, and the legislative. Each of these branches must be separate, or independent from one another, to establish a system of checks and balances to ensure that no institution could become too powerful and despotic.[47] The concept of separation of powers as embodied in the US Constitution was based upon the writings of Montesquieu, who considered the dangers of combining multiple functions in a single governmental authority.[48] Montesquieu, in turn, was influenced by the writings of Locke on the importance of standing laws to avoid arbitrary exercise of governmental power, as judges must make decisions on rights of subjects "by promulgated standing laws" and not "through passion or interest."[49] This idea has been the basis for the concept of the "rule of law" in liberal societies.[50]

44 International human rights bodies have considered the institutional independence of the judiciary in relation to protections from other branches of government on many occasions. See, e.g., Despouy Report (n. 43), paras 18–19; General Comment No. 32 (n. 10), paras 18–19; ECtHR, *Ringeisen v Austria*, App. No. 2614/65, Judgment of 16 July 1971, para. 95; IACtHR, *Apitz Barbera v Venezuela*, Ser. C No. 182, Judgment of 5 August 2008 (Preliminary Objections, Merits, Reparations, and Costs), para. 55; ACHPR, *Media Rights Agenda v Nigeria*, App. No. 224/98, Decision on Merits (6 November 2000), para. 66; IBA Code (n. 43), paras 16, 19–20; Montreal Declaration (n. 43), para. 2.04; Beijing Statement (n. 43), paras 5, 38–40.

45 Human Rights bodies have also established that the separation of powers is neither necessary nor sufficient to achieve independence and impartiality as mandated for by IHRL bodies. Indeed, despite England being the basis of Montesquieu's arguments relating to the separation of powers, the UK until recently was not considered to have held a system of exact separation of powers. It nevertheless had other protections in place to ensure the independence of judges with regard to the influence from other branches of government, guaranteed "both by statute and by the political and legal cultures." ECtHR, *Henryk Urban & Ryszard Urban v Poland*, App. No. 23614/08, Judgment of 30 November 2010, para. 46; Russell (n. 4), p. 302; Helmke & Rosenbluth (n. 11), p. 353; Kornhauser, L. A., "Is Judicial Independence a Useful Concept?" in Burbank & Friedman (n. 14), p. 47.

46 Andenas & Fairgrieve (n. 14), p. 6; Muir Watt, H., "Quelques remarques d'ordre comparative sur la notion d'Accountability apliquée à la justice" in Canivet, Andenas, & Fairgrieve (n. 14), pp. 237–238.

47 Madison, J., The Federalist Papers, No. 51 (1788), reprinted in Hamilton, A., Madison, J., & Jay, J., *The Federalist Papers*, Oxford University Press (2008), pp. 256–260.

48 Montesquieu, C. de S., *The Spirit of the Laws* (1748) as translated and edited by Cohler, A. M., Miller, B. C., & Stone, H. S., Cambridge University Press (1989), Book 11, Chaps 4–6.

49 Locke (n. 5), Pt 1, Chap. XI, para. 136.

50 Helmke & Rosenbluth (n. 11), p. 348.

It is worth pointing out that "institutional independence" may sometimes be used or understood as meaning independence of the investigator from the institution under investigation, for example in the case of an investigator being a member of the military. This is not, however, the meaning that is used here, insofar as the term "military" is not necessarily synonymous with the executive branch of government. Some military judicial members may well be considered part of the judicial branch of government (see Chapter 5, on military chains of command). What matters in each case would be whether the judicial institution, even if part of it is incorporated within the military, is free from undue influence from the executive powers of government. This will be explored further below.

Independence may therefore be seen as originally important *because* it is conducive (if not necessary) to an impartial judge and the rule of law.[51] In turn, the belief that the judiciary will act impartially has been perceived as fundamentally central to the legitimacy of the government and upholding the rule of law. International human rights bodies have established criteria for measuring the independence and impartiality of judges, specifically, that courts, or tribunals and judges must meet four requirements: institutional independence, personal independence, subjective impartiality, and objective impartiality. Under the IHRL requirement for the independence and impartiality of judges and tribunals, it is necessary to meet the four separate (but related) elements of institutional independence, personal independence, as well as both subjective and objective impartiality.

This book has limited its scope specifically to the investigation stage of judicial procedures, in part because there is little written on this specific stage. Nevertheless, it is important to remark at this point that the independence of military judges, courts, and tribunals is a point of contention in academia and practice. At a very superficial level, it may be argued that the concept of "military justice" violates the principle of separation of powers in embodying both the executive and the legislature. It is suggested here the answer may not be so straightforward, as some "military" judges may well be considered as part of the judicial branch of government and have sufficient measures of personal independence. Although this research does not claim to address all the intricacies of military judges and courts, some of these considerations are key to the investigation stage and will be returned to throughout the book.

The independence and impartiality of investigations

The section above clarified that the requirements of independence and impartiality for the judiciary very much tie into the adjudication process, namely in serving the purpose of impartial adjudication. It has also become clear that the perception of independence and impartiality is necessary for trust in the

51 See above, n. 11.

judicial system. For the judiciary, the appearance of justice is as crucial as actual justice itself.

Investigations, however, are usually not part of adjudication – they can be linked to but are separate from the trial stage of judicial procedures. Some investigations may never be linked to an adjudication procedure at all, especially administrative investigations. It is not obvious from the outset therefore that the same standards applicable to judges, courts, and tribunals should apply to investigations. It is also not clear that investigators are necessarily considered part of the "judiciary" in all cases. Rather, it is suggested that the purpose of independence and impartiality of investigations is slightly different: it is to serve the effectiveness of the investigation, which in turn may contribute (or not) to the trial stage.

This section addresses the question of whether investigations need to be independent and impartial, and if so why. It may be put forward that investigations must be independent and impartial as an extension of the fair trial guarantees, but the difficulties in this assertion are set out below. Although it has been found that fair trial guarantees may apply to the investigation stage insofar as they can affect the trial stage, it cannot be said that the same adjudicatory function of the impartial judge is to be found at the investigation stage. Rather, it is suggested that the effectiveness of investigations (as explored in Chapter 3) may require impartiality on behalf of investigators, and that independence serves to support this impartiality. Nevertheless, such standards may very well depend on the context and type of violation. For investigations, the standards of independence and impartiality are very much a means to an end, rather than absolute standards which are required in and of themselves as under fair trial rights.

Do investigations need to be independent and impartial?

Chapter 2 examined how the term "fair trial" is interpreted slightly differently depending on the regional and domestic contexts, and how this has affected the varying focus on the rights of the accused versus the rights of victims under such interpretations. This interpretation can also affect whether or not standards of fair trial are deemed to be applicable to investigations.

Before the ECtHR and Human Rights Committee of the International Covenant on Civil and Political Rights (ICCPR), which take a more restrictive approach to the concept, fair trial rights apply only to the court and trial process. Other stages of the judicial procedure may affect fair trial rights only insofar as they directly affect the court process.[52] The ECtHR has explicitly stated that

52 ECtHR, *Haarde v Iceland*, App. No. 66847/12, Judgment of 23 November 2017, para. 78; "Chapter 6: The Right to a Fair Trial: Part I – From Investigation to Trial" in OHCHR/IBA (n. 38); ICCPR (n. 10), Article 14; General Comment No. 32 (n. 10); Amnesty International, *Fair Trial Manual* (2nd ed.) (2014); Lubell, N., Pejic, J., & Simmons, C., "Guide-

the standards of independence and impartiality as applicable to judges, courts, and tribunals do not apply to investigations.[53] Rather, the standards applicable to investigations are to be derived from the substantive human rights provisions under which the duty to investigate arises.[54] The broader concept of due process before the Inter-American Court of Human Rights (IACtHR), on the other hand, encompasses multiple stages of judicial proceedings, from investigation to trial.[55] The IACtHR has suggested that the criterion of independence and impartiality as broadly part of due process rights does apply to investigations prior to trials.[56] This is evident in its jurisprudence on restrictive military jurisdiction, which has generally extended to investigations as well as trials.[57]

Nevertheless, both regional human rights bodies have come to similar conclusions as to what independence and impartiality means for investigations, and both bodies have used the independence and impartiality of judges to interpret standards applicable to investigations, while adapting them to the context.[58] In particular, both have agreed that what matters is the "overall" independence and impartiality of the investigation, as explored below. It may therefore be concluded that the standards of independence and impartiality as applicable to judges, courts, and tribunals, as required under IHRL standards of fair trial, do not apply *ipso facto* to investigations. Nevertheless, what independence and impartiality of investigators means and how it can be measured may usefully be informed by the extended literature and jurisprudence on the standards applicable to trials, taking into account the different purposes and contexts of investigations.

Although the regional differences do not reflect a common/civil law divide, Chapter 2 explored how some of the approaches of the IACtHR do resemble more closely the civil law systems which make up the majority of States party to the American Convention on Human Rights. This may also be observed with relation to the fact that the investigation and trial stage are not so clearly distinguished in these States. Whereas common law systems clearly separate the functions of investigators (usually police) and that of judges, civil law

lines on Investigating Violations of International Humanitarian Law: Law, Policy, and Good Practice," Geneva Academy/ICRC (2019), Guideline 11, para. 155.

53 ECtHR, *Mustafa Tunç and Fecire Tunç v Turkey*, App. No. 24014/05, Judgment of 14 April 2015, paras 219–225.

54 ECtHR, *Mustafa Tunç and Fecire Tunç v Turkey* (n. 53), paras 219–225.

55 Salmón, E., & Blanco, C., *El derecho al debido proceso en la jurisprudencia de la Corte Interamericana de Derechos Humanos*, Instituto de Democracia y Derechos Humanos y Cooperación Alemana de Desarrollo (2012), p. 29.

56 IACtHR, *Favela Novela Brasilia v Brazil*, Ser. C. No. 345, Judgment of 16 February 2017 (Preliminary Objections, Merits, Reparations, and Costs), para. 185.

57 See Chapter 2.

58 See, e.g., the similar approach on jurisdiction: ECtHR, *Mustafa Tunç and Fecire Tunç v Turkey* (n. 53), paras 223–234; IACtHR, *Favela Novela Brasilia v Brazil* (n. 56), paras 186–191. It is interesting to note that unlike many previous cases involving military investigations, the *Favela Novela Brasilia* case involved police investigations.

systems often have a range of actors involved in investigations which include both police officers as well as "investigative judges" who often oversee the investigation efforts.[59] Civil law systems may therefore be considered to have some form of "judge" already involved at the investigation stage, at least in an overseeing capacity. The different roles of investigators in a military context will be explored further in subsequent chapters, but it is worth remarking that who may be understood to be an "investigator" may vary substantially depending on the domestic system, and may involve police members, prosecutors, and judges.[60] When assessing the independence and impartiality of an "investigator," this justifies even further the need to take a holistic and contextual approach of the whole process, as explored below.

Overall independence and impartiality as serving effectiveness

It may therefore be asked where the standards of independence and impartiality of investigations stem from. Looking back at jurisprudence of human rights bodies, it is clear that the need for independent and impartial investigations was not an extension of the standards applicable to the trial stage, although they may be understood as part of a broader provision of access to justice. In fact, the first allusions to the need for specific standards in investigations of alleged human rights violations did not mention the concept of independence, but focused on the need for impartiality, and often other standards such as promptness or thoroughness.[61] It is suggested that such standards were eluci-

59 Banks, C., & Baker, J., *Comparative, International and Global Justice: Perspectives from Criminology and Criminal Justice*, Sage Publications (2016), p. 105.

60 See ECtHR, *Hanan v Germany*, App. No. 4871/16, Judgment of 16 February 2021, paras 179–181, where the German government explains the structure of the German investigative authorities. See also Cohen, A., & Shany, Y., "Beyond the Grave Breaches Regime: The Duty to Investigate Alleged Violations of International Law Governing Armed Conflicts," *Yearbook of International Humanitarian Law* Vol. 14 (2011), pp. 66–70.

61 Prohibition of Torture: Convention Against Torture and Other Cruel, Inhuman or Degrading Treatment or Punishment, 1465 UNTS 85 (1984), Article 12; Human Rights Committee, *Annadurdy Khadziyev v Turkmenistan*, Communication No. 2252/2013 (24 May 2018), para. 9; *Urmatbek Akunov v Kyrgyzstan*, Communication No. 2127/2011 (7 December 2016), para. 8.3; ECtHR, *Aksoy v Turkey*, App. No. 21987/93, Judgment of 18 December 1996, para. 98, citing *Soering v UK*, Application no. 4038/88, Judgment of 7 July 1989, para. 88. Right to life: UN ECOSOC, Principles on the Effective Prevention and Investigation of Extra-Legal, Arbitrary and Summary Executions (1989), para. 9; UN OHCHR, Manual on the Effective Prevention and Investigation of Extra-Legal, Arbitrary and Summary Executions (1991), Section III.A; International Convention for the Protection of All Persons from Enforced Disappearance (2006), Article 12; ECtHR, *McCann and Others v UK*, App. No. 18984/91, Judgment of 17 September 1995, para. 163; *Nachova and Others v Bulgaria*, Apps. Nos. 43577/98 and 43579/98, Judgment of 6 July 2005, para. 113; IACtHR, *Juan Humberto Sanchez v Honduras*, Ser. C No. 99, Judgment of 7 June 2003 (Preliminary Objections, Merits, Reparations, and Costs), para. 127; *Myrna Mack Chang v Guatemala*, Ser. C No. 101, Judgment of 25 November 2003 (Merits, Reparations, and Costs), paras 173–174; Articles 22 and 23 United Nations Basic Principles on the Use

dated as necessary to achieve the effectiveness of investigations, as elaborated in Chapter 3.

The initial emphasis on impartiality appears to be especially related to the collection of evidence.[62] The establishment of facts (to enable a subsequent determination as to whether or not a violation occurred) requires impartiality in the collection of evidence, and in the way investigative decisions are made (such as whether or not to continue with an investigation). The IACtHR has signalled that this is especially pertinent in cases where investigators are also possible perpetrators.[63] An emphasis on promptness was similarly made, as the passage of time dramatically affects the availability and usability of evidence. Subsequent developments related to the duty to investigate added the requirement of independence as a necessary corollary to the standard of impartiality.[64] Indeed, as seen above with regard to impartial decision-making of judges, the difficulty in verifying an internal behavioural concept has led to the requirement of external guarantees of impartiality, namely, standards of independence.

---

of Force and Firearms by Law Enforcement Officials (1990) make reference to independence more generally with regard to administrative or prosecutorial authorities. UN OHCHR, Basic Principles and Guidelines on the Right to a Remedy and Reparation for Victims of Gross Violations of International Human Rights Law and Serious Violations of International Humanitarian Law, A/RES/60/147 (2005), para. 3(b); Human Rights Committee, "General Comment No. 31: The Nature of the General Legal Obligation Imposed on States Parties to the Covenant," CCPR/C/21/Rev.1/Add. 13 (29 March 2004), paras 15 and 18.

62 E.g., Committee Against Torture, *Gerasimov v Kazakhstan*, Communication No. 433/2010 (10 July 2012), para. 12.5; *Keremedchiev v Bulgaria*, Communication No. 257/2004 (11 November 2008), para. 9.4; *Blanco Abad v Spain*, Communication No. 59/1996 (14 May 1998), para. 8.2; Second Report of the Public Commission to Examine the Maritime Incident of 31 May 2010: Israel's Mechanisms for Examining and Investigating Complaints and Claims of Violations of the Laws of Armed Conflict According to International Law" [Second Turkel Report], p. 126, citing Convention Against Torture (n. 61), Art. 12 and the UN Principles on the Effective Investigation of Torture (n. 61); ECtHR, *Aksoy v Turkey* (n. 61), para. 98. IACtHR, *Myrna Mack Chang v Guatemala* (n. 61), paras 173–174; *Cantoral Huamaní and García Santa Cruz v Peru*, Ser. C No. 167, Judgment of 10 July 2007 (Preliminary Objection, Merits, Reparations, and Costs), para. 133; De León, G., Krsticevic, V., & Obando, L., *Debida diligencia en la investigación de graves violaciones a derechos humanos*, Centro por la Justicia y el Derecho Internacional – CEJIL (2010), p. 29.

63 IACtHR, *Myrna Mack Chang v Guatemala* (n. 61), paras 173–174; Second Turkel Report (n. 62), p. 126.

64 UN OHCHR, Revision of the UN Manual on the Effective Prevention and Investigation of Extra-Legal, Arbitrary and Summary Executions (2016) [Minnesota Protocol], paras 20–22; ECtHR, *McKerr v UK*, App. No. 28883/95, Judgment of 4 May 2001, para. 112; ACHPR, *Sudan Human Rights Organisation & Centre on Housing Rights and Evictions v Republic of Sudan*, App. No. 279/03-296/05, Decision on Merits (27 May 2009), para. 150; Human Rights Committee, *Mamatkarim Ernazarov v Kyrgyzstan*, Communication No. 2054/2011 (7 May 2015), para. 9.6; *Olimzhon Eshonov* v *Uzbekistan*, Communication No. 1225/2003 (18 August 2010), para. 9.6.

The purpose of the given standards of investigations therefore all appear to serve the effectiveness of the investigation.[65] This is evident in the phrasing of the regional human rights courts, which have linked the concept of independence to the effectiveness of investigations.[66] In such contexts, independent and impartial investigators have been found as necessary for the effectiveness of proceedings. Both the ECtHR and the IACtHR have relatively recently brought this focus back to the concept of "effectiveness"[67] by highlighting that investigators do not need to enjoy "absolute independence," they need only to be "sufficiently independent," taking into account the relevant circumstances.[68]

This may be understood as the test of "overall independence and impartiality," which can be phrased in the following way: "Overall, does the investigative body meet sufficient standards of independence and impartiality in order to guarantee the effectiveness of the investigation?" This concept of overall independence and impartiality is contrasted with the "absolute independence" which is required under fair trial rights regarding the independence and impartiality of judges, courts, and tribunals, where all criteria must be met separately. Unlike when examining the independence and impartiality of judges therefore, finding one element which may cast doubt as to the body's independence or impartiality is not sufficient to find a violation of the duty to investigate. Rather, they must be examined separately in each context in light of the purpose of the investigation in question.

Assessing independence and impartiality for investigations

Having seen that the independence and impartiality of investigations are to be assessed by their overall contribution to the effectiveness of the investigations, it is worth examining how these standards may be measured. The standards are to be measured differently to those applicable to judges, courts, and tribunals, insofar as they do not necessarily need to be met separately, as long as they are sufficient to contribute to the effectiveness of the investigation. The independence and impartiality of judges may also be more uniform in application across different trials, whereas the large amount of variation in the type and purposes of investigations may affect what independence and impartiality look

65 See Chapter 3 on the five general principles generally accepted to apply to investigations. Independence, impartiality, thoroughness, promptness, and transparency may thus be understood to all be necessary to contribute to the effectiveness of the investigation.

66 ECtHR, *McKerr v UK* (n. 64), para. 112; ACHPR, *Sudan Human Rights Organisation & Centre on Housing Rights and Evictions (COHRE) v Sudan* (n. 64), para. 150; *Mustafa Tunç and Fecire Tunç v Turkey* (n. 53).

67 ECtHR, *Mustafa Tunç and Fecire Tunç v Turkey* (n. 53), para. 225; *Hanan v Germany* (n. 60), para. 209; IACtHR: *Favela Novela Brasilia v Brazil* (n. 56), para. 190.

68 ECtHR, *Mustafa Tunç and Fecire Tunç v Turkey* (n. 53), paras 223, 249; IACtHR: *Favela Novela Brasilia v Brazil* (n. 56), para. 189.

like. Insofar as independence and impartiality must serve the effectiveness of the investigation, they are to be measured in light of the purpose of the investigation, which in turn is determined by the source of the duty to investigate (as seen in Chapter 3). What independence and impartiality looks like is therefore affected by the specific context and alleged violation in question.

This section suggests that there are three principal ways to assess the overall independence and impartiality of investigations: 1) by assessing the matters of impartiality and implication in the event under investigation; 2) by looking at the independence from those with responsibility in the events in question; and 3) by considering how the standards of independence and impartiality interact with the other applicable standards of an effective investigation.

Is the investigator "implicated"?

It may be considered obvious that an effective investigation requires at the very least that the investigator should not themselves be implicated, namely that the investigators should not be potential suspects or have been involved in the incident under investigation.[69] The concept of an "implicated" individual refers to someone whose individual responsibility may be engaged by the incident under question. In fact, the matter of implication may be considered fundamentally a matter of partiality, insofar as an individual involved in a potentially unlawful act cannot be considered not to have bias or conflict of interest with regard to that act.

Nevertheless, there are various reasons why it is important to address the matter of implication. First, in the context of military chains of command and international criminal law, the matter of personal responsibility for criminal offences is not solely tied to the individual perpetrators. As will be explored further in Chapter 6, commanders may be considered implicated in the possible commission of war crimes which may lead to important considerations for independence and impartiality. There are also other non-criminal forms of responsibility for subordinates which would be important to take into account in assessing who may have engaged responsibility, and therefore potential bias.[70]

69 ECtHR, *Mustafa Tunç and Fecire Tunç v Turkey* (n. 53), para. 222; *Bektaş and Özalp v Turkey*, App. no. 10036/03, Judgment of 20 April 2010, para. 6; *Orhan v Turkey*, App. No. 25656/94, Judgment of 18 June 2002, para. 342; Guidelines on Investigating Violations of International Humanitarian Law (n. 52), para. 103.

70 There are non-criminal offences which may nevertheless involve individual wrongdoing (e.g., disciplinary offences) and which may amount to violations, in which case a similar consideration of implication may arise. The considerations of fair trial applicable at the investigation phase would not be the same as in those of possible criminal proceedings, although if an individual is suspected of (non-criminal) wrongdoing, there may still be a need for a sliding scale of judicial guarantees of protection. In the cases of disciplinary offences (that do not amount to criminal offences), the commander of an individual may have the permission and even obligation to deal with the offence. Annex to the Second Turkel Report (n. 62), p. 683,

Second, and at the other extreme, there is the case where no individual person's responsibility may be engaged. Chapter 3 established that it is not only criminal offences which may lead to violations of either IHRL or IHL, but that investigations are also required for "serious" non-criminal violations, and that these investigations must be effective. Their level of independence and impartiality must therefore be sufficient to guarantee their effectiveness. Some of these possible violations may involve no individual liability at all, but rather relate to systemic problems and/or matters of State responsibility. Because this has not been directly addressed in the literature, it is difficult to provide more than speculative suggestions on what may or may not be required in such contexts. It is conceivable, at least in theory, that some systemic problems with no indication of individual criminal wrongdoing may not necessarily require independent investigations in order to be effective. This is because there may be situations in which the individuals and institutions closest to the incidents may, for reasons of effectiveness, need to be involved in establishing the root causes of the violations and remedying such situations. It would be necessary in such contexts to establish the purpose of the investigation and any possible liabilities (i.e., who may be implicated) in order to assess the required level of independence to achieve impartiality. Oversight and/or supervision by independent authorities in such context may also prove useful in supporting the effectiveness of the investigation.

However, it must be pointed out that there is room to argue that the repetition of a certain type of incident, even if it does not amount to a crime, may be indicative of something more sinister which may require further independence. This will be returned to in Chapter 7.

Independence from those with responsibility

The case law of the human rights bodies on the independence and impartiality of investigators is difficult to generalise, for various reasons: they deal with various human rights violations (therefore the purpose of the investigation can differ); they have evolved over time as new cases arise; and the diverse cases in each region have led to slightly different interpretations. There is, however, a minimum standard which is consistently found in all cases, and which is useful to apply in a cross-cutting manner, namely, that investigators must be "sufficiently independent of the *persons* and *structures* whose responsibility is likely to be engaged."[71] These matters are explored below.

---

para. 50; Kremmydiotis, P., "The Influence of Human Rights Law on the Reform of Military Justice" in Duxbury, A., & Groves, M., *Military Justice in the Modern Age*, Cambridge University Press (2016), p. 322; ECtHR, *Engel and Others v Netherlands*, Apps. Nos 5100/71; 5101/71; 5102/71; 5354/72; 5370/72, Judgment of 8 June 1986, paras 82 and 85.

71 ECtHR, *Mustafa Tunç and Fecire Tunç* v Turkey (n. 53), para. 223 [emphasis added]. This has also been phrased as "the persons responsible for the investigation must be independent from those implicated in the events." *Sergey Shevchenko v Ukraine*, App. No. 32478/02,

The standard that investigators be independent from those whose responsibility may be engaged means that they should not be under undue pressure from those who are implicated. In this context it may be understood as personal independence: that there not be inappropriate pressures (whether positive or negative) on the investigator which may lead them to make decisions based on anything irrelevant. Human rights bodies have specified that such independence requires that there be no hierarchical or institutional influence, as well as practical independence.[72] It is this standard which matters most when looking at the concept of overall independence and impartiality. The ECtHR has found in such cases that it is necessary to examine whether or not, in the given specific circumstances, the institutional connection undermined the effectiveness of the investigation (N.B. This is still a matter of personal, not institutional, independence, as seen above). Both the ECtHR and IACtHR have found on occasion that being a member of the same institution has not in itself undermined the effectiveness of the investigation.[73] While contexts which include institutional connections call for "stricter scrutiny,"[74] it may not, on its own, necessarily violate the required effectiveness of the investigation. This aspect needs to be considered alongside other factors, such as whether there were legitimate doubts about the overall integrity of the investigative process,[75] or whether the nature of the offence related to the exercise of State functions.[76] Specificities related to personal independence in military contexts will be explored further in Chapter 5.

The requirement of independence requires independence not only from "persons" but also "structures" whose responsibility is likely to be engaged. This element is more complicated, and appears to refer to cases in which

Judgment of 4 April 2006, para. 64; *Paul & Audrey Edwards v UK*, App. No. 46477/99, Judgment of 14 March 2002, para. 70; *Mastromatteo v Italy*, App. No. 37703/97, Judgment of 24 October 2002, para. 91; *McKerr v UK* (n. 64), para. 112; IACtHR: *Favela Novela Brasilia v Brazil* (n. 56), para. 189; ACHPR, *Sudan Human Rights Organisation & Centre on Housing Rights and Evictions (COHRE) v Sudan* (n. 64), para. 150.

72 ECtHR, *McKerr v UK* (n. 64), para. 112. The wording "clear independence" was replaced by "practical independence" in subsequent case law citing this case. ACHPR, *Sudan Human Rights Organisation & Centre on Housing Rights and Evictions (COHRE) v Sudan* (n. 64), para. 150. The concept of "practical independence," as opposed to institutional/hierarchical independence could be said to relate to the conduct of investigators irrespective of their formal relationships. Mowbray, A., "Duties of Investigation under the ECHR," *International and Comparative Law Quarterly* Vol. 51 No. 2 (2002), p. 440; *Ergi v Turkey*, App. No. 66/1997/850/1057, Judgment of 28 July 1998, para. 83. The fact of sharing living quarters (which may be considered an element of practical dependence) was not found to affect this. *Jaloud v The Netherlands*, App. No. 47708-08, Judgment of 20 November 2014, para. 189.

73 ECtHR, *Jaloud v Netherlands* (n. 72), para. 189; *Mustafa Tunç and Fecire Tunç* v Turkey (n. 53), para. 254; *Mantog v Roumania*, App. No. 2893/02, Judgment of 11 October 2007, para. 70; *Hanan v Germany* (n. 60), para. 223; *Favela Novela Brasilia v Brazil* (n. 56).

74 ECtHR, *Mustafa Tunç and Fecire Tunç* v Turkey (n. 53), para. 224.

75 ECtHR, *McKerr v UK* (n. 64), paras 127–128.

76 ECtHR, *Mantog c Roumanie* (n. 73), para. 70.

institutions as a whole may be considered to have an element of responsibility for possible violations, and should therefore not be in charge of the investigations. It is not, however, the case that every possible violation committed by a military or police officer must be removed from the military or police as an institution. As seen above, there have been cases where investigations were found to be sufficiently independent because the deaths "did not occur in circumstances which might, *a priori*, give rise to suspicions against the security forces as an institution."[77] This explains the difference in approach to previous case law, where deaths had occurred during "clashes involving the use of force in demonstrations, police and military operations or in cases of violent deaths during police custody."[78] This seems to suggest that in the latter cases there could be suspicion that there is a broader systemic problem within the security institutions, and therefore being "sufficiently independent of the persons and structures whose responsibility is likely to be engaged"[79] would require further independence from these institutions. This will be explored in more detail in Chapter 7.

Nevertheless, it would appear that this concept of institutional responsibility is complicated by a number of factors, not least the endless number of possible permutations it could encompass, but also by the overall requirement of effectiveness, which may take on a different meaning in situations of armed conflict. These issues will be returned to in subsequent chapters.

Independence and impartiality in light of the whole investigation

The requirement of "overall independence and impartiality" means that the above-mentioned requirements of independence and impartiality may not necessarily need all to be present in order for an investigation to be effective. This concept has evolved over time, and is evidenced in more recent cases, which now use the phrasing "for an investigation [...] to be effective, it may *generally* be regarded as necessary" for investigators to be independent from those implicated,[80] as opposed to an absolute obligation. The requirements of overall independence and impartiality means that all circumstances of the possible violation and surrounding context needs to be taken into account, including the promptness, thoroughness, and transparency of the investigation, but also the nature of the alleged violation and the context in which it occurred.

For example, a lack of thoroughness, especially related to the conduct of the investigative bodies, may be seen as aggravating lack of independence,

77 ECtHR, *Mustafa Tunç and Fecire Tunç* v Turkey (n. 53), para. 255.
78 ECtHR, *Mustafa Tunç and Fecire Tunç* v Turkey (n. 53), para. 255.
79 ECtHR, *Mustafa Tunç and Fecire Tunç* v Turkey (n. 53), para. 223.
80 E.g. ECtHR, *Hanan v Germany* (n. 60), para. 206 [emphasis added]. Earlier cases used the phrasing "for an investigation [...] to be effective, it *is* necessary," e.g., *Al-Skeini v UK*, App. No. 55721/07, Judgment of 7 July 2011, para. 167.

such as the failure to carry out certain measures or to punish those responsible if appropriate, giving excessive weight to suspects' statements, failing to explore certain lines of inquiry clearly required, or excessive inertia.[81] The need for promptness may also be linked to independence, insofar as a lack of promptness can create "an appearance of collusion in or tolerance of unlawful acts."[82] The fact that State agents took too long to initiate investigation steps has been seen as undermining the need to maintain public confidence in State institutions.[83] On the other hand, the need for promptness to safeguard evidence and initiate investigative steps has been found to be sufficiently important to justify the use of officials who may not otherwise have met the sufficient degree of independence.[84] A lack of independence can also be found to be aggravated by a lack of transparency, especially in the context in which State agents are involved, as "the true circumstances of the death in such cases are often, in practice, largely confined within the knowledge of State officials or authorities."[85] Additional independence in such cases can be crucial for reasons of trust in State institutions – a matter which brings us back to the perception of justice.

In a similar manner to the need for a perception of independence and impartiality in the context of judges, a need for an appearance of independence and impartiality has also been found for investigations. Whereas for judges this is fundamentally tied to the need for trust in impartial adjudication by judges, in the context of investigations into actions of State agents it is in fact more crucially linked to the need to trust the actions of State agents who have a monopoly of the legitimate use of force.[86] Because direct public scrutiny is not always possible in such contexts, the appearance of independence as a safeguard of trust is all the more important.[87] This need is heightened in the context where there is a general "lack of confidence in the system,"[88] for example where there have been historical tensions between the State body and the affected population. This element has been emphasised in the context of investigations as remedies: where there has already been an established violation by the State, independence can provide an additional safeguard and improve trust

81 ECtHR, *Mustafa Tunç and Fecire Tunç* v Turkey (n. 53), para. 222; *Favela Novela Brasilia v Brazil* (n. 56), para. 188.

82 ECtHR, *Armani da Silva v UK*, App. No. 5878/08, Judgment of 30 March 2016, para. 237; *McKerr v UK* (n. 64), para. 111, 114; *Opuz v Turkey*, App. No. 33401/02, Judgment of 9 June 2009, para. 150.

83 ECtHR, *Armani da Silva v UK*, App. No. 5878/08, Judgment of 30 March 2016, para. 237.

84 ECtHR, *Hanan v Germany* (n. 60), para. 223. The Court in this case cited the "inter-relatedness of promptness and independence."

85 ECtHR, *Leonidis v Greece*, App. No. 43326/05, Judgment of 8 January 2009, para. 67.

86 ECtHR, *Ramsahai and Others v Netherlands*, App. No. 52391/99, Judgment of 15 May 2007, para. 325; *Enukidze & Girgvliani v Georgia*, Application no. 25091/07, Judgment of 26 April 2011, para. 243.

87 ECtHR, *Hugh Jordan v UK*, App. No. 24746/94, Judgment of 4 May 2001, para. 123.

88 ECtHR, *Hugh Jordan v UK* (n. 87), para. 120.

in the system.[89] The failure of the previous investigative authorities can then trigger this additional need for even more independence. These matters will be explored further in Chapters 6 and 7.

It is therefore undeniable that investigations into serious violations of IHL need to be impartial, and this will often require guarantees of independence to secure. Nevertheless, understanding the meaning of these standards for investigations requires assessing their contribution to the overall effectiveness of the investigation in a given context. Assessing an investigator's possible implication in the incident under investigation, their independence from those with responsibility, and their independence in light of the whole investigation are all necessary to assess how they affect effectiveness.

The purpose of the investigation, which is central in assessing its effectiveness, will dictate what constitutes adequate independence and impartiality for an investigation in each case. If the purpose of an investigation is to clarify the facts and maybe charge those involved, the investigators will need to be able to do so effectively, through impartial evidence collection and analysis and decision-making as to the progress of the investigation. Overall independence and impartiality is not the need to ensure institutional and personal independence, substantive and objective impartiality, as in the case of judges and tribunals. Rather, it is a broader contextual assessment which is necessary to determine whether the investigation is overall sufficiently independent and impartial to be effective.

Conclusion

This chapter has explored the concepts of independence and impartiality as applicable to judges, courts, and tribunals, as well as how they may apply to investigations. Exploring the importance of an independent and impartial judiciary is helpful in understanding why these standards are necessary for the rule of law and legitimate governance, but also for clarifying how they relate to one another. It is clear that it is usually the internal behavioural concept of impartiality which matters most for a just judicial outcome in adjudication, yet standards of independence are necessary not only to help promote impartial decision-making, but also to provide a perception of justice and promote trust in a State's judicial system.

When it comes to investigations, it was clarified that it is also impartiality which is crucial for certain steps of the investigation, especially for evidence-gathering and decision-making. Independence can help promote this impartiality and can also help to provide a perception of justice for the proceedings. Nevertheless, the reason independence and impartiality apply to investigations

89 Human Rights Committee, *Mamatkarim Ernazarov v Kyrgyzstan*, Communication No. 2054/2011 (2015), para. 9.6; *Olimzhon Eshonov* v *Uzbekistan*, Communication No. 1225/2003 (2010), para. 9.6.

is not so much related to the fair trial rights applicable to the judiciary. Rather, it is becoming clearer that the standards of independence and impartiality as applicable to investigations are tools to serve their effectiveness.

Whereas judges, courts, and tribunals must meet all requirements of independence and impartiality separately, the term "overall independence and impartiality" as applicable to investigations may be used to distinguish this requirement. For investigations, it will be necessary to consider the specific circumstances of each case to establish what may contribute effectiveness. Such a clarification will enable the exploration of these topics in subsequent chapters, for example what effectiveness means in situations of armed conflict, or in a military context. The overall test is particularly crucial in assessing what may be reasonably expected of States in difficult situations.

Nevertheless, there are also certain questions raised by this chapter which may not be adequately dealt with in this book. For example, it is clear that the rationale for independence and impartiality as tools to achieve justice are based on European political theorists' conceptions of a domestic nation State, and that they are necessary to maintain the trust in the legitimacy of the government. While these terms have been expanded to the international level under IHRL, it nevertheless may lead us to question what legitimacy may mean at an international level, or when multiple States are involved. Why must a State appear to be legitimate to citizens of another State? What would legitimacy look like in such a context? This is particularly important in armed conflict when a State may be involved in a conflict in another State, or even within its own territory against a people who do not recognise the legitimacy of the government in the first place. Some of these concerns will be addressed in Chapter 6, yet it is clear that such questions are not currently adequately addressed in existing legal scholarship.

5 Military institutional challenges to independence and impartiality

Introduction

> *We use words like "honor," "code," "loyalty." We use these words as the backbone of a life spent defending something. You use them as a punch line. I have neither the time nor the inclination to explain myself to a man who rises and sleeps under the blanket of the very freedom that I provide and then questions the manner in which I provide it.*[1]

This quote is part of the famous "You can't handle the truth!" tirade made by Jack Nicholson in the 1992 film *A Few Good Men*, a fictional account of the court martial of a US marine accused of murder. A young JAG [Judge Advocate General] attorney (Tom Cruise, as Lieutenant Kaffee) must expose "the truth" for the proper administration of justice, managing to place Jack Nicholson's character, Colonel Jessep, on the wrong side of the moral compass by the end of the film. But the Colonel's monologue, and the film more generally, raises interesting issues relevant to our topic. The plot uncovers certain dynamics related to toxic culture, a wall of silence, as well as the tensions caused by a perception that "outsiders" do not, and cannot, understand the demands of military life, nor the full meaning of the concept of loyalty.

The unique structure of military institutions does raise various questions in relation to the concepts of independence and impartiality of investigators operating within these institutions. The specific relationships within military hierarchies can create dynamics and influences which may not be found in civilian institutions. This in turn may have implications for the independence of members within such a hierarchy which may not arise in other contexts. Furthermore, it is often perceived that this unique structure creates specific relationships between members of a military institution which may be considered to affect their impartiality. This chapter examines some of the factors characteristic of military institutions which may affect the independence and impartiality of investigators operating within a military context. Some of the

1 Colonel Jessep in *A Few Good Men* (1992), feature film directed by Rob Reiner; Castle Rock Entertainment, USA.

DOI: 10.4324/9781003360223-5

assumptions that are at times made about military institutions, in particular the influences and dynamics presumed to be problematic in military culture, are also deconstructed. It is worth remembering that the effectiveness of an investigation is the yardstick used to assess whether standards of independence and impartiality are overall sufficient, as laid out in the previous chapter. Although the considerations may be similar, this is unlike standards applicable to judges and courts, where the standards must all be met independently, and this may affect the nature of the judicial body differently from the nature of the investigative body.

Military institutions certainly have specificities which must be taken into account in determining the independence and impartiality of investigators, and certain elements of military justice can potentially cause more controversy than some equivalents in civilian justice. Nevertheless, it is important to carefully deconstruct blanket statements as to the ability of military institutions generally to uphold (or not) the required standards of independence and impartiality of investigators.

The effect of military hierarchy on independence and impartiality

A frequently cited concern with the independence and impartiality of military justice systems is related to military hierarchy, especially the impacts of an investigator being in the chain of command. Removing an investigator from the chain of command may not, however, be the quick and easy fix it appears to be. There are various difficulties in examining dynamics of independence and impartiality within military chains of command, starting with the difficulties in defining what constitutes a chain of command, as well as the fact that in some contexts hierarchical relationships may not be problematic, whereas other relationships may be. The nature of the violation may also affect the required independence and impartiality for investigations. Finally, it is also worth considering whether there are any potential negative impacts of "too much independence" on the effectiveness of investigations.

The chain of command

An investigator or judge being "out of the chain of command" has been the turning point of various human rights adjudication cases which have considered military justice matters.[2] Nevertheless, States vary in the way they structure military justice, and have different understandings of what is meant by the chain of command. Within the same armed forces there may be multiple "branches" of command, sometimes under the same single head (e.g.,

2 ECtHR, *Oğur v Turkey*, App. No. 21594/93, 20 May 1999, para. 91. See also *Aktaş v Turkey*, App. No. 24351/94, 24 April 2003, para. 305; *Al-Skeini v UK*, App. No. 55721/07, Judgment of 7 July 2011, para. 171.

the Commander-in-Chief, who may be the political leader of the State). This raises questions with regard to the actual relationships of subordination and command, and how these may impact the personal independence of investigators, as will be explored below.

First of all, it is worth pointing out that it is not the fact that a judge or investigator is in *a* chain of command that is problematic, but it is rather *which* chain of command and *where* in the chain of command the individual holds their place. Even within a civilian justice system, judges and investigators will usually be in some sort of hierarchical structure, and these can have the potential to create problems of independence if junior officers feel under pressure by more senior members to make certain judicial decisions. Independence can be threatened within the judiciary itself through pressures of senior judges over judges lower in their hierarchy through administrative and personnel pressures.[3] These pressures, therefore, are not unique to military hierarchies but rather relate to general requirements of personal independence for judges and investigators to be free from any undue influence.[4]

Rather, what matters for the effectiveness of an investigation is whether the individual with the responsibility to investigate is sufficiently free from undue pressure from the hierarchy of those implicated in the violation. This can be achieved, for example, by having a separate, or parallel, judicial chain of command from the operational chain of command, as explored below. This means that military personnel tasked with investigating should have no relationship of subordination to those carrying out military operations. There are other additional safeguards which can be implemented, such as reporting directly to the judicial instead of executive branch of government, having separate ranking and disciplinary systems, and being financially independent.[5] The European Court of Human Rights (ECtHR) has considered the importance of separate hierarchies even without full judicial independence.[6] Unless the suspect under investigation is a member of the same judicial chain of command (e.g., if a violation is allegedly committed by a military judge or military police), it should not be a problem that the investigator is in *a* chain of command, but rather

3 O'Brien, D. M., & Ohkhosi, Y., "Shifting Judicial Independence from Within: The Japanese Judiciary" in Russell, P. H., & O'Brien, D. M., *Judicial Independence in the Age of Democracy: Critical Perspectives from around the World*, University Press of Virginia (2001).

4 See Chapter 4. This may depend upon the structure of the judiciary and may, for example, be less problematic in States which do not have a career judiciary, in which issues of promotion would not arise.

5 See, e.g., Australian Defence Force Investigative Service in Australia; Canadian Forces Military Police and National Investigative Service in Canada; Military Police Criminal Investigation Department in Israel; Royal Military Constabulary in the Netherlands; Special Investigations Branch of the Royal Military Police in the UK; Military Criminal Investigation Organizations in Army, Navy, and Air Force in the USA.

6 ECtHR, *Ramsahai and Others v Netherlands*, App. No. 52391/99, Judgment of 15 May 2007, para. 343.

whether their chain of command is sufficiently free from undue pressure from the chain of command implicated in the violation.[7]

It will be necessary in every case to consider the unique structure of the domestic chains of command and the possible influences of subordination and other interests in order to assess independence and impartiality in a military institution. What matters is *who* is implicated in the incident being investigated (the hierarchical and practical relation of the investigator to those individuals) and the *nature* of the incident in question. The seriousness of the alleged violation may also affect whether or not an entire chain of command may be considered implicated, as will be explored below.

The impact of subordination and discipline

It is issues of subordination and discipline which have been most explicitly addressed with regard to independence and impartiality within a military context.[8] An impartial investigator is expected to be able to make decisions related to an investigation based only upon relevant facts of the case and relevant law. As seen in Chapter 4, measures to protect personal independence are generally required to protect an investigator's ability to make such impartial decisions. A military investigator may consciously or unconsciously take into account whether their superior may approve or disapprove of the investigative decisions made, especially if such a superior holds disciplinary or administrative powers (including both a negative power, such as demotion, or a positive power, such as promotion) over them. The ECtHR considered problematic in *Sergey Shevchenko v Ukraine* that an investigative body was appointed by the commanding officer of the unit involved in the alleged violation, and acted under his authority, including concerning the conduct of investigative proceedings.[9] In *Oğur v Turkey*, the Court found that the investigation could not be considered independent *inter alia* because the investigating officer was "subordinate to the same chain of command as the security forces he was

7 For allegations of violations committed by military police, a similar arrangement to those for police should be in place, namely an independent police complaints commission. Cordone, C., "Police Reform and Human Rights Investigations: The Experience of the UN Mission in Bosnia and Herzegovina," *International Peacekeeping* Vol. 6 No. 4 (1994); Brereton, D., "Evaluating the Performance of External Oversight Bodies" in Goldsmith, A., & Lewis, C., *Civilian Oversight of Policing*, Hart (2000).

8 ECtHR, *Findlay v UK*, App. No. 22107/93, Judgment of 25 February 1997, para. 75; *Sergey Shevchenko v Ukraine*, App. No. 32478/02, Judgment of 4 April 2006, para. 70; *Arı v Turkey*, App. No. 29281/95, Judgment of 25 September 2001, para. 46; IACtHR, *Palamara-Iribarne v Chile*, Ser. C No. 135, Judgment of 22 November 2005 (Merits, Reparations, and Costs), paras 150–157; *Rodríguez Vera et al. v Colombia* (*the disappeared from the Palace of Justice*), Ser. C No. 287, Judgment of 14 November 2014 (Preliminary Objections, Merits, Reparations, and Costs), para. 447.

9 ECtHR, *Sergey Shevchenko v Ukraine* (n. 8), para. 70.

investigating."[10] Although not necessarily always problematic, if such a superior is considered to have interests in the case, this subordination relationship would be considered a lack of independence because it could affect the subordinate's ability to make impartial decisions. This is a matter of personal independence, as seen in Chapter 4, as subordination and discipline are potential external pressures which may affect an individual's ability to be expected to make an impartial decision.

Being outside the formal chain of command is nonetheless not sufficient to guarantee independence, as *practical* independence is also needed. Issues of rank, in particular, may affect the actual or perceived independence of investigators, even if they are in a different chain of command to those involved in the alleged violation. If investigative personnel rely on favourable assessment reports from their superiors to obtain promotion within the military hierarchy, and if such superiors were to be considered to have an interest in the case under investigation, then investigators of relatively low rank may be susceptible to pressure from such superior officers.[11] In such cases, an individual "may entertain a legitimate doubt about those persons' independence."[12] Issues of how ranking may affect independence are therefore crucial to consider, even within different chains of command. However, such a concern for military investigators (as opposed to judges) must be taken into account within the broader context of the effectiveness of the whole investigation (as explored in Chapter 4), and subsequent cases have found that hierarchical relationships may not always in themselves undermine overall effectiveness.[13]

Other practical dependencies can include the possible interference in an investigation by an implicated individual. In *Al-Skeini v UK*, the Special Investigations Branch (SIB), part of the military police, was part of a separate chain of command "from the soldiers on combat duty whom it was required to investigate."[14] Nevertheless, the ECtHR found (in line with domestic courts) that "during the relevant period, [the SIB was not] operationally independent from the military chain of command."[15] This was because the commanding officer of the unit involved had power over when the SIB should be called in, in closing an investigation initiated by the SIB, and in referring the conclusion of the SIB investigation to the Army Prosecuting Authority.[16] The investigators in this case were therefore not considered practically independent, as the

10 ECtHR *Oğur v Turkey* (n. 2), para. 91. See also *Aktaş v Turkey* (n. 2), para. 305.

11 ECtHR *Sergey Shevchenko v Ukraine* (n. 8), para. 71; see also, *mutatis mutandis* (in the case of military judges), *Arı v Turkey* (n. 8), para. 46; *Mustafa Tunç & Fecire Tunç v Turkey*, App. No. 24014/05, Judgment of 14 April 2015, para. 254; *Hanan v Germany*, App. No. 4871/16, para. 231.

12 ECtHR, *Arı v Turkey* (n. 8), para. 50.

13 ECtHR, *Mustafa Tunç & Fecire Tunç v Turkey* (n. 11), para. 231.

14 ECtHR *Al-Skeini v UK* (n. 2), para. 172.

15 ECtHR *Al-Skeini v UK* (n. 2), para. 172.

16 ECtHR *Al-Skeini v UK* (n. 2), para. 172.

actual interference, or possibility of interference, by the commanding officer could have been considered to influence the decisions taken by the SIB.

Other relationships in a hierarchy: command responsibility and "implication"

It is therefore quite clear that investigators should have no relation of subordination or discipline with those involved in the incident concerned. Yet it is also worth questioning whether or not an investigator being in the same hierarchy, even if superior to an alleged perpetrator, would also *ipso facto* violate the principle of personal independence. In some cases, human rights bodies have found that the investigator being a direct superior, or an immediate colleague, of the possible perpetrator, did put their independence into question.[17] At a very basic level, therefore, being an "immediate colleague" of a possible perpetrator would most likely violate the principle of impartiality and bring up issues of conflict of interest.

But being a superior in the chain of command may also raise concerns of independence and impartiality because a superior may be considered implicated in a violation under the laws of command responsibility. Chapter 3 saw that there are specific obligations incumbent upon commanders for the repression and suppression of violations of international humanitarian law (IHL), *inter alia*, as elaborated under international criminal law and the notion of command responsibility for war crimes. These duties involve a duty either to directly suppress or repress (for example, through disciplinary action) or to report to the competent authority who may effectively suppress or repress the violation.[18] Courts examining the notion have found explicitly in certain cases that a commander has a duty to carry out an effective investigation into war crimes.[19]

Nevertheless, this duty must be considered in light of the developments under international law as seen in Chapter 4 on the independence and impartiality of investigators. It is clear that an investigation into possible criminal liability cannot be carried out by those directly implicated in the violation being

17 ECtHR, *Enukidze & Girgvliani v Georgia*, App. No. 25091/07, Judgment of 26 April 2011, para. 247; *Aktaş v Turkey* (n. 2), para. 301; *Ramsahai v Netherlands* (n. 6), para. 337; *Mustafa Tunç and Fecire Tunç v Turkey* (n. 11), para. 222.

18 Protocol Additional to the Geneva Conventions of 12 August 1949, and Relating to the Protection of Victims of International Armed Conflicts, 1125 UNTS 3 (1977) [API], Article 86; Henckaerts, J.-M., & Doswald-Beck, L., *Customary International Humanitarian Law*, ICRC (2006) [ICRC Customary Law Study], Rule 153.

19 ICTY, *Prosecutor v Pavle Strugar*, IT-01-42-T, Trial Chamber II Judgment of 31 January 2005, para. 376; *Prosecutor v Dario Kordić & Mario Čerkez*, IT-95-14/2-T, Trial Chamber Judgment of 26 February 2001, para. 446; Mettraux, G., *The Law of Command Responsibility*, Oxford University Press (2009), p. 233; Sepinwall, A. J., "Failures to Punish: Command Responsibility in Domestic and International Law," *Michigan Journal of International Law* Vol. 30 No. 2 (2009), p. 256.

investigated.[20] Regardless of the role the commander had in the commission of the possible war crime, the very notion of command responsibility means the commander is implicated in some way, as their responsibility is one of the elements of liability that must be investigated.[21] In such cases the effectiveness of the investigation may very well mandate that it be removed from the responsibility of the commander, and passed on to a further authority. This will most likely be a military or civilian law enforcement agency with a separate chain of command, depending on the domestic system.[22] As international law currently stands, it is reasonable to suggest that in the case of war crimes a commander "discharges their duty to investigate by reporting and referring the case" to the adequate professional body for investigation,[23] rather than investigating themselves. This is reflected to different degrees in the reforms in various military justice institutions with relation to the role of the commander.[24]

The commander nevertheless has a central role in the initial stages of an investigation, including a potentially criminal one in the context of armed conflict. The effective triggering of an investigation in most cases depends upon efficient reporting structures, and potentially implementing certain safeguarding measures at the scene of the incident.[25] Despite not being an independent or impartial authority, there should be sufficient motivations for a commander to carry out such duties effectively, including punishments for failing to do so. The potential cost on the commander for not effectively dealing with possible violations of IHL is high: in the case of war crimes, the commander may be held directly responsible for the commission of these offences. Nevertheless, domestic systems must be structured in such a way that these incentives are

20 "Second Report of the Public Commission to Examine the Maritime Incident of 31 May 2010: Israel's Mechanisms for Examining and Investigating Complaints and Claims of Violations of the Laws of Armed Conflict According to International Law" (Israel, February 2013) [Second Turkel Report], p. 118, paras 66–67; ECtHR, *Mustafa Tunç & Fecire Tunç v Turkey* (n. 11), paras 219–223.

21 Margalit, A., *Investigating Civilian Casualties in Time of Armed Conflict and Belligerent Occupation*, Brill (2018), p. 69.

22 See Margalit (n. 21), pp. 153–183.

23 Margalit (n. 21), p. 65.

24 Margalit (n. 21), pp. 153–183; Hansen, V., "The Impact of Military Justice Reforms on the Law of Armed Conflict: How to Avoid Unintended Consequences" in Duxbury, A., & Groves, M., *Military Justice in the Modern Age*, Cambridge University Press (2016); Goldrick, J., "A Strategic Commander's Perspective" in Lovell, David W., *Investigating Operational Incidents in a Military Context*, Brill (2015). At time of writing, the USA is also considering restructuring its military justice system in this regard. See Paradis, M., "The Impact of Military Justice Reform on Command Responsibility," West Point Lieber Institute, Articles of War (1 June 2021), available at: https://lieber.westpoint.edu/impact-military-justice-reform-command-responsibility/.

25 Lubell, N., Pejic, J., & Simmons, C., "Guidelines on Investigating Violations of International Humanitarian Law: Law, Policy, and Good Practice," Geneva Academy/ICRC (2019) [Guidelines on Investigating Violations of International Humanitarian Law], Guideline 2; Margalit (n. 21), p. 188; *Hanan v Germany* (n. 11), para. 224.

clearly laid out, and that it is in the commander's interest to report and refer cases rather than trying to cover them up.[26] This is particularly crucial in light of the fact that the international concept of commanders as criminally liable for war crimes committed by their subordinates is not always translated into domestic legislation.[27]

There are also difficulties in asserting who constitutes a "commander" for the purposes of command responsibility, and therefore who may be considered "implicated" and not sufficiently independent or impartial. Although in practice it is rarely high-level commanders who are prosecuted for war crimes, in theory, command responsibility for war crimes committed by subordinates can extend all the way "up" the chain of command, including in some cases to the political Head of State.[28] There is no requirement under the notion of command responsibility for the superior/subordinate relationship to be direct or immediate.[29]

Nevertheless, actual responsibility differs in each case, and it is not the case that any individual in a chain of command, even of higher rank, may be found to have command authority and therefore potential liability for war crimes of subordinates.[30] The example has been given of a Chief of Staff, a highly ranked military professional, whose role "is not to exercise command functions, but to assist the commander and to provide him with practical and expert assistance which he might need."[31] There must be some sort of personal "link" between the perpetrator and the commander,[32] namely the ability, obligation, and expectation on the commander in question at the relevant time to take action to prevent or punish war crimes. This is because "criminality does not attach to every individual in this chain of command from that fact alone. There

26 Sepinwall (n. 19), p. 286; Dahl, A. W., "Military Justice and Self-Interest in Accountability" in Bergsmo, M., & Song, T., *Military Self-Interest for Core International Crimes*, Torkel Opsahl Academic Epublisher (2016), p. 26.

27 Sepinwall (n. 19), pp. 255–256; Hansen, V., "What's Good for the Goose is Good for the Gander: Lessons from Abu Ghraib; Time for the United States to Adopt a Doctrine of Command Responsibility Towards Its Own," *Gonzaga Law Review* Vol. 42 No. 3 (2006), p. 349.

28 Finucane, B., "U.S. Recognition of a Duty to Punish War Crimes," *International Law Studies* Vol. 97 (2021), p. 1002; *The German High Command Trial*, reprinted in part in United Nations War Crimes Commission, *Law Reports of Trials of War Criminals* (London, 1949) [High Command case], p. 76. Certain domestic legislation specifies that command responsibility can extend to heads of State. See, e.g., practice of Canada, UK, and Ethiopia in ICRC Customary Law Study (n. 18), Practice Relating to Rule 153.

29 Mettraux (n. 19), p. 146; ICTY, *Prosecutor v Sefer Halilović*, IT-01-48-T, Trial Chamber Judgment of 16 November 2005, para. 63.

30 Mettraux (n. 19), p. 150; High Command case (n. 28), p. 76.

31 Mettraux (n. 19), p. 149 n. 56. See also High Command case (n. 28), p. 86.

32 Mettraux (n. 19), pp. 148–149; Sandoz, Y., Swinarski, C., & Zimmermann, B., *Commentary to the Additional Protocols of 8 June 1977 to the Geneva Conventions of 12 August 1949*, Martinus Nijhoff Publishers (1987) [ICRC Commentary to API], Commentary to Article 86, para. 3544; *Prosecutor v Zejnil Delalić et al.* (*Čelebići case*), IT-92–21-A, Appeals Chamber Judgment of 20 February 2001, para. 303.

must be a personal dereliction."[33] In the normal course of events, a commander higher up in the chain of command is entitled to assume that "details entrusted to responsible subordinates will be legally executed."[34] This is also tied into what the commander "knew or had reason to know," as this "may be harder to establish when the superior stood *at a distance* from the perpetrators both physically or hierarchically in the chain of command."[35]

Therefore, possible implication through command responsibility (which may affect impartiality) may usually be assumed to be relevant only for relatively "direct" commanders, such as field or unit commanders of the alleged perpetrators of war crimes, who in the normal course of duties are expected to be the ones to initiate investigations and/or punish the offences. Commanders who may be higher-ranked, yet do not have such a *de facto* or *de jure* role, including because their responsibilities do not include disciplinary ones, and/or because they are in a "parallel" chain of command, should not usually initially be considered "implicated" in a potential war crime. If such commanders "higher up" in the chain of command are also failing to implement their obligations to punish war crimes, such situations would usually point to repetitive failures in the military accountability system and the presence of systematic impunity. Such situations are particularly difficult to address and would require special considerations to detect in the first place. This will be further addressed in Chapter 7.

Nature of the offence: rotten apples or rotten institutions?

Finally, the nature of the violation may also affect who is considered sufficiently independent and impartial to investigate within a military hierarchy. Chapter 3 established that an investigation must be *overall* sufficiently independent and impartial to be effective, and that this effectiveness is defined by the objective of the investigation. Key to understanding the adequate levels of impartiality of investigations is looking at the nature of the offence at hand and how this will affect the objective of the investigation.

First of all, if a possible violation appears to be "non-serious" in nature, namely, that it does not involve criminal liability, does not affect personal integrity, and is not part of a wider pattern of problems,[36] the type of potential responsibility will affect who may be considered "implicated." The issues with command responsibility and implication are only true for potential war crimes. If it is an administrative violation, it will typically be a commander who is expected to investigate if necessary, and this will very likely be the most effective type of suppression. Nevertheless, in the case of a "serious" non-criminal

33 High Command case (n. 28), p. 76.

34 High Command case (n. 28), p. 76. See also Mettraux (n. 19), p. 239.

35 Mettraux (n. 19), p. 152. See also Finucane (n. 28), p. 1002.

36 See Chapter 3.

violation, higher degrees of independence and impartiality may be required.[37] Although as seen above a commander and even the unit involved may have a role to play in initial investigative steps, the fact that a duty to investigate arises as a matter of international obligation for serious violations of IHL means that such investigations must be carried out in an effective manner. Chapter 4 established that such effectiveness can include a perception of justice, as well as justice itself, a matter which will be returned to below and in Chapter 6. For serious non-criminal violations of IHL, the standards of independence and impartiality of investigations will therefore more closely resemble those required in the case of war crimes.[38]

Chapter 4 also established that there is a need for investigators to be independent not only from persons but also from structures whose responsibility may be in question, in circumstances which "give rise to suspicions against the security forces as an institution."[39] What appears to be important to distinguish in this test is whether the alleged violation was due to a "one-off" offence by an individual police or military person who has acted in breach of orders, or rather an institution-wide practice and/or tolerance of violations which by their very definition puts institutional practice under scrutiny. This "rotten apple" phenomenon is often cited in cases of police or military misconduct by the force of the involved individual. This attempt to explain why the whole institution should not be tarnished is unsurprising considering that both military and police forces need to uphold the public's trust in their ability to legitimately hold a monopoly of the use of force, and therefore have an incentive in suggesting it is just a one-off rather than a deeper-rooted problem. If it is indeed an isolated incident, the levels of independence necessary to achieve impartiality may be considered quite narrow, because there will not be an assumption of collusion amongst colleagues of the same institution.

Although it is of course possible that individuals act in breach of orders, and that their institutions would seek to bring them back in line, claims of "rotten apples" are often met with scepticism.[40] The situation in which the "security forces as an institution" is under suspicion appears to imply that the violation is due to a systemic problem, where the root cause is in fact something deeper, for example related to training, institutional culture, or other systemic factors. It is crucial for institutions to consider these systemic issues at the root of problematic behaviours, whether it is before or after incidents of misconduct come to light. In the case of alleged abuses committed by the Royal Ulster Constabulary

37 Guidelines on Investigating Violations of International Humanitarian Law (n. 25), paras 169 and 181.

38 Guidelines on Investigating Violations of International Humanitarian Law (n. 25), para. 181.

39 *Mustafa Tunç and Fecire Tunç v Turkey* (n. 11), para. 255.

40 I am slightly averse to the "rotten apple" analogy – an apple rarely rots alone, and you can have a rotten apple from a rotten tree, spreading fungal disease, or infestation. In all cases it would be best to check if there is a deeper (systemic) root cause to the problem rather than declaring it an isolated case.

in Northern Ireland in the *Brecknell v UK* case, or the Honduran armed forces accused of enforced disappearances in the *Velásquez Rodriguéz* case, what was being alleged was not a one-off offence by an individual, or a few individuals, but rather an institution-wide practice and/or tolerance of violations which by very definition put institutional practice under scrutiny. In such cases, independence from the "structures whose responsibility may be in question" may require independence from the military. This will be further examined in Chapter 7, but it is key to note that in considering adequate levels of independence and impartiality it is necessary to consider who or which entity is under scrutiny.

Too much independence? The matter of expertise

A final element related to the matter of structural independence within military investigations is that of competence and expertise in investigating. "Independence" often means a removal from those involved in an incident under scrutiny, but this can also mean a removal from those with an operational understanding of the case. Dahl has cautioned that "if independence means distance – in organisation, geography and mentality – one may find oneself in a situation where the independent bodies lack understanding of military affairs. If such lack of understanding leads to unwarranted sentences or acquittals, it is time to pull the brakes."[41] The caution in this case relates to the need for technical expertise in military investigations, including into violations of IHL. In order to carry out an effective investigation, an investigator needs to know not only the relevant legal issues but also military technical expertise. Examples have been given of various technical expertise central to any investigation into air strikes,[42] which are arguably today some of the most controversial investigations. In the same piece, Dahl highlights the importance of military expertise in investigating by reference to a case where a civilian investigator would have been more likely to acquit a possible war crime because of lack of understanding of artillery distances.[43] These are some of the criticisms launched against the most independent investigations, for example those carried out by organisations external to the military or even outside the State involved.

41 Dahl (n. 26), p. 27; Heng, B., Liivoja, R., Ng, D., & Oswald, B., "Military Justice in Comparative and International Perspective: A View from the Asia Pacific," *Journal of International Peacekeeping* Vol. 20 (2016).

42 Schmitt, M. N., "Investigating Violations of International Law in Armed Conflict," *Harvard National Security Journal* Vol. 2 (2011), p. 84; Dahl (n. 26), pp. 27–28; "In a high-tech environment such as in air and missile warfare, the demands for expertise are substantially higher. An investigator who does not understand, for example, weapons options, fusing guidance systems, angle of attack, optimal release altitudes, command and control relationships, communications capabilities, tactical options, available intelligence options, enemy practices, pattern of life analysis, collateral damage estimate methodology, human factors in a combat environment, and so forth, will struggle to effectively scrutinise an air strike."

43 Dahl (n. 26), p. 27.

The ECtHR has considered various facets of the obligation of competence in military matters in relation to investigations.[44] Although it was rejected as sufficient reason to employ military judges in the case involving the trial of civilians,[45] in another case involving police officers involved in the adjudication of a case concerned with fellow police officers, the ECtHR found sufficient reason to employ such expertise. In this case, the ECtHR found that

> the fact that an expert works for the police does not in itself force us to believe him incapable of acting with the desired neutrality. To judge otherwise would unacceptably limit in many cases the possibility, for tribunals, to turn to expert opinions, taking into account, for example, the fact that [...] policemen often have particular competence in the matter of fingerprinting.[46]

Expertise in police or military matters may therefore be a factor contributing to the need for "less" independence in specific cases, although their involvement must be adequately safeguarded.[47]

Nonetheless, the view that *only* military personnel may investigate or prosecute cases involving military matters is also misplaced. In fact, the difficulty of evidence-collection can remain even with internal military investigations (see below on the "wall of silence" phenomenon). Furthermore, civilian criminal courts often have to "decide cases involving complex professional contexts (say, instances of medical malpractice)" and it has been pointed out more than once that military operations need not be any different from these cases which require the assistance of specific experts or *amicus curiae*.[48] An independent investigator may be provided with information by a technical specialist who need not meet the standards of independence and impartiality. Many States have, in fact, "opted for a model of concurrent jurisdiction," wherein practical considerations are taken into account such as "the ability to prosecute most efficiently and effectively in the circumstances of the case," and that in all models "the effective investigation and prosecution of offences committed by military members may require some civilian–military collaboration and coordination."[49]

44 *Mustafa Tunç and Fecire Tunç v Turkey* (n. 11).

45 *Incal v Turkey*, App. No. 41/1997/825/1031, Judgment of 9 June 1998, para. 70.

46 *Emmanuello v Italy* (1999), App. No. 35791/97, Decision on Admissibility of 31 August 1999, p. 7 [my translation].

47 *Ramsahai v Netherlands* (n. 6), para. 344.

48 Heng et al. (n. 41), p. 135. See also Collins, P., *The Military As a Separate Society: Consequences for Discipline in the United States and Australia*, Lexington Books (2019), pp. 23, 36. Although it is worth pointing out that even those who advocate for abolition recognise that special understanding may be required in cases which have occurred in the heat of combat, such as where allegations of murder or other criminal conduct have occurred on the battlefield (p. 35).

49 Heng et al. (n. 41), p. 135.

In many civilian cases, "expert witnesses are often called upon to explain forensic details that may shed light upon what the accused may or may not have done or intended to do."[50] For example, the Norwegian system provides for prosecutors specialised in military matters who "occasionally have to explain important aspects of the case to the court – aspects that would have been known to the court if its members had some basic military experience."[51] It is possible, therefore, that in some cases a division of tasks and responsibilities may be an important way of addressing the standards of independence and impartiality, while meeting the requirements of competence and expertise. In all cases, any investigative authority must undoubtedly hold the relevant legal, forensic, and military expertise to effectively investigate. Just as investigations must be sufficiently independent and impartial to achieve effectiveness in investigating, there may be some situations in which there may be "too much" independence for the investigation to be effective.

It is clear that an investigator being either subordinate or superior to the individual under investigation in a chain of command can be problematic for their personal independence. It is increasingly becoming apparent in State practice that serious violations of IHL such as war crimes are being removed from the direct chain of command of the unit involved.[52] There can also be no practical relationship of subordination or discipline, even outside the formal chain of command. Nevertheless, the adequate standards will depend on the nature of the violation, who may be implicated, and the structural hierarchies in each specific context. The need for independence and impartiality must also be balanced with the need for competence, although they need not necessarily be mutually exclusive.

Military culture: Loyalty, camaraderie, and the wall of silence

The section above considered elements characteristic of military institutional structures which may be seen as affecting the personal independence of military investigators, namely, the relational pressures which may affect their ability to make impartial decisions. Nevertheless, it cannot be said that all the concerns surrounding military investigations are strictly related to observable structural issues. All of the above concerns can be addressed through structural changes, as has been done in various States which have created specific structural guarantees of independence for military judicial officers. Beyond the institutional and practical factors mentioned above, there remains a certain discomfort in some situations around military institutions investigating and trying members of their "own" armed forces.

50 Dahl (n. 26), p. 27.

51 Dahl (n. 26), p. 27.

52 See, e.g., State practice analysed in the Annex to the Second Turkel Report (n. 20), as well as conclusions in the report (p. 140). Waters, C., "Democratic Oversight Through Courts and Tribunals" in Duxbury & Groves (n. 24).

This section seeks to explore the more intangible concerns which arise in the context of military personnel investigating violations committed by members of the armed forces. For this, it is necessary to answer the question of whether there are factors necessarily present, or more likely to be present, in military life which may affect the independence and impartiality of military investigators. Elements related to military culture which are often attributed to undermining the impartiality of military investigators are considered, in particular the concepts of loyalty, camaraderie, and the phenomenon of the "wall of silence" which has often been found to be present in large-scale cover-ups of violations committed by military personnel. This section necessarily borrows from other disciplines, in particular sociology, ethics, and psychology, in order to address themes which go beyond the scope of current legal understanding. It is also usefully informed by studies on police culture, which are more common, and where very similar issues have been identified.[53] This chapter does not seek to add to the literature in these disciplines, but rather seeks to draw on the existing expertise in order to understand and clarify their legal implications.

Good and bad loyalty

It is indisputable that loyalty plays a key role in military institutions. What is less obvious is how such loyalty may negatively, or positively, affect different aspects of behaviour and the administration of justice within the military. One end of the argument suggests that because military personnel are loyal, they cannot be impartial. In the *Palacio de Justicia v Colombia* case, the Inter-American Court of Human Rights (IACtHR) found that because the armed forces are "an institution based on the principles of loyalty and subordination," active-duty officers therefore "lack the necessary independence and impartiality to try cases of members of the same institution implicated in human rights violations against civilians."[54] These principles of loyalty and subordination were seen as directly responsible for the lack of independence and impartiality of the military personnel who were supposed to hold their colleagues to account. The IACtHR found that "active-duty officers are neither independent nor able to deliver impartial judgments against members of the same Armed Forces."[55] This argument suggests that military judges will necessarily seek to protect the personal interests of their colleagues out of a sense of institutional loyalty, and beyond the interests of justice. In terms of the standards of independence and impartiality as explored in Chapter 4, this internal behavioural bias will therefore undermine their ability to make impartial decisions.

53 Coleman, S., "Case Study 2: Good Loyalty and Bad Loyalty" in Skerker, M., Whetham, D., & Carrick, D., *Military Values*, Howgate (2019), p. 96.

54 IACtHR, *Palacio de Justicia* (n. 8), para. 447, citing expert opinion of Guzmán.

55 IACtHR, *Palacio de Justicia* (n. 8), para. 447. See also *Durand & Ugarte v Peru*, Ser. C No. 68, Judgment of 16 April 2000 (Merits), para. 126.

Nevertheless, the conclusion that military justice systems *de facto* violate the principles of independence and impartiality is not found in other human rights bodies,[56] even though militaries before these bodies are also institutions "based on the principles of loyalty and subordination." The matter is further complicated by the fact that the counterargument may also be put forward, namely, that the right type of loyalty to an institution may in fact have the opposite effect on impunity. This argument suggests that rather than military personnel being more likely to want to "conceal their part in the situation or to downplay the seriousness of the alleged crime," it would in fact be in the interests of the military to hold a soldier accountable and to "isolate him or her from the armed forces as a whole by describing the soldier as a 'bad apple' and thus restore the public image of the armed forces."[57] In this sense, it has been suggested that "it is not the case that any military court will be inherently sympathetic to members of the military committing gross violations of human rights and that it will be inclined to mitigate punishment because of the position of the accused."[58] Professional militaries in particular are expected to behave in a manner quite opposite to this, as "abuse of one's rank or position has classically been treated as a greater breach of trust" in such contexts.[59] To properly understand the impact of loyalty on independence and impartiality, it would therefore be necessary to be able to distinguish the "good" from the "bad" loyalty, and also to understand the scope of the loyalty in question to understand its sphere of influence.

It is tempting to suggest in such cases that "it just depends on which military," yet this does not help us in comparing systems, or understanding when an institution may be changing for better or worse. Furthermore, examples of loyalty causing issues of accountability may arguably be found in every single State in the world, and not only in military institutions. The question of whether an individual with judicial functions (whether judging or investigating) is able to make impartial decisions with relation to cases in which members of the same institution are under scrutiny is not unique to military institutions. Such cases have been studied in the cases of police, medical, and even

56 ECtHR, *Cooper v UK*, App. No. 48843/99, Judgment of 16 December 2003, para. 115; *Grieves v UK*, App. No. 57067/00, Judgment of 16 December 2003, para. 69; *Findlay v UK* (n. 8), para. 73; UN Human Rights Committee, "General Comment No. 32: Article 14: Right to Equality Before Courts and Tribunals and to a Fair Trial," CCPR/C/GC/32 (23 August 2007), para. 22.

57 Rowe, P., "How Well Do International Human Rights Bodies Understand Military Courts?" in Duxbury & Groves (n. 24), p. 28.

58 Gibson, M. R., "International Human Rights Law and the Administration of Justice Through Military Tribunals: Preserving Utility While Precluding Impunity," *Journal of International Law and International Relations* Vol. 4 No. 1 (2008), pp. 41–42; Gleeson, P., "Subject Matter Jurisdiction of Military Courts: Remarks by Mr. Patrick Gleeson," *Expert Consultation on the Administration of Justice Through Military Tribunals* (2014), p. 7.

59 Gibson (n. 58), pp. 41–42; Gleeson (n. 58), p. 7; Pariselle, J., "La Justice militaire française à la lumière de son histoire," *Military Law & Law of War Review* Vol. 19 (1980), p. 299.

judicial bodies (where the actions of another judge may be under scrutiny).[60] It is therefore worth exploring how in fact loyalty may in itself undermine the impartiality of investigators, and what this may depend on.

The need for loyalty

The concept of loyalty is espoused as a key military value in professional militaries around the world.[61] It is formally encouraged within military institutions as part of official training as a desirable and positive factor in a professional military and need not necessarily have a negative impact on conduct. Alongside other military values such as discipline and obedience, it is considered vital to promote teamwork and "the desire, in extremis to make the ultimate sacrifice if the team needs you to."[62] Loyalty can be understood to embody both loyalty to one's direct team ("horizontal loyalty") as well as loyalty upwards "to the chain of command, the broader institution, the government, state and people" ("vertical loyalty").[63] Both are considered crucial to the effectiveness of military operations:

> without vertical loyalty, to the state and its people, personnel are unlikely to go into battle at all, and once there are unlikely to focus on achieving the mission they have been entrusted with. Without horizontal loyalty, troops in the field may well focus on self-preservation, rather than on protecting each other.[64]

Loyalty is also likely to arise informally as a consequence of various factors of military life, although it is not at all unique to military institutions.[65] A specific type of shared identity and close bonding is formed "by those who lived and fought side-by-side in extreme and austere conditions,"[66] and the presence of personal danger may lead to the creation of "close semi-familial relations that military personnel share with those with whom they have served."[67] Such a group identity is particularly reinforced in tightly knit groups, perhaps even

60 See, e.g., *Belilos v Switzerland*, App. No. 10328/83, 29 April 1998, para. 66.

61 Whetham, D., "Loyalty" in Skerker, Whetham, & Carrick (n. 53), p. 82.

62 Whetham (n. 61), p. 82.

63 Whetham (n. 61), p. 82.

64 Coleman (n. 53), p. 95.

65 Similar considerations may be found in other groups that face danger and share the same risks, such as in the police, firefighters, and first responders. Ouellet, M., Hashimi, S., Gravel, J., & Papachristos, A. V., "Network Exposure and Excessive Use of Force: Investigating the Social Transmission of Police Misconduct," *Criminology and Public Policy* Vol. 18 No. 3 (2019), p. 690.

66 McCormack, P., "Case Study 1: Levels of Loyalty: Country, Service, Mission, Troops" in Skerker, Whetham, & Carrick (n. 53), p. 93.

67 Coleman (n. 53), p. 94.

more so in special operations teams.[68] Group identity in general "can have a profound impact on behaviour, both good and bad."[69] It need not, therefore, necessarily be bad, and the camaraderie it creates is a value "held in high regard in the military."[70] Arguably, the presence of "a strong *positive* identity" can be in itself "an excellent defence against ethical drift away from appropriate conduct."[71]

Toxic loyalty and separatism

Yet it is implicit in many criticisms of military justice systems that the loyalty found in some military environments can lead to an environment that promotes impunity. It is a criticism also found in police forces for the same reasons.[72] This form of loyalty which may be seen as affecting behaviour in a negative way may be termed as "toxic loyalty," and is often associated with other characteristics, such as hypermasculinity, a "warrior mentality," hazing or initiation rites, excessive alcohol consumption, and generally being expected to live up to "a rogue, irreverent and scruffy stereotype."[73] This may be aggravated in specialised units, such as Special Forces units, which operate in particularly harsh conditions and with heightened standards of secrecy.[74]

In some cases, such a group identity and subculture can lead to a feeling of separatism and exceptionalism, whereby members believe themselves to be exempt from the broader laws and regulations.[75] At the very least, the internal codes of behaviour and morals established informally by the lived experiences of members within that group supersede the external laws and regulations.[76] Such a feeling of exemption from the usual rules of society may be exacerbated in contexts where personnel feel that the laws and policies they are supposed to implement are disconnected from the lived realities on the ground, for example where orders and policies lead to ineffective, or even unethical, results

68 Whetham, D., "Special Operations Command: Leadership and Ethics Review," Annex A to Chapter 3.03, Inspector-General of the Australian Defence Force Afghanistan Inquiry Report (2020) [Brereton Report], pp. 517–518.

69 Whetham (2020) (n. 68), p. 517.

70 Heng et al. (n. 41), p. 137.

71 Whetham (2020) (n. 68), pp. 517–518.

72 Ouellet et al. (n. 65), p. 679.

73 Whetham (2020) (n. 68), p. 513; Ouellet et al. (n. 65), pp. 676–677.

74 See United States Special Operations Command, "United States Special Operations Command Comprehensive Review" (23 January 2020). In the case of alleged murders carried out by Navy SEALs in the USA, Corn mentioned a difficulty surrounding the fact that "the SEALs are a community that circles to protect its own, and it might be a little bit challenging to get people to be forthcoming with information." Ward, A., "Two SEAL Team 6 members. An Army Green Beret. A murder," *Vox* (13 November 2017), available at: www.vox.com/world/2017/11/7/16604484/seal-team-6-navy-army-green-beret-murder.

75 Whetham (2020) (n. 68), p. 512; Collins (n. 48), p. 6; Ouellet et al. (n. 65), p. 679.

76 Whetham (2020) (n. 68), p. 513; Ouellet et al. (n. 65), p. 679.

on the ground.[77] This can lead units to develop "a law unto themselves" with negative (and potentially unlawful) behaviours becoming "permissible and equated with being a good and effective soldier."[78]

Impact on investigations

The impact of this type of separatism on the effectiveness of investigations is twofold. On the one hand, it may lead members of a unit to believe that ethically, and perhaps even militarily, the right thing to do is to cover up misconduct by their peers. This "wall of silence" or "closing of ranks" against investigators can be found in situations where the investigator (military or not) *is* in fact independent and outside of the "loyalty sphere," as their actions may be hindered by the loyalty of the group to which the individual being investigated belongs. This "selective memory loss" was blamed for the cover up of abuse by British soldiers in Iraq in the Baha Mousa scandal,[79] and a similar picture emerged from the Australian Brereton report of the conduct of Australian troops in Afghanistan.[80] It is also a phenomenon found, and studied much more broadly, in police forces.[81] Such actions are in fact also a form of loyalty, albeit "not the form of loyalty the senior command of the Army, or a majority of the country, found acceptable."[82] This is not *per se* a matter of independence and impartiality of the investigators, but affects rather an investigator's ability to access and collect evidence. It may also affect the ability for investigations to be triggered in the first place, as individuals will be less likely to report misconduct by their peers.[83] This is extremely problematic for the administration of justice in military contexts yet cannot be addressed by providing more independence; in fact, it would appear the more independent an authority would be, the more the ranks would close.

On the other hand, the concept of loyalty could raise issues of independence and impartiality in the case where the investigator is included as part of the same scope of toxic loyalty as the person being investigated. If this toxic loyalty means that the sub-group has developed a separatist mentality, with its own regulations and codes, it could be expected that an investigator may hold bias towards those under investigation, usually leading them to act more favourably towards their peers, above the interests of justice. In such a case, it would seem necessary

77 Whetham (2020) (n. 68), p. 510; Olsthoorn, P., "Military Virtues and Moral Relativism" in Skerker, Whetham, & Carrick (n. 53), p. 5.

78 Whetham (2020) (n. 68), p. 516.

79 McCormack (n. 66), p. 88.

80 Whetham (2020) (n. 69), p. 504.

81 Ouellet et al. (n. 65), p. 679.

82 McCormack (n. 66), p. 90.

83 See, in the context of the likelihood for police members to report misconduct by their peers, Allen, C., "Ethics and Army Leadership: Climate Matters," *Parameters* Vol. 45 No. 1 (2015), p. 76.

to provide further independence so as to ensure impartiality. This precise phenomenon is what the IACtHR found in the case of Colombian military investigators covering up for human rights violations committed by their peers.[84]

The scope of loyalty: "unit, corps, God, country"?

It is clear that such subcultures that believe their members to be above the law are not an acceptable part of society. The historical example of such behaviour amongst the clergy in Europe is given as one where such separatism has come to be seen as unacceptable and has been abolished.[85] Were this to be an unavoidable or prevalent situation in military institutions, the calls for the abolition of military judicial separatism is reasonable. It is also clear that the negative effects of such dynamics go beyond impunity for violations of international law, as they can also lead to discrimination, bullying, higher risks of suicide, and negative impacts on military discipline. It may also have devastating effects on an individual's attempt to return to civilian life.[86]

What is not clear, however, is whether this type of toxic loyalty is necessarily found in every military institution, and at every level. Furthermore, if it is to be suggested in some cases that independence is necessary to solve such problematic loyalties, it would be necessary to determine the scope of the problematic loyalty in question. Is a military member expected to be problematically loyal to their unit members, their battalion, service, the armed forces as a whole? The question may not necessarily be answered by simply replacing a military investigator with a civilian one; indeed, even broader/alternate scopes can be envisioned, such as nationality, ethnicity, religion, or political affiliation. Although this chapter is concerned with the loyalties which arise specifically in the context of the military, it is worth considering that problematic loyalty affiliations are not confined to the armed forces.[87] For example, some of the issues concerned with these broader categories are considered in Chapter 6 in the context of impartiality in ethnic conflicts.

An example has been given of possible "sub-universes" within the UK armed forces, which may be "repeatedly divided until for the private soldier, the smallest social grouping is the section of eight soldiers."[88] In the smallest

84 IACtHR, *Palacio de Justicia* (n. 8), para. 447, citing expert opinion of Guzmán.

85 Collins (n. 48), pp. 6 and 10.

86 Collins (n. 48), pp. 18–19. See also on the impact of bullying and hazing, Doward, J., "Key army reports 'hidden' from new Deepcut inquest," *The Guardian* (24 February 2019), available at: www.theguardian.com/uk-news/2019/feb/23/deepcut-barracks-geoff-gray-army-reports-hidden-from-inquest.

87 For an examination of potential cross-institutional toxic loyalty between public prosecutes and gendarmerie in Eastern Turkey in the 1990s, see Reidy, A., Hampson, F., & Boyle, K., "Gross Violations of Human Rights: Invoking the European Convention on Human Rights in the Case of Turkey," *Netherlands Quarterly of Human Rights* Vol. 15 No. 2 (1997).

88 McCormack (n. 66), p. 92.

sub-universe, it is understandable that in one same unit, where individuals have been living and fighting alongside each other (possibly in situations of life or death), the possibility of bias is very strong. The direct relationship to those under scrutiny may be said to affect the subjective impartiality of an investigator, that is that they have such a relation to the person under investigation that it cannot be considered possible not to be biased in some way. Such an individual should not be expected to make impartial decisions. The ECtHR considered such a case of direct relationship in *Ramsahai v The Netherlands*, where it found it problematic that essential parts of the investigation were carried out by the same police force ("direct colleagues") to which the accused officers belonged.[89] The IACtHR found such a direct affiliation in *Favela Nova Brasilia v Brazil*, where the investigative agents were charged with investigating their "colleagues of the same institution and the same unit."[90]

This, however, becomes more complex as the "scope" of proximity is broadened. The loyalty mentioned in the *Palacio de Justicia* case before the IACtHR includes loyalty to the entire "armed forces," or "military." What is implied is that one member of the armed forces will be necessarily sympathetic to another, no matter their relation to each other, and regardless of the nature of the offence.[91] Similar considerations have been found in other IACtHR cases.[92] In line with its stricter approach to independence in cases involving the military, the IACtHR has stated that an investigation must be led by an independent organ "different from the police force involved in the incident, such as a judicial authority or the Public Minister."[93] The scope before the ECtHR is less clear cut, but it has considered in some cases that a broad institutional affiliation was found to undermine impartiality. In *Brecknell v UK*, the ECtHR criticised the fact that the initial investigations were carried out by the very same body that was implicated in the allegations, namely that officers of the Royal Ulster Constabulary had allegedly been "heavily involved" in the incidents which they were tasked to investigate.[94] The Royal Ulster Constabulary, being an entire police force (in Northern Ireland), the membership in this case is broad. In other cases, the Court found that specific affiliations were aggravating factors to a more generic affiliation.[95]

89 ECtHR, *Ramsahai v Netherlands* (n. 6), para. 335.

90 IACtHR, *Favela Novela Brasilia v Brazil*, Ser. C. No. 345, Judgment of 16 February 2017 (Preliminary Objections, Merits, Reparations, and Costs), para. 216 [my translation].

91 IACtHR, *Palacio de Justicia* (n. 8), para. 447, citing expert opinion of Guzmán.

92 *Velásquez Rodríguez v Honduras*, Ser. C No. 4, Judgment of 29 July 1988 (Merits), para. 180. *Mapiripán Massacre v Colombia*, Ser. C No. 134, Judgment of 15 September 2005 (Merits, Reparations, and Costs), para. 190(h). *Cabrera Garcia y Montiel Flores v Mexico*, Ser. C No. 220, Judgment of 26 November 2010 (Preliminary Objection, Merits, Reparations, and Costs), para. 86.

93 *Favela Novela Brasilia v Brasil* (n. 90), para. 187 [my translation].

94 ECtHR, *Brecknell v UK*, App. No. 32457/04, Judgment of 27 November 2007, para. 76.

95 *Aktaş v Turkey* (n. 2).

Some of the intangible concerns associated with military culture and the likelihood of the wrong kind of loyalty affecting the administration of justice may be caused and addressed by leadership within the armed forces. At a very basic level, if members of armed forces are expected first of all to possess "vertical" loyalty to their institution and State, these higher echelons need to ensure they endorse and promote the right type of culture and values within their ranks. If leaders of a State's armed forces uphold an "ethic in which some lives [are] valued and others not," then it is no surprise that loyalty in such cases could lead to the "dehumanisation of millions of people."[96] In many military dictatorships where there is no or little pretence that respect for international law is valued, it is not loyalty within the armed forces which will need to be addressed to promote accountability. Furthermore, even if violations of international law are not the official or explicit values of the leadership, but such acts are implicitly ordered and/or tolerated, the effect may be similar (see in this regard Chapter 7).

There are even more indirect ways in which the leadership of the armed forces may affect the likelihood of miscarriage of justice, including "placing disproportionate pressure on unit commanders to produce results,"[97] for example with regard to the number of "victories" against the enemy. That such orders may lead to "false positives" is well documented in various cases.[98] Linked to this is the need for trust by military personnel in the values and legitimacy of the leadership of the armed forces. Leaders must be shown the make the right decisions, punish wrongdoers when they are reported, and be in touch with the realities on the ground. The armed forces also need to train their personnel to understand which type of loyalty is expected of them.

The role of appearances

It is therefore suggested that broad military affiliation is insufficient on its own to automatically undermine the principle of impartiality. The scope of toxic loyalty is different in every case, and beyond the immediate unit level, it would be difficult to generalise across different systems. How then can it be established whether military investigators are more likely to behave partially, in favour of other military members under investigation? Chapter 4 examined how regional human rights courts found that subjective impartiality, namely the actual impartial decision-making of the individual, is to be assumed unless there is proof to the contrary. Such proof of bias may be established, for example, through demonstrating that members of a particular group have

96 McCormack (n. 66), p. 90.

97 Palau, M., "The 'false positives' scandal that felled Colombia's military hero," *The Guardian* (19 November 2020), available at: www.theguardian.com/world/2020/nov/19/colombia-false-positives-killings-general-mario-montoya-trial.

98 E.g., the "false positives" in Colombia, as described in Palau (n. 97), or the use of "throw-downs" in Australia, as described in Whetham (2020) (n. 69), p. 511.

pre-established viewpoints, specific prejudices, or the presence of stereotyping of matters under investigation.[99] If such factors are suspected and/or found to be present, subjective impartiality may be questioned. Objective impartiality, on the other hand, must be demonstrated in personal and institutional safeguards such as those explored above, but also through the general provision of an appearance of impartiality.

Chapter 4 considered that for courts, what is at stake when it comes to matters of appearance of impartiality is "the confidence which the courts in a democratic society must inspire in the public and above all, as far as criminal proceedings are concerned, in the accused."[100] Many of the criticisms of military justice systems may well be focused on the lack of perception of independence and impartiality, albeit in some cases accompanied by an actual lack of structural and practical independence and impartiality. The judgments cited above, finding that the military as a whole encompassed a form of toxic loyalty, also found a combination of flawed measures that overall led the military justice system to fail in its obligations.[101] In a case involving police members on a board of inquiry, the ECtHR found that the fact that the police board member could return to other departmental duties meant that "the ordinary citizen will tend to see him as a member of the police force subordinate to his superiors and loyal to his colleagues. A situation of this kind may undermine the confidence which must be inspired by the courts in a democratic society."[102] In *Castillo Petruzzi v Peru*, the IACtHR found that the "faceless" character of the judges (combined with the fact that judges could not recuse themselves) meant that "defendants have no way of knowing the identity of their judge and, therefore, of assessing their competence."[103] It is therefore the appearance of the judges in this case which was problematic, and not their actual competence (or lack of it). The African Commission on Human and Peoples' Rights (African Commission) has found that the fact that members of tribunals belonged to the executive branch of government meant that "its composition alone create[d] the appearance, if not actual lack, of impartiality," and this "regardless of the character of the individual members."[104]

99 IACtHR, *Palamara-Iribarne v Chile* (n. 8), para. 146; IACtHR, *Atala Riffo and Daughters v Chile,* Ser. C No. 239, Judgment of 24 February 2012 (Merits, Reparations, and Costs), para. 234; *Duque v Colombia,* Ser. C No. 310, Judgment of 26 February 2016 (Preliminary Objections, Merits, Reparations, and Costs), para. 163.

100 *Incal v Turkey* (n. 45), para. 71.

101 This included flaws in the preliminary steps on the scene of the crime, in particular in the way forensic evidence was collected and analysed, and a failure to correct early flaws in subsequent reviews. See *Palacio de Justicia* (n. 8), para. 434.

102 *Belilos v Switzerland* (n. 60), para. 67.

103 IACtHR, *Castillo Petruzzi et al v Peru*, Ser. C No. 59, Judgment of 30 May 1999 (Merits, Reparations, and Costs), para. 133.

104 ACHPR, *Constitutional Rights Project (In Respect of Wahab Akamu, G. Adega and Others) v Nigeria*, App. No. 60/91, Decision on Merits (22 March 1995), para. 14; *Constitutional*

The role of appearances for investigations is perhaps less clear cut than it is for judges, courts, and tribunals, as it is just one of the elements which must tie into the entire "overall" independence and impartiality regarding the effectiveness of the investigation. Yet it has been pointed out that showing an appearance of independence and impartiality is particularly important in cases where an investigation procedure may itself be "open to doubt" and "not amenable to public scrutiny."[105] This is of particular relevance for military operations in situations of armed conflict, where transparency and public scrutiny is often limited for security reasons. The appearance of independence and impartiality is a safeguarding tool in situations in which the very actions of the State are under scrutiny, as "what is at stake here is nothing less than public confidence in the State's monopoly on the use of force."[106] On the other hand, the credibility of investigations and trust in military justice systems may be enhanced by institutional safeguards.[107]

The matter of appearances of independence and impartiality of military justice systems is difficult to generalise. The argument that a military justice system "appears" to lack independence and impartiality just because it is part of the same (very broad) institution as those being tried appears too broad an argument to be universally applicable. A dissenting judge in the ECtHR *Öcalan* case suggested that to consider that just because a member of a court was a military judge meant that the whole court could not appear independent and impartial would be "to take the 'theory' of appearances very far."[108] Indeed, suggesting such would be to rule out any possibility of military adjudication, despite the fact that the Human Rights Committee, ECtHR, and African Commission at least (if not the IACtHR) have maintained that military courts *in principle* can carry out independent and impartial decisions.

Yet in some cases in which the military justice system has a history and/or reputation of failing to adequately carry out justice, such broad categorisations may hold. It is worth remembering how the "test" of appearances is to be carried out: according to the ECtHR and IACtHR at least, such a test of appearances relies on the point of view of a "reasonable observer,"[109] most probably understood as a member of the domestic society to which the military court belongs. It cannot, therefore, solely be the perspective of the accused, the victim, or even a section of society. In taking into account the IACtHR's recent broad dismissal of military justice in general it is important to bear this

Rights Project (In Respect of Zamani Lakwot and Six Others) v Nigeria, App. No. 87/93, Decision on Merits (22 March 1995), paras 13–14.

105 ECtHR, *Hugh Jordan v UK*, App. No. 24746/94, Judgment of 4 May 2001, para. 123.

106 ECtHR, *Ramsahai and Others v Netherlands* (n. 6), para. 325.

107 Dahl (n. 26), p. 26.

108 Mowbray, A., "Duties of Investigation under the European Convention on Human Rights," *International and Comparative Law Quarterly* Vol. 51 No. 2 (2002), p. 182, citing dissenting opinion, para. 6.

109 General Comment No. 32 (n. 56), para. 21. See Chapter 4.

in mind. Not only have the institutional safeguards as mentioned above been lacking in these specific cases, but more generally within the context of historic impunity it is not unreasonable to suggest that a "reasonable observer" in, say, Colombia, Mexico, or Argentina at certain times has had good reasons to doubt the appearance of independence and impartiality of military judges.

A crucial point to make at this stage is that effective investigations can matter very much to the perception of justice (and mental health) not only of the victims of violations, but also to the members of the militaries involved. It has been remarked that military personnel, too, also have "the need to look ourselves in the mirror and be content with what we see."[110] The need to believe that the institutions and the causes they are fighting for are just, will be undermined if violations of laws and regulations are not effectively investigated or punished. In this sense, effective accountability can aid in establishing a moral compass for those involved in difficult operations. This has been highlighted by various retired military personnel who have commented on anecdotal evidence of the impact of the perception of justice on soldiers.[111] This need to believe in the legitimacy of the missions one is involved in is necessary to foster discipline and obedience, and to legitimise the use of lethal force and potentially losing one's life.[112] Personnel who trust in their leadership and believe in the legitimacy of their work are also more likely to work better.[113] Furthermore, botched investigations often mean that further inquiries and other judicial and non-judicial proceedings will be carried out, which has the potential not only of being judicially questionable, but also possibly putting the witnesses (including military personnel) through the same traumatic experiences over and over again.[114] It is essential that investigations, as far as possible, are done correctly the first time.

This section identified that loyalty can impact on impartiality, and separately that it can also impact on the willingness of military personnel to report or bear witness regarding violations committed by their peers. Both of these factors can undermine the effectiveness of investigations for different reasons, and a series of different problems which can accompany the presence of toxic loyalty were also mentioned. Yet, increasing independence does not solve all the problems associated with ineffectiveness of investigations caused by this type of toxic loyalty. A broader contextual approach will be necessary to contribute

110 Stringer, J. J., "Conclusion" in Skerker, Whetham, & Carrick (n. 53), p. 366.

111 Dahl (n. 26), pp. 23–25; Stringer (n. 110), p. 366.

112 Whetham (2019) (n. 61), p. 83.

113 Allen (n. 83); Whetham (2019) (n. 61), p. 83.

114 Hampson, F., "An Investigation of Alleged Violations of The Law of Armed Conflict," *Israel Yearbook on Human Rights* Vol. 46 (2016), p. 2; Watkin, K., "Accountability fatigue: A human rights law problem for armed forces?" *Just Security* (November 2018), www.justsecurity.org/61318/accountability-fatigue-human-rights-law-problem-armed-forces-petraeus-united-kingdom/.

to an effective investigation, including by considering the role of appearances in investigations.

Conclusion

This chapter has deconstructed and addressed the different ways in which military investigations lack, or are perceived to lack, independence and impartiality. It has corroborated the premise at the introduction of this book that there is nothing inherent in military institutions which necessarily compromises their capability of being independent and impartial. That is not to say that there are not specific factors which must be taken into account. Military institutions do contain unique structures of influence which must be considered when assessing how an investigator operating within this institution is to meet the required standards of independence and impartiality necessary for an effective investigation. In general, it is necessary for an investigator to be structurally and practically independent from those implicated in the incident under investigation, and this will often mean being outside of the direct chain of command of those involved. What "implicated" in a violation means may be affected by the notion of command responsibility. Furthermore, an investigator needs to be "competent," as well as independent and impartial, and this may have implications on the choice of investigator, who will need at least military knowledge, if not experience.

There are further elements within military life which are perceived to affect a military investigator's ability to act impartially. This chapter scrutinised some of the criticisms of lack of impartiality with regard to military members investigating or judging "themselves," and found that these criticisms do not point to one particular specific scope of bias. They have ranged from investigators investigating their direct colleagues (within the same unit) to those investigating members simply of the same institution. It was posited that institutional affiliation in itself cannot be sufficient to establish presence or lack of impartiality in an investigator, but rather that the context as a whole, including the nature of the offence, the military culture, and the general national context within which the military is operating will all contribute to assessing the appropriate levels of independence and impartiality of military investigations. The following chapters will go on to consider in more detail further contextual elements which may affect independence and impartiality of military investigations.

6 The impact of armed conflict on independence and impartiality

Introduction

Critics of the maintenance of a separate system of military justice have remarked that most of contemporary military experience occurs in a peacetime environment, and therefore that referring to the exceptionalities of combat environment is redundant in considering how military affairs should be attended.[1] It is indeed important that legal and practical measures intended for war and armed conflict not be used in situations of peace, something that is crucial in protecting populations from overreach by State powers. Nevertheless, even if it may not be the majority of military experience, it is still necessary to consider how such powers *can* legitimately operate in conflict situations, however rare they may be, as situations of armed conflict do not suspend the need for lawful administration of justice. As this book is concerned with violations of international humanitarian law (IHL), a situation of armed conflict is presupposed, and not all of the arguments made here may therefore hold in times of peace. A State must, however, prepare, in times of peace, for lawful and just procedures which may be triggered in times of conflict.

Investigators may face practical difficulties which are unique, or particularly aggravated, in situations of armed conflict, especially in the collection and analysis of evidence and in the resources available to them.[2] Armed conflict can also affect the independence and impartiality of investigations, either in the fulfilment or the interpretation of the standards. Considerations related to the extraterritoriality of the operations, the conflict-specific jurisdiction or the security situation in combat scenarios can all affect who legally or physically can investigate. This chapter explores how the standards of independence and

1 Collins, P., *The Military As a Separate Society: Consequences for Discipline in the United States and Australia*, Lexington Books (2019), pp. 20 and 25.

2 Lubell, N., Pejic, J., & Simmons, C., "Guidelines on Investigating Violations of International Humanitarian Law: Law, Policy, and Good Practice," Geneva Academy/ICRC (2019) [Guidelines on Investigating Violations of International Humanitarian Law], Guideline 8; Schmitt, M. N., "Investigating Violations of International Law in Armed Conflict," *Harvard National Security Journal* Vol. 2 (2011), p. 55.

DOI: 10.4324/9781003360223-6

impartiality of investigations may be affected by practical and theoretical challenges related to situations of armed conflict, and how the law can be used to address these challenges.

Reasonableness in armed conflict

Chapter 3 established that the standards applicable to effective investigations into violations of IHL must be measured in a similar way to those under international human rights law (IHRL) and international criminal law (ICL), namely in assessing whether all *reasonable means* were put into the investigation in light of its objective. The choice of means, including the choice of investigator and the allocation of resources, is therefore subject to a test of "reasonableness." This section addresses in more detail how this assessment of reasonableness in an armed conflict situation must inform how the standards of independence and impartiality are put into practice in light of the overall effectiveness of investigations. It is suggested that in the context of IHL, what is "reasonable" may be understood in light of caveats found in other areas of this body of law, namely of the need to balance considerations of humanity with that of military necessity. It is necessary to clarify this concept in order to subsequently examine how it applies in addressing conflict-related obstacles to independence and impartiality.

Reasonableness in fulfilling international legal obligations

The concept of reasonableness in international law does not have a single definition, and its interpretation necessarily varies depending on the context.[3] It is used in various "primary rules" in treaty texts,[4] including in multiple human rights treaties,[5] but is also used in the interpretation and application of primary rules.[6] Any test assessing reasonableness must "be adapted in response to the particularities in the area of law and the factual situation at issue."[7] The concept of reasonableness in the means employed for an investigation therefore not only depends upon the practical context (including the presence, type, and location of armed conflict), but also of the body of

3 Corten, O., "Reasonableness in International Law," *Max Planck Encyclopedia of Public International Law*, Elsevier (2013), para. 24; ICJ, "Interpretation of the Agreement of 25 March 1951 Between the WHO and Egypt," Advisory Opinion (20 December 1980), para. 49; ECtHR, *Wemhoff v Germany*, App. No. 2122/64, Judgment of 27 June 1968, para. 10.

4 Corten (n. 3), para. 3.

5 International Covenant on Civil and Political Rights, 999 UNTS 171 (1966), Art. 9, Art. 10.2, Art. 14; European Convention for the Protection of Human Rights and Fundamental Freedoms, ETS 5 (1950) [ECHR], Art. 6.

6 ICJ, "Barcelona Traction, Light and Power Company, Limited (*Belgium v Spain*)," Judgment of 5 February 1970, para. 93; Optional Protocol to the International Covenant on Economic, Social and Cultural Rights, Annex, Art. 8(4).

7 Corten (n. 3), para. 24.

law under which the duty arises. What is "reasonable" in such cases must therefore be interpreted in line with the body of law under which the investigation is being carried out. Furthermore, what is "reasonable" must be distinguished from what is "possible." It may be *possible* for a State to do a certain action, for example by halting all war-fighting efforts to conduct an investigation in a high-security combat situation, but it may not be *reasonable* for the State to do so. What is reasonable in such cases should be assessed by the circumstances at the time.

IHRL bodies have taken into account armed conflict situations in determining how various human rights treaty obligations are to be fulfilled in a reasonable manner.[8] In relation to investigations, "what is required of States varies according to the circumstances, both the situation in general at the time and the specific context in which the incident arises."[9] States must therefore take "the reasonable steps available to them" in conducting an investigation,[10] taking into account, for example, "circumstances of generalised violence, armed conflict or insurgency."[11] The five general principles of an effective investigation are not absolute principles, but are to be interpreted within a specific context, based on what was possible at the time and reasonable expectations.[12] This is seen, *inter alia*, in the way in which the "means not results" test has been applied, as seen in Chapter 3. A State has a degree of flexibility in which means it uses and how it applies the five general principles, as long as they are reasonable within the circumstances in contributing towards an effective investigation. In the context of armed conflict, it has also been suggested that the procedural duty to investigate must be applied "realistically."[13] A State therefore has an obligation to invest reasonable means into securing the independence and impartiality of investigations, taking into account the context at hand and how the employed means can contribute to the overall effectiveness of the investigation.

8 Gowlland-Debbas, V., & Gaggioli, G., "The Relationship Between International Human Rights and Humanitarian Law: An Overview" in Kolb, R., & Gaggioli, G., *Research Handbook on Human Rights and Humanitarian Law*, Elgar Publishing (2013); Margalit, A., "The Duty to Investigate Civilian Casualties during Armed Conflict and Its Implementation in Practice," *Yearbook of International Humanitarian Law* Vol. 15 (2012), p. 68.

9 Hampson, F., "An Investigation of Alleged Violations of The Law of Armed Conflict," *Israel Yearbook on Human Rights* Vol. 46 (2016), p. 19; Margalit (n. 8), p. 68.

10 ECtHR, *McShane v UK*, App. No. 43290/98, Judgment of 28 May 2002, para. 96; *Al-Skeini v UK*, App. No. 55721/07, Judgment of 7 July 2011, para 164.

11 ECtHR, *Al-Skeini* (n. 10), para. 164. See also IACtHR, *Moiwana Community v Suriname*, Ser. C No. 124, Judgment of 15 June 2005 (Preliminary Objections, Merits, Reparations, and Costs), para. 153; ACHPR, *Zimbabwe Human Rights Forum v Zimbabwe*, App. No. 245/02, Decision on Merits (15 May 2006), paras 154 and 175.

12 Guidelines on Investigating Violations of International Humanitarian Law (n. 2), para. 34.

13 ECtHR, *Al-Skeini* (n. 10), para. 168; *Hanan v Germany*, App. No. 4871/16, Judgment of 16 February 2021, para. 224.

Similarly, under ICL, the obligation upon commanders is that they take all "necessary and reasonable measures" to repress war crimes.[14] The notion of what is "reasonable" for a commander to do with regard to repression of war crimes within a conflict situation was in fact one of the turning points in the *Bemba* Appeals case before the International Criminal Court (ICC). The ICC Appeals Chamber stated that "it is not the case that a commander is required to employ every single conceivable measure within his or her arsenal, irrespective of considerations of proportionality and feasibility," but only what is "*reasonable* under the circumstances."[15] The Court laid out parameters to assess reasonableness, "such as the operational realities on the ground at the time."[16] In this context, "Commanders are allowed to make a cost/benefit analysis when deciding which measures to take," including by taking into consideration "the impact of measures to prevent or repress criminal behaviour on ongoing or planned operations."[17] Nevertheless, although they are allowed to choose "the least disruptive measure," it must "reasonably be expected that this measure will prevent or repress the crimes."[18] It was therefore reminded that the objective of the investigation must be kept in mind in the choice of means; the chosen means must still be able to effectively prevent or repress war crimes, even if this is not achieved in the most efficient way.[19]

Reasonableness in IHL as balance between military necessity and humanity

The concept of "reasonable" investigative measures into violations of IHL are usefully informed by the above-mentioned references to IHRL and ICL. Nevertheless, IHL may provide us with a further element in understanding what may be "reasonable" in investigative means for violations of IHL. Various provisions of IHL use the concept of "feasibility" rather than "reasonableness," a concept which has developed a specific definition based upon reservations to Article 87 of Additional Protocol I (API) by various State parties.[20] In the context of the obligation to take feasible precautions in attack, "feasible" precautions are generally understood as those "which are practicable or practically possible taking into account all circumstances ruling at the

14 ICTY, *Prosecutor v Vujadin Popović et al.*, IT-05-88-A, Appeals Chamber Judgment of 30 January 2015, para. 1932; ICC, *The Prosecutor v Jean-Pierre Bemba Gombo,* App. No. ICC-01/05-01/08, Trial Chamber III Judgment (21 March 2016), para. 197.

15 ICC, *The Prosecutor v Jean-Pierre Bemba Gombo*, App. No. ICC-01/05-01/08, Judgment in the Appeals Chamber (2018), para. 169.

16 ICC, *Bemba* Appeals (n. 15), para. 170.

17 ICC, *Bemba* Appeals (n. 15), para. 170.

18 ICC, *Bemba* Appeals (n. 15), para. 170

19 See Chapter 7 on the matter of potentially being "unable" to investigate due to the circumstances and reasonable expectations.

20 Boothby, B., *The Law of Targeting*, Oxford University Press (2012), p. 173; Gill, T., & Fleck, D., *The Handbook of the International Law of Military Operations*, Oxford University Press (2010), p. 353.

time, including humanitarian and military considerations."[21] This concept and definition of feasibility is also used in other contexts in API related to conduct of hostilities,[22] and has also been taken up in the Protocol III on Prohibitions or Restrictions on the Use of Incendiary Weapons,[23] and in the Protocol II on the Convention on Prohibitions or Restrictions on the Use of Certain Conventional Weapons.[24]

Although the concept of feasibility is principally used in the contexts of conduct of hostilities, it is a concept which ties into the very core of IHL. The very existence of IHL is "a compromise based on a balance between military necessity, on the one hand, and the requirements of humanity, on the other."[25] It is therefore suggested that this balance is useful in understanding the "reasonableness" in other contexts of IHL, such as in the way investigations into alleged violations are carried out. What is considered "reasonable" in the context of IHL is therefore dictated by the core of the body of law, thus taking both military necessity and humanity as the balancing factors in understanding the content of this reasonableness. When a State is faced with decisions of prioritisation of resources, or security risks for their personnel in investigating, both these elements must therefore be used in finding the adequate way forward.

It must be caveated that not all provisions of IHL are subject to the concept of reasonableness, and some treaty provisions and their interpretation contain absolute obligations or prohibitions, for example the prohibition of torture of detainees. The concept of reasonableness only applies to certain treaty and implementation provisions, for example for the means put into an investigation, or in the application of Article 87 API, as mentioned above.

How to measure reasonableness in independence and impartiality

States therefore have an obligation to put in the reasonable means necessary to carry out an effective investigation into violations of IHL. What is to be considered "reasonable" will be assessed *inter alia* by the situation on the ground, including both humanitarian and military considerations. This section considers what this may mean for the choice of investigators, and the way in which the standards of independence and impartiality are fulfilled.

21 Henckaerts, J.-M., & Doswald-Beck, L., *Customary International Humanitarian Law*, ICRC (2006) [ICRC Customary Study], Rule 15.

22 Protocol Additional to the Geneva Conventions of 12 August 1949 and relating to the Protection of Victims of International Armed Conflicts, 1125 UNTS 3 (1977) [API], Arts 41(3), 56(2), 57(2)(a), 58, 78(1), 86(2).

23 Protocol on Prohibitions or Restrictions on the Use of Incendiary Weapons (Protocol III) (10 October 1980), Art 1(5).

24 Protocol II, annexed to the Convention of 10 October 1980 on Prohibitions or Restrictions on the Use of Certain Conventional Weapons, Art. 3.

25 Sandoz, Y., Swinarski, C., & Zimmermann, B., *Commentary to the Additional Protocols of 8 June 1977 to the Geneva Conventions of 12 August 1949*, Martinus Nijhoff Publishers (1987) [ICRC Commentary to API], Commentary to Article 35, para. 1389.

Chapter 4 set out that the standards of independence and impartiality as applicable to investigations are to be measured in light of their contribution to the overall effectiveness of that investigation. They are not absolute principles in and of themselves but must be examined in each context and in light of the purpose of the investigation in question. The context of armed conflict will be one element of the context which must be taken into account in establishing what an "effective" investigation may look like. Situations of armed conflict, as will be seen below, may affect who can and should investigate, and in some cases may mean the use of less independent measures than those used in peacetime. Nevertheless, such measures must be reasonable in each context, and will need to demonstrate that they are still contributing to the overall effectiveness of the investigation.

Crucial to adapting to conflict-related challenges is advance preparation by States for situations of armed conflict and extraterritorial military operations. The concept of effectiveness, including that of good faith, implies a certain element of due diligence. States are expected to make reasonable arrangements, for example prior to a conflict or to deployment, to mitigate all difficulties which can be foreseen. It is necessary, for example, for a State to adequately prepare for jurisdictional and practical considerations which may arise in investigating possible violations committed during extraterritorial operations,[26] as will be seen below. It also means that sufficient safeguards of independence and impartiality need to be set up for whatever investigative authority is mandated to operate in such circumstances. Were a State to fail to set up adequate due diligence mechanisms for foreseeable operations, it may well fail to meet standards of international law.

Even with adequate prior preparation, there may be situations in armed conflict which affect the ability of the foreseen independent and impartial investigative authority to operate. For example, situations of ongoing hostilities may mean that law enforcement personnel are not able to access the scene of a possible violation. Or, as will be seen below, the situation may require prompt disciplinary action on behalf of a commander who is not an independent and impartial authority. It can be envisioned that in such circumstances a decision may be made that it is not feasible to use the investigative body or techniques which may have been used in other situations, such as in non-combat settings. The legitimacy of these decisions must be assessed based upon the standard of reasonableness, and whether the decision was made in light of all of the circumstances at the time. If less independent and impartial measures must be taken due to conflict-related reasons, the overall effectiveness of the investigation may be met with other measures, such as subsequent detailed scrutiny and review of the proceedings. This in turn brings us back to the need for adequate preparation prior to conflict, as commanders and other authorities who may be required to step in in exceptional circumstances must have adequate training in how to deal with such situations.

26 Guidelines on Investigating Violations of International Humanitarian Law (n. 2), para. 133.

This section has clarified the standard of "reasonableness" that should be applied in assessing whether reasonable means were put into achieving an effective investigation under IHL. The importance of clarifying this standard at this point is to enable a proper assessment of the exceptional measures which may be used in situations of armed conflict. States must consider which investigators will most contribute to the overall effectiveness of investigations in such difficult contexts and provide sufficient resources in preparation and carrying out of military operations to ensure these investigators can legally and practically function.

Legal and practical obstacles to independence and impartiality in armed conflict

There are both legal and practical obstacles which may affect the choice of investigator in armed conflict. On the one hand, the laws applicable in situations of armed conflict may affect who may legally investigate, especially in terms of extraterritorial jurisdiction, and occasionally in cases of triggering specific exceptional domestic legislation. On the other hand, armed conflicts can also pose real practical obstacles to any investigator, especially in terms of accessing the scene of incidents, and this can affect who in practice is able and/or willing to investigate.

Jurisdiction: the impact on independence

Jurisdictional specificities related to extraterritorial operations and times of war can affect the scope of military jurisdiction, and these jurisdictional specificities can in turn affect the choice of investigator, and therefore the standards of independence and impartiality. For extraterritorial operations, various questions can arise with regard to criminal jurisdiction over offences committed by members of the armed forces, and the availability of experts and equipment to carry out investigations. In many jurisdictions, a criminal investigation in peacetime and within a State's own territory may be carried out by an entirely civilian police force. However, many States also have specific jurisdictional arrangements for offences committed abroad or committed in times of armed conflict or "war." Much of the discussion of these topics in existing literature has not necessarily separated the trial versus the investigation stage in such jurisdictional considerations. This section highlights how this division is extremely important in considering the proper administration of justice. Furthermore, it briefly addresses the matter of investigations into non-criminal violations, which are often not contemplated in discussions on jurisdiction, even though they also affect the implementation of IHL.

Extraterritorial jurisdiction

If a conflict is occurring outside the territory of a State, the matter of jurisdiction over offences committed by a State's armed forces is crucial to consider in the fight against impunity. Under IHL, States have an obligation to exercise jurisdiction over war crimes committed by their armed forces, whether or not they are committed on their territory.[27] This means they must have a legal and practical way of enforcing criminal jurisdiction over actions of their armed forces even if committed abroad.[28] They will also want to exercise criminal jurisdiction over other offences than war crimes for matters of domestic justice as well as disciplinary control. Additionally, Chapter 3 saw that there is a need to suppress all other violations of IHL which may not be criminal in nature, for example through administrative and/or disciplinary sanctions.

Such "service jurisdiction" over members of armed forces abroad is not uniform, even across similar legal systems.[29] The example of common law systems is often highlighted, as systems which are "generally reluctant to claim extraterritorial reach."[30] In such contexts, special (military) service jurisdiction of members of the armed forces is the only way in which the States such as the UK, USA, and Canada can exercise criminal jurisdiction over actions of their military abroad.[31] It is worth considering, however, whether this special service jurisdiction necessarily needs to be military. Laws can be changed, as has been done, for example, for specific types of extraterritorial offences such as child sexual exploitation in common law States.[32] An argument has been made in the case of Australia that specialised civilian courts could instead "travel with the military to war zones just like other professional civilians, such as medical and training personnel."[33] However it is not only common law States which use military jurisdiction for extraterritorial jurisdiction. Even other legal systems, which may be able to exercise jurisdiction *ratione personae* over their citizens abroad for criminal offences, will have specific legislative provisions for service jurisdiction over members of its armed forces abroad, including in

27 Geneva Convention (I) for the Amelioration of the Condition of the Wounded and Sick in Armed Forces in the Field, 75 UNTS 31 (1949) [GCI], Art. 49; Geneva Convention (II) for the Amelioration of the Condition of Wounded, Sick and Shipwrecked Members of Armed Forces at Sea, 75 UNTS 85 (1949) [GCII], Art. 50; Geneva Convention (III) Relative to the Treatment of Prisoners of War, 75 UNTS 135 (1949) [GCIII], Art. 129; Geneva Convention (IV) Relative to the Protection of Civilian Persons in Time of War, 75 UNTS 287 (1949) [GCIV], Art. 146; API (n. 22), Art. 85. For customary law, see ICRC Customary Study (n. 21), Rule 158.

28 The same or similar considerations will apply in military operations abroad which may not amount to an armed conflict, such as some peacekeeping operations. The specificities of non-conflict extraterritorial operations are not covered in depth here.

29 Liivoja, R., "Service Jurisdiction under International Law," *Melbourne Journal of International Law* Vol. 11 No. 2 (2010).

30 Liivoja (n. 29), p. 309.

31 Liivoja (n. 29), p. 309.

32 E.g., in the UK for sexual offences against children, certain terrorism-related offences, fraud, and bribery; see Crown Prosecution Service, Legal Guidance: 'Jurisdiction' (updated 7 November 2019), available at: www.cps.gov.uk/legal-guidance/jurisdiction; Liivoja (n. 29), 310; Collins (n. 1), p. 33.

33 Collins (n. 1), p. 32.

some cases accompanying civilians.[34] In at least some of these cases, such service jurisdiction is under the remit of military jurisdiction, although in other cases it may be hybrid military/civilian.[35] Some of the practical reasons for this will be returned to below.

It must be emphasised at this point that much scrutiny over military jurisdiction has focused on the courts and trial stage of judicial procedures. In some contexts, the fact that a State may have exclusive "civilian" jurisdiction over members of their armed forces is referring to the nature of the courts where such cases will be examined. The pretrial procedures, especially initial investigative steps, may, however, be carried out by military personnel. This very fact was examined in the *Hanan v Germany* case before the European Court of Human Rights (ECtHR). Germany has "for historical reasons [...] deliberately refrained from reintroducing a separate military justice system after 1949,"[36] and therefore

> the responsibility for investigations of criminal offences potentially committed by German soldiers lay in all cases and exclusively, with civilian law enforcement agencies and civilian criminal law courts, irrespective of whether the potential offences have been committed within Germany or abroad.[37]

Nevertheless, Germany does have a military police accompanying the armed forces which can (and must) carry out investigations in cases of alleged violations. In the *Hanan* case, there was in fact no legal authority for the civilian authorities to investigate on the ground.[38] It is therefore expected to a certain degree that it will be military personnel that are carrying out at least the preliminary steps of a judicial process on the ground, such as the investigation.[39] This goes back to difficulties as to what is meant by a "military justice" system. Germany is understood to have a purely civilian justice system, yet military police do exist, and their involvement in the investigation was a point of concern for the applicants in the *Hanan* case. It is therefore not only common law jurisdictions which exercise some sort of military jurisdiction abroad, and

34 Liivoja (n. 29), p. 310.

35 Heng, B., Liivoja, R., Ng, D., & Oswald, B., "Military Justice in a Comparative and International Perspective," *Journal of International Peacekeeping* Vol. 20 (2016), p. 135.

36 ECtHR, *Hanan v Germany* (n. 13), para. 179.

37 ECtHR, *Hanan v Germany* (n. 13), para. 179.

38 ECtHR, *Hanan v Germany* (n. 13), para. 180. This was due to "the multilevel nature of the military deployment in Afghanistan under the delegation of United Nations Security Council powers, which did not entail legal powers for the civilian law enforcement authorities of the troop-contributing States to pursue criminal investigations of their own on Afghan territory (other than through international legal assistance)."

39 Dahl, A. W., "Military Justice and Self-Interest in Accountability" in Bergsmo, M., & Song, T., *Military Self-Interest in Accountability for Core International Crimes*, Torkel Opsahl Academic EPublisher (1st ed.) (2016), p. 28.

especially when looking at the investigation stage, many States do in fact use military personnel for preliminary processes of criminal investigations.

It is therefore important that States consider how the administration of justice will be carried out in extraterritorial settings when considering the effective implementation of IHL. In all cases, the adequate standards of independence and impartiality need to be installed within the justice system, which is able to operate abroad, whether it be military or civilian. There are also other reasons to employ military justice systems abroad, such as for the effective suppression of non-criminal violations, as addressed in Chapter 2. If the military judicial authorities will have a larger role to play in conflict and/or extraterritorial operations than in other situations, sufficient structural and legislative arrangements should be in place to ensure the overall independence and impartiality within these military authorities. As explored above, currently most systems involve military police in at least parts of the judicial procedure, even if there is subsequent recourse to civilian courts. In all cases, this requires training all military personnel for how they must deal with a possible violation in different contexts.[40] Consideration of how an investigation may be carried out into a possible violation where the State does not have ground control of the scene of the incident, for example in the case of aerial bombardment, needs also to be taken into account.[41] Nevertheless, even brief involvement of military personnel may be problematic if there are systematic problems within the military institution as a whole. Such scenarios will be addressed in Chapter 7.

"War" jurisdiction

One other important element which can affect the jurisdictional scope of military justice institutions is the use of exceptional legal powers in times of "war" or other situations of emergency. Such jurisdictional specificities often include an expansion of military jurisdiction geographically, such as where military judicial procedures may be held, and the expansion of military jurisdiction *ratione materiae* and *ratione personae*.[42] In various common law States, for example, it is frequent to find permissive use of field courts martial in such cases, where military courts may be set up anywhere they may be needed.[43]

40 Guidelines on Investigating Violations of International Humanitarian Law (n. 2), Guideline 2.

41 Guidelines on Investigating Violations of International Humanitarian Law (n. 2), para 139.

42 See, generally, Reports of the International Society for Military Law and Law of War [ISMLLW Reports] from the Seminars on Military Jurisdiction of 2001 and 2011, contributions for the following States: Algeria, Cameroon, Democratic Republic of the Congo (DRC), Kenya, Mali, Rwanda, Senegal, Sudan, Tunisia, Uganda, Zimbabwe, Peru, USA, India, Iran, Israel, Pakistan, Singapore, Austria, Belgium, Czech Republic, Denmark, France, Hungary, Finland, Ireland, Italy, Lithuania, Netherlands, Norway, Spain, Portugal, Switzerland, UK.

43 E.g., Senegal: "in times of crisis (war, insurrection …) the special jurisdictions can be set up in other places than in Dakar, within the internal limits of the national territory" (ISMLLW Report 2001 (n. 42), Vol. II, p. 69 [my translation]). Uganda: "The military legal system of Uganda provides for Field Court Martial which operate only in circumstances where it is

Some States have specific wartime Military Penal Codes,[44] whereas others will include offences which may only be committed in times of war.[45] In some cases, the scope of offences as well as the scope of persons under military jurisdiction will be expanded in times of war or other emergency, such as over specific types of civilians.[46] In Hungary and Finland, military courts can be set up in wartime, whereas in peacetime there only exists military council in civilian courts.[47] In the case of Austria, the invocation of war powers provides for the creation of military jurisdiction abolished in peacetime.[48] In many cases, offences committed during times of war are punished more severely, and more leeway is given to commanders in the scope of disciplinary measures which may be used to punish offences.

---

impracticable for the offender to be tried by the other military courts of original jurisdiction. Such circumstances can only arise in war time" (ISMLLW Report 2001 (n. 42), Vol. II, p. 31). Zimbabwe: "The military legal system has no real distinction in wartime versus peacetime except for the convening of [Field General Courts Martial]" (ISMLLW Report 2001 (n. 42), Vol. II, p. 117). Israel: "A Field Court Martial was set up only under special circumstances (wartime) and is not a permanent institution" (ISMLLW Report 2001 (n. 42), Vol. I, p. 201).

44 E.g., Italy: "in times of war the application of the Wartime Military Penal Code is foreseen" (ISMLLW Report 2001 (n. 42), Vol. I, p. 209 [my translation]).

45 DRC: some crimes only exist in times of war. See, *inter alia*, Code Pénal Militaire, Arts 127–132. Belgium: specific provisions in Military Penal Code for wartime with some offences only possible in war (ISMLLW Report 2011 (n. 42), p. 458). Czech Republic: some crimes can only be committed during wartime (ISMLLW Report 2011 (n. 42), p. 237). Denmark: expanded jurisdiction in war (ISMLLW Report 2001 (n. 42), Vol. I, p. 110). Finland: some offences only applicable during wartime (ISMLLW Report 2001 (n. 42), Vol. I, p. 151). Italy: Wartime Military Penal code provides extension of military jurisdiction (ISMLLW Report 2001 (n. 42), Vol. I, p. 209). Spain: some offences specific to wartime, extended military jurisdiction (ISMLLW Report 2001 (n. 42), Vol. I, p. 116). Switzerland: if State or army face major danger, the field of application of the Military Penal Code is extended *ratione materiae* and *ratione personae* (ISMLLW Report 2011 (n. 42), p. 404). Turkey: some crimes only exist in wartime (ISMLLW Report 2001 (n. 42), Vol. II, p. 105).

46 Singapore: in wartime, civilians accompanying or following military operations are subject to military law (ISMLLW Report 2011 (n. 42), p. 388). Finland: some civilians covered by military penal code in wartime (ISMLLW Report 2001 (n. 42), Vol. I, p. 151). France: extension of persons covered by jurisdiction; Hungary: in cases of state of emergency/war jurisdiction over persons and acts extended (ISMLLW Report 2011 (n. 42), p. 249). Netherlands: extension of military jurisdiction over specific civilians (ISMLLW Report 2011 (n. 42), p. 351). Norway: jurisdiction extended in war (ISMLLW Report 2001 (n. 42), Vol. II, p. 21). Spain: military jurisdiction extended to specific civilians (ISMLLW Report 2001 (n. 42), Vol. I, p. 116). Switzerland: if State or army face major danger, the field of application of the Military Penal Code is extended *ratione materiae* and *ratione personae* (ISMLLW Report 2011 (n. 42), p. 404); UK: possibility of martial law with courts martial to try civilians if law and order breaks down in UK territory ("Second Report of the Public Commission to Examine the Maritime Incident of 31 May 2010: Israel's Mechanisms for Examining and Investigating Complaints and Claims of Violations of the Laws of Armed Conflict According to International Law" (Israel, February 2013) [Second Turkel Report], Annex, p. 767).

47 Hungary: ISMLLW Report 2011 (n. 42), pp. 287–291; Finland: ISMLLW Report 2001 (n. 42), p. 152.

48 Austria: ISMLLW Report 2001 (n. 42), p. 69.

The use of wartime or other exceptional jurisdiction which affects the scope of military justice raises various concerns regarding the administration of justice: first that they are politically, and not factually, triggered measures; and second that the use of "exceptional" measures can mean that their fairness and legality are not scrutinised or tested in peacetime.

The concept of "war" as conceived of in such statutes is not usually equivalent to armed conflict in the factual sense of the term as understood to trigger, for example, the application of IHL. Situations of war or other public emergencies which may trigger such jurisdictional changes are often initiated by official declarations of war authorised by governmental authorities, meaning that they are political, not factual, triggers.[49] Although in many cases they are not frequently used (Italy, for example, has not used its wartime jurisdiction since the Second World War),[50] there has been problematic triggering of such specific jurisdictions for political ends. Abuses become clear in such cases, if jurisdictional changes are used as excuses not to apply existing laws.[51]

Second, the use of such "exceptional" jurisdiction in times of war (which is to be expected to remain an exception) can raise concerns around the efficiency or adequacy of systems which are created *ad hoc*. If the infrastructure

49 E.g., France: declaration of war authorised by Parliament (ISMLLW 2011 Report (n. 42), p. 249); Ireland: war cannot be declared or participated in except with assent of Irish Parliament (Dáil Éireann) (ISMLLW Report 2011 (n. 42), p. 304). Italy: "In case of serious threat to territorial integrity, a declaration of war enabled the Parliament to award necessary powers to the government." (ISMLLW Report 2001 (n. 42), Vol. I, p. 209. Israel: "In which armed forces are taking part in military action and Government or MOD declare that due to state of war different set of rules concerning military courts is engaged" (ISMLLW Report 2001 (n. 42), Vol. I, p. 201). DRC: "Mobilisation of armed forces ordered by the President of the Republic," Art. 29 Code judiciaire militaire. USA: "'Time of war' means period of war declared by US Congress or the President's factual determination that the existence of hostilities warrants finding that time of war exists" (ISMLLW Report 2001 (n. 42), Vol. I, p. 140). Belgium: "Mobilisation of the army by royal decree with support of government" (ISMLLW Report 2011 (n. 42), p. 458). Czech Republic: traditional notion of war limited to IACs (ISMLLW Report 2011 (n. 42), p. 237). Denmark: war-specific rules apply when Denmark is: at war; in imminent danger of war when MOD made public announcement thereof; when military unit deployed against foreign forces seeking with hostile intent to invade Danish territory or attacked outside Danish territory (ISMLLW Report 2001 (n. 42), Vol. I, p. 110). Italy: "In case of serious threat to territorial integrity, a declaration of war enabled the Parliament to award necessary powers to the government." (ISMLLW Report 2001 (n. 42), Vol. I, p. 209). Netherlands: "an armed conflict in which the Kingdom of the Netherlands is involved either in case of individual or collective self defence, or to restore international peace and security" (ISMLLW Report 2011 (n. 42), p. 351). Norway: when nation is at war, including war having been declared or the nation being under armed attack. Will apply for units abroad if by royal decree (ISMLLW Report 2001 (n. 42), Vol. II, p. 21). Portugal: declaration of war between Portugal and a foreign State (ISMLLW Report 2011 (n. 42), p. 377).

50 ISMLLW Report 2001 (n. 42), Vol. I, p. 209.

51 Sheeran, S., "Reconceptualizing States of Emergency Under International Human Rights Law: Theory, Legal Doctrine, and Politics," *Michigan Journal of International Law* Vol. 34 No. 3 (2013), p. 492.

is not in place during peacetime, and is only instituted in times of crises, it is more likely to be susceptible to procedural flaws. In Austria, for example, it has been pointed out that there are no legal provisions for setting up a military justice system in wartime.[52] Following the Russian invasion in 2022, Ukraine has debated whether to reinstall military courts, which were abolished in 2010.[53] A system which is not tested during peacetime may struggle to uphold legal standards in times of crisis. It is a fact of international law that the existence of war or any other political situation of emergency does not lead to the suspension of the law, although it may lead to different application. As this book focuses on violations of IHL, it is concerned only with situations in which an armed conflict exists, therefore only with potentially "exceptional" circumstances. The standards as laid out in previous chapters must therefore be met in any circumstance, albeit subject to the accepted caveats of reasonableness. Any institutions being used for the administration of justice in such exceptional times must therefore also meet the required standards of fair trial, and investigations into alleged violations by such institutions must also be effective.

With regard to the independence and impartiality of investigators, the change of jurisdiction may affect who investigates. Military justice institutions (including the investigative authorities) may be called upon to deal with offences and persons which would, in peacetime, be allocated to civilian jurisdiction. In such cases, the investigative authority must also fulfil the required standards under IHL and IHRL. This means it needs to be overall sufficiently independent and impartial for investigations to be effective. A State must ensure, in times of peace, that the structures which it can legally call for in situations of emergency are able to function competently and fairly. In this regard, States which use military jurisdiction even in peacetime may actually be better prepared for situations of emergency if it means that the system is tried and tested and may even have been under scrutiny of various domestic or international bodies with regard to fair trial rights and general administration of justice.[54]

Access to the scene and security: who can investigate?

Ongoing armed conflict may affect the security situation on the ground of a potential violation, as well as general access to the scene, which may in turn

52 ISMLLW Report 2001 (n. 42), p. 69 "there are, however, also neither any legal provisions nor even theoretic concepts or intentions for setting up a system of military jurisdiction for wartime."

53 Nuridzhanian, G., "Prosecuting War Crimes: Are Ukrainian Courts Fit to Do It?" *EJIL: Talk!* (22 August 2022), available at: www.ejiltalk.org/prosecuting-war-crimes-are-ukrainian-courts-fit-to-do-it/.

54 Arnold, R., "Military Criminal Procedures and Judicial Guarantees: The Example of Switzerland," *Journal of International Criminal Justice* Vol. 3 (2005), p. 764.

affect the choice of investigator. In high-risk security situations, it may be that civilian police are not able, or willing, to come to the scene of the incident, or at least not with the promptness necessary for an effective investigation. In the *Halilović* case before the ICTY, a situation arose in which the civilian police, who had jurisdiction, were not physically able to access the scene of the incident.[55] In other cases, civilian police may not want to travel to high-risk security areas. In the *Hanan v Germany* case before the ECtHR, the German government put forward that "the security situation at the material time would not have allowed sending civilian prosecutors or police officers to the place of the incident in order to conduct independent investigations" and that requiring civilian authorities to always investigate in such contexts would be "unrealistic and potentially counterproductive."[56] The Court agreed that the alleged delay and lack of independence indeed had to be examined "against the background of ongoing hostilities in the bomb release area."[57]

Enabling safe access of investigators to a scene may also require the expenditure of significant resources to provide (military) security for the transport and operation of the investigation.[58] In Australian operations in Afghanistan, this expenditure of resources on gathering evidence in unsafe areas appeared to generate frustration amongst soldiers who perceived that some of these assets should instead be used for "'real' operations."[59] The presence of armed conflict may thus affect the availability of technical resources for investigating, or the way in which resources are prioritised. In a situation in which hostilities are ongoing and resources may be scarce, it is a cost calculation that will surely have to be taken into account.

Access to the scene by investigators also affects the requirement of promptness for initiating investigative steps, and in many combat environments, the most prompt investigative authority may not be the most independent or impartial.[60] This affects not only the prompt securing of evidence, but also the ability to mitigate the spread of indiscipline in the case of potential deliberate misconduct by soldiers.[61] In such situations, a commander may have to take prompt disciplinary action which in non-combat environments may have been dealt with in a more formal (for example, criminal) proceeding. The context

55 ICTY, *Prosecutor v Sefer Halilović*, IT-01-48-T, Trial Chamber Judgment of 16 November 2005, paras 663–664.

56 ECtHR, *Hanan v Germany* (n. 13), para. 181.

57 ECtHR, *Hanan v Germany* (n. 13), para. 223.

58 Dahl (n. 39), p. 28; *Hanan v Germany* (n. 13), paras 27, 223.

59 Whetham, D., "Special Operations Command: Leadership and Ethics Review," Annex A to Chapter 3.03, Inspector-General of the Australian Defence Force Afghanistan Inquiry Report (2020) [Brereton Report], p. 523.

60 See ECtHR, *Hanan v Germany* (n. 13), para 223, where the Court commented on "interrelatedness of promptness and independence."

61 Hansen, V., "The Impact of Military Justice Reforms on the Law of Armed Conflict: How to Avoid Unintended Consequences" in Duxbury, A., & Groves, M., *Military Justice in the Modern Age*, Cambridge University Press (2016), p. 126.

in such situations may therefore affect the type of procedures, as what may be required "under hostile fire" may differ from "in the relative safety of large, hardened bases, or stateside garrisons."[62]

Finally, it is necessary to point out that the presence of ongoing hostilities may affect judicial proceedings even by military personnel. A study of US Courts Martial in Afghanistan and Iraq found that

> the full-bore application of military justice was impossible in the combat zone. In practice, deployed commanders and judge advocates exercised all possible alternatives to avoid the crushing burdens of conducting courts-martial, from sending misconduct back to the home station, to granting leniency, to a more frequent use of administrative discharge procedures.[63]

The arguments that a military procedure is more effective than a civilian one may in such circumstances not be convincing.[64] However, as mentioned above, in such cases it is still necessary to distinguish what is feasible at the investigation stage versus the trial (e.g., court martial) stage. While courts may be delayed, sent home, or use technology such as video links,[65] it is not the case that most investigative steps can be thus adapted.

There will not be one solution to addressing the practical challenges to independent and impartial investigations in armed conflict. However, States should be held accountable for whether they in good faith put in the reasonable means for an effective investigation at the time. Such reasonable measures most likely include training military commanders how to act in situations of emergency with regard to possible violations of IHL when the usual investigators may not be able or willing to access the scene.[66] It would also include documenting and justifying why the usual investigative measures could not be taken, and increased transparency on such procedures would aid in proving the good faith element necessary to assessing the effectiveness of investigations.[67] Chapter 7 will consider that in the case of a State being unable genuinely to carry out an effective investigation, it may have a responsibility to request international assistance for the implementation of its obligations under IHL.

Jurisdictional specificities may arise in situations of armed conflict which may affect who investigates, and therefore raise questions regarding their independence and impartiality. However, insofar as all such specificities are

62 Collins (n. 1), p. 27.
63 Collins (n. 1), p. 28.
64 Collins (n. 1), p. 28.
65 Collins (n. 1), pp. 28–34.
66 See Guidelines on Investigating Violations of International Humanitarian Law (n. 2), Guideline 2.
67 See Guidelines on Investigating Violations of International Humanitarian Law (n. 2), Guidelines 1, 10 and paras 141, 173, 184.

foreseen in domestic legislation, States have an obligation to ensure that these procedures would function fairly in practice. For our purposes, this would mean ensuring that the structural guarantees of independence and impartiality as established in previous chapters need to be set up in all existing and foreseen systems. However, there are also practical obstacles which can arise as a result of armed conflict which can affect the choice of investigator. In such contexts, what is important is that reasonable means are put into investigative efforts to contribute towards its effectiveness. Such obstacles can sometimes be foreseen, and it is also important for States to ensure their personnel are properly prepared for such contexts. In all situations, military personnel should be adequately trained as to how to act in exceptional circumstances in accordance with their domestic and international responsibilities.

Legitimacy in armed conflict: impact on the perception of independence and impartiality

Finally, there are elements related to specific types of armed conflict which may affect the perception of independence and impartiality of investigations. Chapter 4 established that the concepts of independence and impartiality of courts and judges are tied to the Nation State-centric concept of the legitimacy of a government in the eyes of the people over whom it is governing. This is also the reasoning behind the need for "appearance" of independence and impartiality and the need to maintain public trust in the judicial system. Independence and impartiality as applicable to investigations serve a different purpose to those standards applicable to judges, but they nonetheless derive from the same need to maintain public trust in the State's monopoly of the use of force and judicial authority. Yet such a rationale raises problems in contexts which may transcend the Nation State in various ways, for example in an international setting where the "public" may not all be citizens of the investigating State, or when a State is made up of different religious, ethnic, or other groups, some of whom may not feel represented by the State forces.

Whose side are you on?

A State carrying out military operations abroad may be welcome or unwelcome by the territorial State and its civilian population. The legitimacy of an armed intervention will depend on many political and factual matters specific to each conflict, may not be uniform across the territory, and may evolve over time. Nevertheless, doubtless most situations of foreign armed intervention or occupation will at some point or another raise issues of legitimacy, and armed violence is frequently based on these legitimacy crises. Although not the focus of this book, the possible legitimacy problems of the administration of justice within occupied territories can clearly be seen though military courts trying "enemy" civilians.[68] Similar concerns can arise for the investigation and prosecution of the State's own personnel for violations committed against the occupied population; "when war crimes and other core crimes are allegedly committed by the occupying power in the course of occupation, prosecution by the same State may raise concerns with respect to the impartiality and independence in particular of military tribunals."[69] These legitimacy problems and perceptions of injustice arise despite the obligation occupying States have in prosecuting such crimes.

Even within one State these issues of legitimacy can arise. In the case of an internal armed conflict where a minority may not feel it is represented by the State, the legitimacy of the State apparatus may even be the cause of the armed conflict. As seen in Chapter 4, belief in the legitimacy of the State is crucial for the rule of law. Such crises of legitimacy arise not only in situations of armed conflict but are also frequently cited in cases where the police and or judicial powers may be seen to discriminate against a certain minority group. The test of "objective impartiality," namely the perception of impartiality by a reasonable observer, is therefore of particular relevance in assessing issues of legitimacy.[70]

The perception of independence and impartiality of a judicial officer may be compromised if the institution to which they belong is considered to take "sides," in preference to or against the accused, in line with the position of that institution in the conflict. In the case of military justice institutions, this may be particularly aggravated by the fact that a branch of the same institution will most likely be actively engaged in hostilities within the conflict. The Inter-American Court of Human Rights (IACtHR) commented on this in a Colombian case in which the judges were members of the National Police, who were the "very same military forces engaged in fighting the insurgent groups" and "charged with prosecuting their peers for executing civilians," finding that this caused the proceedings to be flawed from the outset.[71] A similar finding was issued by the European Court of Human Rights (ECtHR), which found that the leader of a political party considered to be a terrorist party by the government should understandably "have been apprehensive

68 "The officials deciding your fate are essentially your enemies." Ashly, J., "Israel's military courts 'humiliating charade' for Palestinians," *Al Jazeera* (26 February 2018), available at: www.aljazeera.com/features/2018/2/26/israels-military-courts-humiliating-charade-for-palestinians. See also McBride, M., "Separate and unequal: Inside Israel's military courts, where the only defendants are Palestinians," *Haaretz* (28 March 2017), available at: https://archive.ph/Tme1T; B'Tselem, "The Military Courts," 11 November 2017, available at: www.btselem.org/military_courts.

69 Santalla Vargas, E., "Military or Civilian Jurisdiction for International Crimes? An Approach from Self-Interest in Accountability of Armed Forces in International Law" in Bergsmo & Song (n. 39), p. 414.

70 See Chapter 4.

71 IACtHR, *Las Palmeras v Colombia,* Ser. C No. 67, Judgment of 4 February 2000 (Merits), para. 53.

about being tried by a bench which included a regular army officer belonging to the military legal service."[72]

What is assumed in these cases by both regional human rights Courts is that the ideological considerations involved in a conflict will be so important across the whole institution that it must be assumed to affect their impartiality in relation to the other side of the conflict. This issue may be tied to problems associated with institutional loyalty as seen in Chapter 5. It must be remarked that in the cases above, membership of a military institution was only one element amongst many other flaws which was taken into account in assessing the inappropriateness of the proceedings.[73]

Addressing legitimacy concerns

The above-mentioned legitimacy challenges affect the administration of justice in armed conflict generally, and there are elements specific to the requirements of judges and courts which cannot be addressed within the scope of this book. Such issues of international administration of justice are also raised in the context of international courts and are receiving increasing interest through studies of an "international rule of law" which transcends traditional domestic conceptions of justice.[74] But they also raise important questions related to the perception of independence and impartiality of investigations in armed conflict. The requirements of an effective investigation as developed in previous chapters may be used in an attempt to begin answering how some of these legitimacy concerns may be addressed for investigations.

As international law currently stands, States may still legally use military jurisdiction in various situations, including to investigate violations of IHL, yet they should also be aware of the tensions present through the use of such systems. In all cases, States will need to make reasonable adjustments to mitigate the lack of appearance of independence and impartiality. Such measures may include increasing transparency of the proceedings, increasing participation of victims or those affected by alleged violations, and generally improving communication with affected communities.[75] Nevertheless, what is "reasonable" in such cases, taking into account the resources, conflict, and

72 ECtHR, *Öcalan v Turkey*, App. No. 46221/99, Judgment of 12 May 2005, para. 113; Mowbray, A., "Military Judges and the Right to a Fair Trial: Was *Öcalan* Fair?" *Human Rights Law Review* Vol. 6 No. 1 (2006), p. 178.

73 In *Las Palmeras v Colombia* (n. 71), the prosecutors were "suspected material authors of the acts," and the general context of impunity and systematic failures in the military judicial system was also important. In *Öcalan* (n. 72) there was held to be a violation of the right of *habeas corpus* and other elements of fair trial other than independence and impartiality.

74 See, e.g., Wohlwend, D., *The International Rule of Law: Scope, Subjects, Requirements*, Edward Elgar Publishing (2021); McCorquodale, R., "Defining the International Rule of Law: Defying Gravity?" *International and Comparative Law Quarterly* Vol. 65 No. 2 (2016).

75 Guidelines on Investigating Violations of International Humanitarian Law (n. 2), Guidelines 5, 10, and para. 174.

general political situation may not lead to a situation in which the accused or victims perceive the justice system as independent, impartial, or generally just. Furthermore, the issue of the "reasonable observer," whose perception matters in such contexts, is further complicated by the diversity of potential communities involved. What may appear independent to one section of the population may not to another.

In contexts in which objective impartiality may not be achieved through existing mechanisms, States may have a responsibility to consider further measures of independence in order to achieve meaningful justice. Such mechanisms can include involving existing domestic oversight mechanisms, creating domestic *ad hoc* systems, and involving international oversight or adjudicatory mechanisms. These will be further explored in Chapter 7, but it is worth mentioning that it is possible that conceptions of justice in armed conflict situations may need to be considered beyond legal (especially criminal) measures. The role of investigations in disseminating truth, and potentially providing reparations, may have an important role to play in contributing towards a more wholesome conception of justice in armed conflicts.[76]

Legitimacy concerns can arise with regard to investigations in situations of armed conflict, especially (but not only) if investigations are carried out by military bodies. There are some measures which can be used to mitigate such concerns, such as increasing transparency and communication surrounding investigation procedures and results. The subsequent chapter will explore further ways in which a commitment to accountability may be enhanced through additional domestic and international safeguards for independence. Yet such measures may not always be sufficient to improve the legitimacy of procedures, especially for members of the "opposite side" of the armed conflict (who will often be the ones affected by possible violations of IHL). States have an obligation to implement reasonable means to improve this perception of justice, as well as safeguarding the actual independence and impartiality of investigators. However, it is unlikely that achieving a perception of justice in situations of armed conflict will solely be restricted to legal proceedings.

Conclusion

The context of armed conflict can affect the independence and impartiality of investigations, both directly in the choice of investigator available as well as more indirectly through issues of legitimacy often found in situations of conflict. The way in which investigations must be carried out in such contexts is necessarily dictated by the concept of effectiveness, which includes an element of "reasonableness." What is "reasonable" in armed conflict may mean that

76 Simmons, C., "Whose Perception of Justice? Real and Perceived Challenges to Military Investigations in Armed Conflict," *International Review of the Red Cross* Vol. 102 No. 914 (2021), p. 821.

less efficient measures, including those which may be considered unacceptable in peacetime, may be legitimately employed if they contribute towards an effective investigation.

This chapter has seen that jurisdictional peculiarities in situations of armed conflict or "war," as well as in military operations carried out abroad, may affect who is legally able to investigate. Other situations, especially in ongoing hostilities, may affect who is practically able to access the scene. States have a responsibility to prepare by ensuring that adequate measures are put into place for independent and impartial investigators to be able to operate in such situations. Furthermore, adequate training should be given to other individuals who may be called upon exceptionally to carry out investigative measures in certain circumstances, in particular to commanders. In all cases, the object and purpose of the investigation must be borne in mind; in the case of war crimes, it will be the prevention and repression of such war crimes, including but not limited to their criminal prosecution. A commander may well make decisions in certain cases to initiate prompt disciplinary action prior to any judicial involvement in order to prevent the repetition of a certain behaviour, even if this is not what would normally be done in situations of peace.

The elements of legitimacy of investigative officers in various situations of armed conflict, including occupation or internal armed conflicts, are much more problematic to overcome, and transcend the legal field. States still have an obligation to do what is reasonable to mitigate the perception of lack of independence and impartiality in such cases, taking into account as much as possible how appearances may affect the perception of justice. If the circumstances require less independent and impartial means to be employed for legitimate reasons related to the armed conflict, the effectiveness of proceedings will need to be ensured through other safeguarding measures.

7 When it goes wrong

Failures to investigate, patterns of violations, and systematic impunity

Introduction

On 18 January 1989, 15 judicial officials who were investigating crimes committed in the area of La Rochela, Colombia, were rounded up and shot by a group of gunmen, allegedly acting with the cooperation and acquiescence of State agents.[1] The officials were investigating the alleged detention, torture, disappearance, and murder of civilians by the Army.[2] During military and civilian investigations into the attack, which lasted 18 years, judges, witnesses, and next of kin were threatened and intimidated.[3] Seven individuals were convicted, including only one State-agent, a sergeant in the Colombian army.[4] This incident was part of a broader systematic persecution of judicial officials during the Colombian armed conflict, which included threats, kidnappings, personal attacks, disappearances, and murders.[5] In proceedings before the Inter-American Court of Human Rights, the Court found that the "systematic patterns" behind the crime continued to exist after the incident and the investigation.[6]

During the Troubles in Northern Ireland, the UK government introduced Operation Demetrius in 1971, allowing for "extrajudicial measures of detention and internment of suspected terrorists," mostly suspected members of the IRA.[7] Interrogation techniques used on the internees included what would become known as the "five techniques," including sensory deprivation and overload, deprivation of sleep, food, and water, and forced stress positions, which was found to amount to "inhuman and degrading treatment" by the European Court of Human Rights (ECtHR).[8] The UK claimed that the case

1 IACtHR, *La Rochela Massacre v Colombia*, Ser. C No. 163, Judgment of 11 May 2007 (Merits, Reparations, and Costs), para 2.
2 IACtHR, *La Rochela Massacre* (n. 1), para. 75.
3 IACtHR, *La Rochela Massacre* (n. 1), para. 165.
4 IACtHR, *La Rochela Massacre* (n. 1), para. 154.
5 Centro por la Justicia y el Derecho International (CEJIL), "La Rochela," available at: https://cejil.org/en/case/la-rochela-2/.
6 IACtH, *La Rochela Massacre* (n. 1), para. 158.
7 ECtHR, *Ireland v UK*, App. No. 5310/71, Judgment of 18 January 1978, para. 34.
8 ECtHR, *Ireland v UK* (n. 7), para. 168.

DOI: 10.4324/9781003360223-7

should be considered inadmissible before the ECtHR because the individuals involved had not exhausted the remedies available to them domestically.[9] In response, the Court found that the practice involving these five techniques represented "an accumulation of identical or analogous breaches which are sufficiently numerous and inter-connected to amount not merely to isolated incidents or exceptions but to a pattern or system,"[10] This mattered, because the presence of such repeated acts tolerated by high-level State officials meant *de facto* that "administrative enquiries would either not be instituted, or, if they were, would be likely to be half-hearted and incomplete."[11] Individuals would therefore be unable, and should not be expected, to find domestic redress for the violations committed.[12]

Sometimes things go terribly wrong, over and over again. Many of the cases that come to mind when thinking of flagrant misconduct of justice by military bodies are not related to individual cases but involve a repeated pattern of behaviour or impunity. Rather than throwing in the towel for such "broken" systems, it is suggested that these too can be considered from an angle of independence and impartiality, but that they require specific considerations because of the scale of violations, and the consequences of a failure to investigate leading to impunity. In such contexts, it is worth paying attention to the patterns of violations being committed, which are often indicative of a failure to investigate, and can sometimes lead to inferences on the responsibility of those involved. This, in turn, should indicate what levels of independence and impartiality are required for an investigation into these violations to be considered effective. In the most serious cases, patterns of violations can be indicative of systematic impunity, which can lead to international intervention in various forms.

Previous chapters have so far mostly focused on specific factors that may affect the independence and impartiality of investigations, and how, in theory, these factors may be addressed for investigations to be effective. This chapter explores contexts in which a narrow focus is not sufficient to address all the concerns of lack of independence and impartiality with regard to some violations of international humanitarian law (IHL). It suggests that there are certain situations in which even with a properly constituted military justice system, the effectiveness of an investigation will nevertheless be compromised by the broader context in which violations are committed. This chapter explores unique elements which may affect independence and impartiality of investigations into patterns of problems or patterns of violations, including the role of a failure to investigate in causing or aggravating such patterns.

9 ECtHR, *Ireland v UK* (n. 7), para. 156.

10 ECtHR, *Ireland v UK* (n. 7), paras 159 and 168.

11 ECmmHR, *Ireland v UK*, *Yearbook of the European Court of Human Rights*, Series B, Vol. 23-1 (1976–1978), p. 394; ECtHR, *The Greek Case*, *Yearbook of the European Court of Human Rights* (1972), p. 194.

12 ECtHR, *Ireland v UK* (n. 7), para. 159.

A failure to investigate as a form of responsibility

Human Rights bodies have highlighted the crucial role of effective investigations in refuting any claims that a government is acquiescing in or tolerating violations.[13] Investigations are often a necessary part of the effective redress for one-off violations *inter alia* because they serve towards guaranteeing non-repetition for future violations (as explored in Chapter 3). If an investigation into violations serves in part to deter the commission of future such violations, conversely the failure to investigate can lead to the repetition of similar violations in the future. A failure to investigate can constitute endorsement or at the very least tolerance for the commission of the violations in question and can send a signal to perpetrators (past or future) that their actions will not be punished by the State. In this context, the repetition of violations and endorsement or tolerance of these violations feed into each other in a cycle which will often lead to widespread and gross violations. This can have implications on the responsibility of those who had a duty to investigate, and ultimately on the standards of independence and impartiality.

Individual responsibility

At an individual level, a commander may be held responsible for violations committed by their subordinates if they fail to investigate such violations. A commander who knowingly fails to effectively investigate (and, if relevant, punish) perpetrators can be seen as implicitly accepting or endorsing the violation, and sends the implicit message that it is all right to commit such violations in the future.[14] This is the case, for example, in cases where a commander may "turn a blind eye" to, or be "willfully ignorant" of events.[15] It is also true when they carry out investigations which they know will not be effective.[16] They can therefore become responsible for the violations they failed to investigate, but also any subsequent violations which may occur as a result of the prior failure to investigate. In the case of war crimes, command responsibility can include criminal liability for the war crimes themselves.[17]

13 E.g., ECtHR, *Avsar v Turkey*, App. No. 25657/94, Judgment of 10 July 2001, para. 406.

14 Sepinwall, A. J., "Failure to Punish: Command Responsibility in Domestic and International Law," *Michigan Journal of International Law* Vol. 30 No. 2 (2008), p. 294.

15 Hansen, V., "The Impact of Military Justice Reforms on the Law of Armed Conflict: How to Avoid Unintended Consequences" in Duxbury, A., & Groves, M., *Military Justice in the Modern Age*, Cambridge University Press (2016), p. 110.

16 See Chapter 3.

17 This is a matter of debate under international law and is not necessarily how it is interpreted in national doctrine. See Sepinwall (n. 14), pp. 255–256; Hansen, V., "What's Good for the Goose is Good for the Gander: Lessons from Abu Ghraib: Time for the United States to Adopt a Doctrine of Command Responsibility Towards Its Own," *Gonzaga Law Review* Vol. 42 No. 3 (2006), p. 349.

It is not, however, the case that a commander will be held responsible in such a way for every failure to investigate. In the case of war crimes, a commander may be held liable for a failure to investigate an alleged crime in two instances: where they had direct knowledge of a crime or where they "had information which should have enabled them to conclude in the circumstances at the time" that a crime may have been committed.[18] The concept of "knowledge" ties into the matter of intent, or as a form of *mens rea*. It is what makes the difference between a genuine mistake or negligence and the deliberate sending out of a message of endorsement or tolerance for violations.

State responsibility

At a State responsibility level, the obligations to investigate are broader than for individual commanders, and the implications for responsibility are more complex. Unlike commanders and their subordinates, a State is responsible for all violations committed by its agents, even if they effectively investigate and redress the violations.[19] A State can, however, become responsible for something *further* if it does not investigate such violations once it has become aware of them. A failure to investigate in such cases can form a violation of both primary and secondary rules of State responsibility (see Chapter 3). In the case of a repetitive failure to investigate serious violations, this can even lead to an aggravated form of State responsibility with implications on the action which may be taken by other States to cease such violations (see below).

A State's failure to investigate as a form of responsibility is important because explicit and public announcements of a policy to commit violations are rare; "governments no longer commit [violations] as a matter of overt policies. Their sins are those of omission or tolerance as they fail to rein in deeply-entrenched and often politically-popular abuses against marginalised social sectors."[20] It is exceptional that explicit policy can be demonstrated as such. Instead, it has been found that when a State does not act to put an end to, redress, and not-repeat a violation (for example, by failing to investigate),

18 Protocol Additional to the Geneva Conventions of 12 August 1949, and Relating to the Protection of Victims of International Armed Conflicts, 1125 UNTS 3 (1977) [API], Art. 86(2). This latter concept is understood as the concept of "constructive knowledge" (Dinstein, Y., *The Conduct of Hostilities Under the Law of International Armed Conflict*, Cambridge University Press (3rd ed.) (2016), p. 311) and has been phrased as that they "had reason to know" (Henckaerts, J.-M., & Doswald-Beck, L., "Customary International Humanitarian Law," ICRC (2006) [ICRC Customary Study], Rule 153) and "should have known" (UN War Crimes Commission, *Law Reports of Trials of War Criminals*, Vol. IV, pp. 85, 123, 117, 35) or that "they are at fault in having failed to acquire such knowledge" (Dinstein, p. 310).

19 European Commission of Human Rights, *Ireland v UK*, *Yearbook of the European Court of Human Rights*, Series B, Vol. 23-1 (1976–1978), p. 393.

20 Neild, R., "Confronting a Culture of Impunity: The Promise and Pitfalls of Civilian Review of Police in Latin America" in Goldsmith, A., & Lewis, C., *Civilian Oversight of Policing: Governance, Democracy and Human Rights*, Hart (2000), p. 254.

it is endorsing or at the very least tolerating such violations, and this entails specific responsibility on behalf of the State.

Institutional implication

This raises the question of what independence and impartiality of investigators means when the investigative authorities themselves may be considered to be implicated, and the consequences of this on the redress mechanisms for such violations. As seen in Chapter 4, the effectiveness of investigations requires at the very least that the investigative authorities must not have been personally implicated in the violation under investigation. The chapter also established that institutional affiliation is not necessarily an obstacle to the overall independence and impartiality in isolated cases. The ECtHR found in the case of *Mustafa Tunç and Fecire Tunç v Turkey* that the suspicions against a military conscript were "not related to his particular status as a gendarme or as a member of the armed forces,"[21] and the military as a whole institution was therefore overall sufficiently independent and impartial to effectively investigate the case.

However, the case is different if it is "the security forces as an institution" which are suspected of being at the root cause of the violations,[22] such as in the cases of deaths arising "from clashes involving the use of force in demonstrations, police and military operations or in cases of violent deaths during police custody."[23] In the examples given, the security forces as a whole institution may be considered to be implicated, because rather than a one-off isolated incident due to the actions of one "bad apple," deaths during demonstrations or in custody may very well point towards a pattern of problems implicating the institution. In order to effectively examine the root causes of such serious incidents, the investigator may need to be outside of any implicated institution. In *Avsar v Turkey*, the ECtHR found that the investigation could not be considered effective because it failed to take into account the role of the security forces in the killing of the victim, and therefore "to what extent the incident was premeditated and whether, as alleged, it formed part of the unlawful activities carried out with the connivance and acquiescence of the authorities at that time in the south-east of Turkey."[24] The suggestions that there was a pattern of problems implicating military institutions is what draws the distinction between this case and the *Tunç* case.

This element of institutional implication is relevant not only for direct involvement in the giving of orders, but also in the case of a failure to investigate by this institution. It was established above that a failure to effectively

21 ECtHR, *Mustafa Tunç and Fecire Tunç v Turkey*, App. No. 24014/05, Judgment of 14 April 2015, para. 255.

22 ECtHR, *Mustafa Tunç and Fecire Tunç v Turkey* (n. 21), para. 255.

23 ECtHR, *Mustafa Tunç and Fecire Tunç v Turkey* (n. 21), para. 255.

24 ECtHR, *Avsar v Turkey* (n. 14), para. 406.

investigate can be construed as instigation, acquiescence, or tolerance of violations, which can entail aggravated regimes of responsibility at both the individual and State levels. It also means that a failure to investigate implicates the individuals or institutions who have failed in the commission of the pattern of violations, and at the very least leaves suspicions open as to their active or passive involvement in the offences. Therefore, in the case of violations involving the failure to investigate, the principle of effectiveness requires for the cases to be removed from these institutional structures which have failed.

Furthermore, institutional implication is not confined to military institutions, but any institution which may have a responsibility to investigate, for example in the case of judges who failed to order investigations,[25] or legal institutions if legal advice may be at the root cause of the violations. An individual soldier being investigated for targeting a civilian may well be adequately dealt with by their direct commander and the usual system of military justice. Nevertheless, if the soldier targeted the civilian following rules of engagement (ROE) which suggested this was lawful or acting upon legal or policy advice within their unit, the investigation must take into account this broader context in effectively investigating.[26] If it transpires that these unlawful ROE were issued by lawyers within the military institution who may also have a role in investigating these incidents, the matter of independence and impartiality becomes even more relevant.[27]

A repetitive failure to investigate violations can therefore constitute a form of responsibility on behalf of those with the duty to investigate. A commander who fails to investigate violations committed by their subordinates may be held liable for these and subsequent violations, in particular in the case of war crimes. A State may fall under the regime of aggravated State responsibility following a repetitive failure to investigate certain most serious violations, and this has implications on actions which other States may take in bringing an end to such violations. A failure to investigate can lead to institutional implication, requiring any subsequent investigations to be removed for the institution that had a responsibility to investigate.

Patterns of problems affecting independence and impartiality

At both the individual and State responsibility levels, a failure to investigate therefore affects who or what institution may be considered "implicated" in a

25 See "Los exjueces mendocinos, condenados a prisión perpetua," *Mendoza Post* (26 July 2017), available at: www.mendozapost.com/nota/67963-los-exjueces-mendocinos-condenados-a-prision-perpetua/.

26 Cohen, A., & Shany, Y., "Beyond the Grave Breaches Regime: The Duty to Investigate Alleged Violations of International Law Governing Armed Conflicts," *Yearbook of International Humanitarian Law* Vol. 14 (2011), p. 55.

27 This is a frequent criticism of the Israel Military Advocate General's Corps. See B'Tselem, "Whitewash Protocol: The So-Called Investigation of 'Operation Protective Edge'" (2016), p. 3.

violation and affect the independence and impartiality of redress mechanisms. The biggest problem with a failure to investigate, however, is when it is not an isolated incident, but is rather part of a broader pattern of problems, potentially leading to repeated violations.

Patterns of violations can affect the effectiveness of investigations in different ways, depending on what is causing them. In some cases, they are symptomatic of a failure to investigate, which will affect institutional implication as explored above. In others, patterns of violations may be the result of an explicit or implicit policy, or because problematic biases (such as toxic loyalty explored in Chapter 5) are affecting the impartiality of investigators. Finally, there are situations in which patterns of problems are caused by technical systemic problems which may not affect independence and impartiality, but these contexts must still be investigated effectively.

Patterns of violations implying a failure to investigate

Those who fail in their responsibility to investigate violations can be seen to be contributing to a more widespread context of repeated violations and impunity by tolerating and causing a pattern of violations. As seen above, this is true at both the individual and State responsibility levels and can cause institutional implications affecting the independence and impartiality of investigators. A pattern of problems or violations can therefore be symptomatic of a failure to investigate at some level – an element that has been elucidated both by international criminal courts for command responsibility and human rights regional courts for State responsibility.

Under command responsibility, the repetition of incidents in itself can contribute towards what a commander "should have known," even without evidence of direct knowledge of their commission. The Second World War Tribunals considered in various cases the link between acts that had been repeated and the responsibility of the commander whom it could be inferred "knew, or should have known," and formed the basis of what is understood as the "constructive" (as opposed to actual) knowledge of atrocities being committed.[28] In the Yamashita case, an American military tribunal found that "the atrocities were so numerous, involved so many people, and were so widespread that the accused's professed ignorance is incredible."[29] In the trial of *Major Karl Rauer and Six Others*, a British military court considered whether prison officials could be held directly responsible for the shooting of multiple prisoners of war, whom they were told had attempted to escape the

28 Finucane, B., "US Recognition of a Commander's Duty to Punish War Crimes," *International Law Studies* Vol. 97 (2021), p. 1004.

29 General Headquarters, U.S. Army Forces, Pacific, Office of the Theater Judge Advocate, Review of the Record of Trial by a Military Commission of Tomoyuki Yamashita, General, Imperial Japanese Army, 26 December 1945, pp. 81–83.

camp over consecutive days. The court found the officers not guilty of the first charge, but of all subsequent shootings. This may have been because "it was less reasonable for these officers to believe after the second incident that the prisoners involved were shot while trying to escape than it was after the first, and that measures should have been taken after the first shootings to prevent a repetition."[30] This constructive knowledge was subsequently expanded substantively in the jurisprudence of the *ad hoc* international criminal courts.[31]

This analysis of constructive knowledge under command responsibility is useful to consider in the context of patterns of violations. A commander's role is a crucial one in initiating effective investigative procedures for violations of IHL, and it is therefore right that the consequences of a failure to investigate at an individual level should be harsh. The due diligence obligation of a commander may include looking out for patterns of problems amongst their subordinates (within what is reasonable). While there may be cases which are hard to detect and attribute to constructive knowledge, other cases of flagrant repetition of violations, such as the repetitive shooting of prisoners of war, have been used to attribute responsibility to a commander for the commission of such violations because it implies a repetitive failure in their investigative responsibilities.

Similarly, at a State responsibility level, human rights bodies have found that a State's tolerance of violations may be inferred through observation of a pattern of repeated violations, which leaves no room for a State to claim it did not "know." This is so even for cases where it could not be demonstrated that the acts themselves were even committed by State agents. States have been found responsible for human rights violations through the very fact that the acts were widespread and repeated.[32] The repetition and widespread nature of violations can mean that "it is inconceivable that the higher authorities of a State should be, or at least should be entitled to be unaware of the existence of such a practice" due to the "accumulation of identical or analogous breaches."[33]

A pattern of incidents or violations can therefore be symptomatic of a failure to investigate. In turn, this can have implications on the independence and

30 *Trial of Major Karl Rauer and Six Others*, British Military Court, Wuppertal, Germany (18 February 1946), as recorded in United Nations War Crimes Commission, *Law Reports of Trials of War Criminals* Vol. IV (1948), pp. 113–117).

31 See, e.g., ICTY, *Prosecutor v Zejnil Delalić et al.* (*Čelebići case*), IT-92-21-A, Appeals Chamber Judgment of 20 February 2001, para. 677; *Prosecutor v Tihomir Blaškić*, IT-95-14-T, Trial Chamber Judgment of 3 March 2000, para. 332.

32 IACtHR, *Velásquez Rodríguez v Honduras*, Ser. C No. 4, Judgment of 29 July 1988 (Merits), paras 147–148; Roht-Arriaza, N., "State Responsibility to Investigate and Prosecute Grave Human Rights Violations in International Law," *California Law Review* Vol. 78 (1990), p. 470; Siatitsa, I.-M., "'A Serious Violation of International Human Rights Law' – An Attempt to Clarify a Crucial Provision of the Arms Trade Treaty," *European Journal of Human Rights* Vol. 5 (2015), p. 621; CAT, Report on Nepal under Article 20, A/67/44, Annex XIII, p. 299, para. 97.

33 ECtHR, *Ireland v UK*, App. No. 5310/71, Judgment of 18 January 1978, para. 159.

impartiality of investigations as seen above, as the institutional implication may lead to the need for further independence in order to achieve effectiveness.

Policy-related violations: undue pressure from above

Patterns of incidents or violations can also be caused by policy-related violations, namely violations which are caused by an implicit or explicit policy by higher levels of authority (e.g., of the military or other parts of the executive branch).[34] Incidentally, policy-related violations can also lead to a failure to investigate, depending on the type of policy.

If there is an explicit or implicit policy to commit violations, this can put pressures on individuals and/or institutions to behave in a certain way with regard to their judicial responsibilities. For example, if the plan or policy is originating from high levels of authority, it is possible that they may place undue pressure upon investigators as individuals or judicial institutions as a whole. This is fundamentally an issue of institutional and personal independence as explored in Chapter 4, as those with a responsibility to investigate can be put under undue pressure in their investigative duties. The Inter-American Court of Human Rights (IACtHR) has considered such cases where the possible perpetrators included individuals who were "above" the investigators and judicial authorities in hierarchy and authority, therefore enabling them to exert undue pressure on them.[35] Nevertheless, the level of authority is not sufficient to establish lack of independence, as guarantees against undue pressure can be legally and practically in place. For example, in systems in which a strict separation of powers is present, the policy of a high-level executive may not affect the independence of the judiciary. Even within hierarchies there may be safeguards against undue interference, such as the prohibition of unlawful command influence in US military law.[36]

In the case of a pattern of incidents or violations, it is therefore necessary to consider whether or not an explicit or (more likely) implicit policy may be causing this. This in turn will affect the effectiveness of any investigation into such violations, most likely requiring more independence.

The scope of problematic biases affecting the impartiality of investigators

There is a further possible element which may lead to patterns of violations, namely that investigators may be affected by problematic biases affecting their

34 Lubell, N., Pejic, J., & Simmons, C., "Guidelines on Investigating Violations of International Humanitarian Law: Law, Policy, and Good Practice," Geneva Academy/ICRC (2019) [Guidelines on Investigating Violations of International Humanitarian Law], Guideline 15.

35 IACtHR, *La Rochela Massacre v Colombia*, Ser. C No. 163, Judgment of 11 May 2007 (Merits, Reparations, and Costs), para. 165; *Manuel Cepeda Vargas v Colombia*, Ser. C No. 213, Judgment of 26 May 2010 (Preliminary Objections, Merits, Reparations, and Costs), para. 118.

36 USA, Uniform Code of Military Justice (1951), Art. 37.

impartiality as explored in Chapter 6. If the root cause of a pattern of violations is a widespread belief or campaign regarding a certain segment of the population, or a certain type of offence, it is possible that those with a responsibility to investigate and prosecute may themselves be affected by this bias. This could be the case, for example, if the investigators believe the interests of the individual soldiers to be above those of the law, or if they hold a bias against an ethnic or religious section of the population who are the victim of the alleged violation. If the biases are ones entrenched within a society, for example racism, sexism, classism, or other forms of discrimination, they may very well permeate through the judicial system to the point of leading to biased results.[37] This may be even more complicated if the judicial institutions are effectively used as a political tool, where judicial decisions have an impact on the political reality.[38]

Nevertheless, such biases are difficult to assume or to test; Chapter 4 saw that actual impartiality in general is near impossible to measure, and it is therefore more useful to consider objective impartiality, or the perception of impartiality, which includes considering whether a reasonable observer would perceive the investigator to be impartial. Difficulties remain as to who constitutes a reasonable observer in the context of discrimination against a minority, or in an international context, as explored in Chapter 6. Addressing such biases would require, in a peaceful democratic society, the education of judicial authorities, or overhaul of a judicial structure. In the case of armed conflict where the bias may be endorsed by the executive branch and supported by popular opinion and may even be tied into root causes of the armed conflict, it would be very difficult to remedy at a domestic level.

Systemic problems that don't affect independence and impartiality

Finally, it is worth mentioning that not all patterns of problems will necessarily cause problems of independence and impartiality in investigating, especially if these are linked to technical systemic problems. The term "systemic" is one used in various contexts, including in relation to military operations, to denote an issue which is affecting a system as a whole. There can, for example, be systemic issues in the way training is given, the way a weapon functions, or the way resources are distributed to detainees.[39] The concept of systemic problems

37 Mahoney, K., "Judicial Bias: The Ongoing Challenge," *Journal of Dispute Resolution* Vol. 2015 No. 1 (2015), p. 46.

38 Hajjar, L., *Courting Conflict: The Israeli Military Court System in the West Bank and Gaza*, University of California Press (2005), p. 130 describes prosecutors' discomfort at their duties in a military justice system in occupied territories "on what was effectively the front line of the military administration's efforts to crush the uprising by using harsh punishment to deter resistance."

39 Guidelines on Investigating Violations of International Humanitarian Law(n. 34), Guideline 13.

does not necessarily point to any intent or maliciousness in its existence, and it may not necessarily lead to violations of the law. For example, if a systemic issue with a weapon causes it to miss a target and cause unexpected civilian damage which is excessive in relation to the military advantage gained, this is not *per se* a violation of the principle of proportionality. The commander (and other actors involved in) launching the weapon would have had to be aware of the malfunction (or possible malfunction) and therefore "expect" excessive civilian harm in order for it to constitute a violation. Other systemic problems may lead to violations in and of themselves, for example through a systemic problem in national doctrine leading to problematic legal interpretation of what constitutes a combatant, which may lead to the violation of the principle of distinction.

It is suggested that States do have an obligation to investigate systemic problems in military operations, and there are many non-legal reasons to investigate systemic issues, related to operational effectiveness.[40] Nevertheless, in the case of systemic problems, there is no implication that any actor or State is attempting to hide or cover up misconduct, and there is not necessarily any lack of good faith on the part of authorities. For this reason, matters of implication or undue pressure affecting the independence and impartiality of investigators should generally not come into play. Furthermore, such systemic problems are more likely to be effectively investigated using domestic systems of justice and redress, as long as a State recognises its obligation to do so. However, the detection of systemic problems can be challenging and difficult to do from within the affected units. For this to be possible, it is necessary for States to have domestic systems of monitoring and review to be able to pick up on systemic problems in the first place.[41] A certain degree of independence may be necessary for such systems to be effective, insofar as they need to be able to have a cross-cutting view of all potential factors at play.[42] States also need to acknowledge and respond in good faith when external actors (such as courts or civil society) point to possible systemic problems.

Finally, it is worth pointing out that if systemic problems are not effectively investigated, they are likely to lead to more serious patterns of serious violations. It was established above that a failure to investigate can lead itself to responsibility, and that the repetition of incidents can lead to implied "knowledge" on behalf of both individuals and States. It is in the interest of States to investigate and correct issues, even if they are not violations of international law, before they become something more serious.

40 See Chapter 3; Guidelines on Investigating Violations of International Humanitarian Law (n. 34), paras 26–29.

41 Hampson, F., "An Investigation of Alleged Violations of The Law of Armed Conflict," *Israel Yearbook on Human Rights* Vol. 46 (2016), pp. 8–10; Guidelines on Investigating Violations of International Humanitarian Law (n. 34), para. 182.

42 Guidelines on Investigating Violations of International Humanitarian Law (n. 34), para. 178.

The existence of patterns of violations can therefore affect the independence and impartiality of investigations in a different manner than "one-off" violations, especially if there has also been a failure to investigation. This can be because of institutional implication, because high-level policies put undue pressure on the investigators, or because the scope of problematic biases involves investigators. Some patterns of problems may be caused by systemic problems which do not affect independence and impartiality, but these also need to be effectively investigated in order not to become more serious.

Achieving independence and impartiality when investigating patterns of violations

If there is a potential pattern of violations, usually indicated by a repetition of similar incidents, this may therefore have implications on the required standards of independence and impartiality. The conclusions from Chapter 4 demonstrated that what is important for investigations is whether they are deemed overall sufficiently independent and impartial to be effective. This requires taking into account the specific context of the violations under investigation, and the specific relation of the investigators to those involved in the alleged violations. The standards of independence and impartiality of investigations into patterns of violations are theoretically no different to those applicable to isolated violations – they also need to be sufficiently independent and impartial overall to be effective. Nevertheless, the context of patterns of violations can affect independence and impartiality in ways which are different to isolated cases, and these factors can also be particularly difficult to detect from the outset. This is because achieving effectiveness in investigations into patterns of violations often requires cross-cutting procedures capable of identifying the pattern of problems and the scope of problematic influences on investigators. This should then enable identification of the functional obstacles to independence and impartiality (personal and institutional) but creating meaningful justice in the context of patterns of violations can also require establishing a perception of independence and impartiality.

The need for cross-cutting investigation in the context of a pattern of problems

To provide effective remedies for patterns of violations, it is necessary to establish the level at which such violations are being committed in order to guarantee an investigator's ability to operate without undue pressure or influence. This ties into the matter of the scope of the investigation,[43] and more generally to its effectiveness. Chapter 3 saw that in order to be effective, an investiga-

43 This can also be considered as a matter of thoroughness – an investigation into a violation cannot be considered thorough if it does not take into account all relevant lines of inquiry. See, e.g., IACtHR, *Ibsen Cárdenas and Ibsen Pena v Bolivia* (2010), para. 237(a); Pasqualucci, J.

tion needs to be able to achieve its purpose, including identifying the nature of the violation, possible perpetrators, and ways to redress the violation. In the context of patterns of violations, effectively identifying the root cause of the violation will require cross-cutting analysis of all potential causes of the violation and its general context.[44]

The need for a cross-cutting investigation in the context of a pattern of problems has an implication on the choice of investigator for reasons of expertise but also of independence and impartiality. The usual investigative authorities for isolated violations may not have access to information enabling cross-cutting analysis. They may also not be sufficiently independent to be able to make decisions upon the implication of authorities who may be superior to them in any way. This is especially true in cases which implicate a military and/or judicial hierarchy. This may result in the investigation and prosecution of low-level perpetrators of violations, named as "bad apples" within a system, without taking into account the real root causes of the violations which may be in higher echelons of authority.

The IACtHR has found investigations ineffective precisely because they failed to take into account the context and patterns of violations which would have enabled recognising the pressures exerted on the investigators and judicial authorities. In the *Rochela Massacre* case, the IACtHR found that the investigation was ineffective, *inter alia* because it failed to acknowledge that the investigators and judiciary were themselves threatened by power structures which had orchestrated the killings.[45] For this reason, the Court found that an effective investigation must take into account "the patterns of operation of the complex structure of individuals who executed the massacre."[46] In *Manuel Cepeda Vargas*, the IACtHR reiterated that the investigation could only be considered effective "if it is carried out based on an overall view of the facts that takes into account the background and context in which they occurred and that seeks to reveal the participation structure,"[47] and that part of the State's obligation to investigate includes determining "the patterns of collaborative action."[48]

The ECtHR has also highlighted the importance of drawing inferences between a pattern of violations. In *Sakir v Greece*, the ECtHR noted that the police treated a racist attack as an isolated incident and failed to place the case within the context of other similar reports, thus hindering the possibility

M., *The Practice and Procedure of the Inter-American Court of Human Rights*, Cambridge University Press (2nd ed.) (2013), p. 225.

44 Reidy, A., Hampson, F., & Boyle, K., "Gross Violations of Human Rights: Invoking the European Convention on Human Rights in the Case of Turkey," *Netherlands Quarterly of Human Rights* Vol. 15 No. 2 (1997), p. 164; IACtHR, *Ibsen Cárdenas and Ibsen Peña v Bolivia* (n. 43), para. 237(a); Pasqualucci (n. 43), p. 225.

45 IACtHR, *La Rochela Massacre* (n. 35), para. 165.

46 IACtHR, *La Rochela Massacre* (n. 35), para. 165.

47 IACtHR, *Manuel Cepeda Vargas* (n. 35), para. 118.

48 IACtHR, *Manuel Cepeda Vargas* (n. 35), para. 119.

of drawing the links between the racist incidents. The failure to adequately address the true scope of the violations in this context meant that the State could not "avoid all appearance of complicity or tolerance of the illegal acts."[49] In *H.B. v Hungary*, the Court similarly noted that the authorities failed to take into account the "specific context" of the anti-Roma rally in which the acts took place, which was indispensable to an effective investigation "given that it was not an isolated incident but formed part of the general hostile attitude against the Roma community" in the area.[50]

This, however, raises difficulties: it is not always obvious from the outset of an investigation that the case in question may be considered part of a broader pattern of problems (as opposed to isolated incidents), and it may be unclear at what level a plan, policy, or tolerance may be occurring (in order to establish the required levels of independence and impartiality). In the absence of being able to know or guess the results of an investigation before it has commenced, due diligence requirements would mean setting up monitoring and oversight mechanisms which have the responsibility to detect such patterns and take appropriate action in such cases.[51] It may also mean carrying out preliminary investigations or inquiries in order to establish the relevant scope of a subsequent effective investigation.

Removing obstacles to independence and impartiality at a functional level

In order to establish a sufficiently independent and impartial investigation into patterns of violations, it will be necessary to remove any obstacles to this independence and impartiality, by identifying any sources of undue pressure and ensuring they cannot interfere.

For criminal investigations this can be done by removing the investigative authority from the implicated institution to another existing institution. As seen in previous chapters, there are sometimes investigatory bodies independent from the operational chain of command (the chain of command which would have been involved in the commission of the violations) within military justice systems.[52] In other States, civilian and military justice systems may have concurrent jurisdiction over certain types of offences, and it may be possible to challenge the decision to investigate and try a case before the military jurisdiction. However, alternative jurisdiction is not always possible before domestic

49 ECtHR, *Sakir v Greece*, App. No. 48475/09, Judgment of 24 March 2016, para. 72 [my translation].

50 ECtHR, *R.B. v Hungary*, App. No. 64602/12, Judgment of 12 April 2016, para. 72.

51 Hampson (n. 41), p. 14.

52 See Chapter 5.

legal systems,[53] and there may be political situations or traditions which *de facto* mean such challenges will very rarely be successful.[54]

In such cases, there may be *ad hoc* or special prosecutorial authorities able to independently investigate. Such *ad hoc* procedures will often usually occur following scrutiny and pressure by civil society or international or regional bodies, or during transitions in government. Special prosecutorial authorities for specific types of offences can be an effective way to combat impunity for systematic violations by providing further independence.[55] Such systems are, however, rare and complex, and their success may be very unpredictable due to their *ad hoc* nature. Furthermore, for a domestic system to work there must be at least some level of governmental will to redress past violations, and in the case of gross and systematic violations it is often only possible after transition to a new government.[56] Their use can also appear arbitrary if they are established only in some contexts, for example when there is sufficient media attention and/or it aligns with political interests.

53 In the USA, UK, and Canada, for example, civilian courts do not necessarily have jurisdiction over criminal offences committed by members of their armed forces abroad (unless such offences fall within a narrow category of select offences). Liivoja, R., "Service Jurisdiction Under International Law," *Melbourne Journal of International Law* Vol. 11 No. 2 (2010), p. 310.

54 Margalit, A., *Investigating Civilian Casualties in Time of Armed Conflict and Belligerent Occupation*, Brill (2018), p. 215.

55 In Colombia, there exists a specific Human Rights Unit of the Prosecutor General's Office that can review specific cases which may involve IHRL violations and which historically have been very linked to systematic violations. This office has the power to challenge the military jurisdiction and order the opening of criminal investigations (IACtHR, *Santo Domingo Massacre v Colombia*, Ser. C No. 259, Judgment of 14 November 2014 (Preliminary Objections, Merits, and Reparations), para. 90). More recently, the Special Jurisdiction for Peace has been established which aims, *inter alia*, to establish who must be tried for serious violations of IHL and IHRL (Consejería para los derechos humanos, "Preguntas y respuestas sobre el Sistema Integral de Verdad, Justicia, Reparación y no Repetición" (2017) available at: www.derechoshumanos.gov.co/Prensa/2017/Paginas/170405-Preguntas-respuestas-sobre-Sistema-Integral-Verdad-Justicia-Reparacion-Repeticion.aspx). In Guatemala, the government in talks with the UN decided to establish the "International Commission Against Impunity in Guatemala" in 2006 (Roht-Arriaza (n. 32), p. 82). Similarly, in El Salvador, a prosecutor for the defence of human rights was set up to oversee "police misconduct on the most serious abuse resulting in loss of life and high-profile cases," and this to demonstrate that "police were not above the law and could be held accountable by the judiciary and civilian authorities." (Neild (n. 20), p. 241). Nepal has a special investigation and trial body which has jurisdiction over cases relating to corruption, theft, torture, and disappearance (Nepalese Army Act 2006 ss. 119(1) and (3). See Jha, U. C., "The Reform of Military Justice in South Asia" in Duxbury and Groves (n. 15), p. 188). In the UK, following allegations of gross misconduct of military operations in Iraq, the Iraq Historic Allegations Team was opened, which had to deal with individual criminal cases as well as systemic problems with the military justice system. Damrosch, L. F., "Gross and Systematic Human Rights Violations," *Max Planck Encyclopaedia of Public International Law*, Elsevier (2011), para. 18.

56 Damrosch (n. 55), para. 18.

Finally, it is worth mentioning that it may not always be possible or desirable to set up criminal investigations that are sufficiently independent. This can be because of the above-mentioned difficulties in determining the scope of the problems and therefore the necessary scope of independence. In this context, non-criminal investigative procedures such as inquiries may be useful tools in properly mapping out the context and scope of the violations, and they may, in some cases, leave open the possibility of future criminal proceedings.[57] On their own, military or civilian inquiries will usually not be sufficient to redress widespread patterns of serious violations of international law, and will encounter many problems. They often take years to complete, at great public cost, and do not always receive the public perception of accountability they may have set out to achieve.[58] Nevertheless, they can be important tools for effective "lessons-learned" exercises within the armed forces, and can also increase public trust within such institutions.

Creating meaningful justice: perception of independence and impartiality

To achieve meaningful justice it may be necessary to place particular emphasis on the perception of independence and impartiality for investigations into patterns of violations. Chapter 4 saw that this concept is very much tied into the trust in the judicial institutions to fairly adjudicate by society as a whole. If it is

57 The British Army commissioned an inquiry into "Cases of Deliberate Abuse and Unlawful Killing in Iraq in 2003 and 2004 (as reported in "Second Report of the Public Commission to Examine the Maritime Incident of 31 May 2010: Israel's Mechanisms for Examining and Investigating Complaints and Claims of Violations of the Laws of Armed Conflict According to International Law" (Israel, February 2013) [Second Turkel Report], p. 737). Similar systems of internal Boards of Inquiry can be found in other common law States. In the UK, public inquiries may be ordered under the Inquiries Act of 2005 to deal with systemic issues when "there is a need to address them from a wider perspective, [as] civil and criminal proceedings – even if carried out properly – may not suffice" (Margalit (n. 54), pp. 207–208). In the USA, congressional inquiries may be opened, as was done in the case of Abu Graib (Second Turkel Report, Annex, pp. 496, 515). Israel can carry out Commissions of Inquiry, such as was done into the Gaza flotilla incident (Second Turkel Report, p. 309; Lesh, M., "A Critical Discussion of the Second Turkel Report and How It Engages With the Duty to Investigate Under International Law," *Yearbook of International Humanitarian Law* Vol. 16 (2013), p. 121). In Germany, a parliamentary inquiry was initiated in a case where public military officials were suspected of mismanaging an investigation in Afghanistan (Second Turkel Report, Annex, p. 839). In the Netherlands, Parliamentary Inquiries may be opened, including to review military operations, to establish the facts and background surrounding a particular incident or situation (other than criminal liability) (Second Turkel Report, Annex, pp. 900, 910). In Nigeria, the President established in 2017 a Judicial Commission to review compliance of the Armed Forces with human rights obligations and rules of engagement, especially in local conflict and insurgency situations with Boko Haram. "Osinbajo inaugurates judicial committee to review military compliance with human rights," *The Guardian Nigeria* (5 August 2017), available at: https://guardian.ng/news/military-osinbajo-inaugurates-judicial-committee-to-review-human-rights-abuse/.

58 Margalit (n. 54), p. 209.

security forces such as the military (and/or the police) who may be implicated in the violations, it is also about trust in the State's monopoly of the use of force. Both of these concepts of trust are crucial to maintaining legitimacy and effective rule of law within a nation State. It may therefore be necessary to provide additional guarantees of independence and impartiality than are functionally necessary in the context of a pattern of repeated violations. For example, following repeated allegations that soldiers are abusing detainees, a military investigator may be functionally sufficiently independent and impartial to investigate the matter. Nevertheless, the perception of independence and impartiality requiring a reasonable observer to trust in the objective impartiality of the investigator may mean that the investigator must be placed outside of the military institution.

Examples of mechanisms which may be used to increase independence for the purpose of improving trust in the justice system include oversight mechanisms such as ombudsmen and complaints commissions for security forces. They can serve as an extra avenue for receiving information about possible violations committed by State agents, but also to increase public trust in State institutions.[59] The role and effectiveness of ombudsmen in overseeing the administration of justice by security forces can fluctuate greatly from one system to another,[60] and they can often only issue findings and forward cases to courts rather than directly address issues themselves.[61] International oversight mechanisms also exist, as UN and other entities often work in monitoring democratic accountability, *inter alia*, the independence of the judiciary.[62]

The usual difficulties with establishing a perception of independence and impartiality remain, and, as seen in Chapter 6, may be aggravated in situations of armed conflict. In the context of patterns of violations where the mistrust may be widespread through society and even internationally, the requirement of a perception of justice may be a strong tool for advocating for increased independence. However, there is a further difficulty in investigating and prosecuting cases in which any State organ has been implicated. A State accused of committing patterns of serious violations of international law will usually deny the presence of such, as it implies a degree of seriousness and implication

59 Goldsmith & Lewis (n. 20), p. 1. In Canada, there is the Military Police Complaints Commission (MPCC), which is one of the few permanent civilian mechanisms to oversee military investigations (Margalit (n. 55), p. 219; Second Turkel Report, Annex (n. 57), p. 613). In the UK, Her Majesty's Inspectorate of Constabulary (HMIC) was set up explicitly to "strengthen the independence and effectiveness of the [Royal Military Police]" Margalit (n. 54), p. 220). In Israel, there are various bodies which can deal with complaints by civilians and organisations regarding the actions of soldiers, police, or other security forces (including prison services) (Second Turkel Report (n. 57), pp. 285–309).

60 Neild (n. 20), p. 237; Rose-Ackerman, S., "Corruption and Post-Conflict Peace Building," *Ohio Northern University Law Review* Vol. 34 No. 2 (2008), p. 437.

61 Neild (n. 20), p. 237.

62 E.g., Transparency International and the World Bank; Rose-Ackerman (n. 60), p. 441; McLaughlin, R., "The Emerging Paradigm for Operational Incident Investigation" in Lovell, D., *Investigating Operational Incidents in a Military Context*, Brill (2015), pp. 215–216.

which most governments are not willing to be associated with.[63] The exception to this is if there is a change of government, especially in a transitional setting where a new government may be willing to recognise the systematic nature of the violations committed by the previous government.

Investigations into patterns of violations do not require different standards of independence and impartiality than into isolated violations: they need to be overall sufficiently independent and impartial to be effective. Establishing meaningful independence and impartiality means removing subjective obstacles and creating a perception of independence and impartiality. Nevertheless, establishing what this means in the context of a pattern of problems necessarily requires a more cross-cutting approach, which may be difficult to instigate if mechanisms of monitoring and due diligence are not installed to detect such patterns. Furthermore, there will always be difficulties in investigating and prosecuting cases in which any State organ has been implicated.

Investigative mechanisms to redress patterns of violations will vary greatly depending upon the type and level of violation, and the domestic legal infrastructure. It is important for States to have in place existent mechanisms with increased independence, including those able to carry out criminal investigations, in case the normal judicial systems fail. In extreme cases, it may be necessary to set up *ad hoc* institutions, often with the support and oversight of international mechanisms. Setting up domestic systems of oversight and increased independence is important to fulfil a State's international obligations, but also to secure trust in a State's ability to carry out justice, including through military justice systems where present.

Systematic impunity and measures of last resort

A final note must be made regarding situations in which systematic impunity prevents domestic investigative mechanisms from being effective at all. This may be with regards to all violations, but in most cases it will be related to a specific type of violation, for example violations of a certain nature (e.g., sexual abuse), or against a specific type of person (e.g., an ethnic or religious group). In such cases, the levels of independence and impartiality required for an investigation to be effective may well be at the international level. This section explores briefly the concept of systematic impunity and the implications for redress. Although the responsibility will still be on States to domestically investigate such violations, there are contexts of systematic impunity in which international mechanisms have been foreseen to be the only potential redress available.

The international legal system may be understood as based upon the premise that isolated violations do occur, insofar as redress mechanisms for such

63 "Where allegations of serious violations are made, as in the Turkish cases, the official response is almost inevitably one of denial." Reidy, Hampson, & Boyle (n. 44), p. 169. See also Cohen & Shany (n. 26), pp. 77–78.

violations (including investigations) are provided for in primary and secondary norms of international law. Nevertheless, this international legal system is also based on the premise that at some level there will be good faith efforts to put an end to and redress these violations. When such good faith efforts are non-existent, particularly difficult challenges arise in the implementation of international law. It is suggested here that the concept of systematic impunity is useful in addressing the appropriateness of investigations in response to violations of IHL insofar as there is a link between the presence of such impunity and the inability and/or unwillingness of domestic justice systems to deal with the violations in good faith. This is because unlike "one-off" violations, or even some patterns of problems which are duly investigated, the concept of systematic impunity implies an element of official policy or tolerance in the commission of the violations which will in some cases lead judicial systems to be unable or unwilling to remedy such violations. The international community can be faced with the challenge of balancing the particularly serious consequences of systematic impunity with the importance of State sovereignty upon which the international legal system is built.

Systematic impunity in the international legal regime

Evidence can be found under international law indicating that the presence of systematic impunity will have an implication on the adequate forum in which to bring such violations to justice. Interpretative bodies have found that the repetitive failure to redress serious violations can mean that other States may take action to do so, and/or that individuals need not seek to exhaust domestic remedies that are obviously ineffective.

The International Law Commission (ILC) Articles on State Responsibility paid particular attention to the systematic failure of a State to fulfil certain obligations with regards to peremptory norms (for example, the prohibition of torture), by attaching specific consequences to the commission of such violations.[64] Article 40 states that a breach of international law is to be considered particularly serious if it "involves gross or systematic failure by the responsible State to fulfil the obligation" arising under a peremptory norm.[65] The Articles on State Responsibility suggest that other States have specific responsibilities with regard to repetitive commission or tolerance of violations, and refer *inter alia* to the non-applicability of the rule of exhaustion of domestic remedies by human rights bodies (as explored below).[66] The consequences can be a particularly serious breach of a State's international obligations and mean specific scrutiny and action by the

64 International Law Commission, Articles on Responsibility of States for Internationally Wrongful Acts (2001) [Articles on State Responsibility], Arts 40–41.

65 Articles on State Responsibility (n. 64), Art. 40(2).

66 Articles on State Responsibility (n. 64), Commentary to Art. 40, para. (7), citing ECHR, *Ireland v UK* (n. 19).

international community to bring about a lawful end to the commission of such violations.[67] What measures may be taken by other States, beyond needing to be lawful, are unspecified within the ILC Articles, and the commentary recognises that "the legal regime of serious breaches is itself in a state of development."[68]

International human rights law (IHRL) bodies have also explored in depth the failure of domestic systems to redress systematic violations, principally through activities of the UN and the regional human rights bodies in attempting to overcome barriers to State sovereignty in some of the worst cases of impunity. Discussion at the UN began in the 1960s in relation to "consistent patterns of gross violations of human rights" which were deemed "so serious as to merit a special treatment by the human rights organs of that organization."[69] This was particularly important in the context of the possible tension present within the UN Charter between Article 56 on the obligation to take action to promote the observance of human rights and Article 2(7), which prohibits the UN in intervening "in matters which are essentially within the domestic jurisdiction of any state."[70] Faced with situations of apartheid and systematic racial discrimination in southern Africa and Latin America, certain human rights bodies argued that contexts of "gross and systematic" violations could not be within the domestic jurisdiction of the State, as the domestic systems of judicial redress would almost by definition be ineffective.[71] In such situations, therefore, victims of human rights violations could not expect to find domestic redress,[72] and international action of one form or another would therefore be necessary to promote the observance of human rights. These considerations led to UN ECOSOC resolutions 1235 and 1503 to the Human Rights Commission, with equivalent procedures eventually inherited by the Human Rights Council (HRC).[73] These resolutions enable the HRC and bodies to take specific action in these contexts, such as placing such violators under specific scrutiny and developing thematic procedures addressed to monitor these violations.[74] The concept of systematic violations was subsequently analysed by specific UN treaty bodies in order to establish whether the pattern of violations was such that a special inquiry procedure needs to be initiated by the relevant committee into the situation.[75]

67 Articles on State Responsibility (n. 64), Art. 41.

68 Articles on State Responsibility (n. 64), Commentary to Art. 41, para. 14.

69 Medina Quiroga, C., *The Battle of Human Rights: Gross, Systematic Violations and the Inter American System*, Martinus Nijhoff Publishers (1988), p. 7.

70 Damrosch (n. 55), para. 2.

71 Damrosch (n. 55), para. 2.

72 Medina Quiroga (n. 69), p. 10.

73 Damrosch (n. 55), para. 9.

74 Damrosch (n. 55), para. 3. This is potentially applicable to all UN member States, regardless of ratification.

75 Convention Against Torture and Other Cruel, Inhuman or Degrading Treatment or Punishment, 1465 UNTS 85 (1984) [CAT], Article 20; Optional Protocol to the Convention on the Elimination of All Forms of Discrimination Against Women, UNTS 2131 (1999), Article

Cases can be found in each regional human rights system which explore the implications of the presence of patterns of violations condoned by State authorities. In many cases, this has implications on the need to exhaust domestic remedies. As was seen in Chapter 3, the subsidiary nature of regional human rights bodies (as well as arguably many international bodies) means that they step in only when the domestic systems have failed, and often when they have failed once to uphold certain obligations and failed again to remedy the violations. Regional human rights bodies have found that the systematic practice of violations may enable broad-sweeping statements on the ineffectiveness of domestic systems of justice (including investigations).[76] In such cases it is not necessary to show on a case-by-case basis that the investigation (or broader judicial proceeding) was ineffective, but that there is a broader contextual flaw within the administration of justice which needs rectifying. In some cases, this means that victims of such violations are not required to seek to exhaust domestic remedies, as such remedies would necessarily be ineffective.

International criminal law (ICL) as a body of law was developed precisely because domestic systems failed to redress the most serious crimes, as "international crimes such as genocide, crimes against humanity, and war crimes, are collective and typically state-sponsored criminal offences" and "often they will not be prosecuted or punished by the state of commission."[77] The non-working of domestic judicial systems, either through bad faith or inability, is crucial to the concept of the International Criminal Court (ICC) gaining jurisdiction under the complementarity principle of the Rome Statute. This principle makes explicit that domestic sources of redress are to be given priority and encouraged (see Chapter 3). This very fact gives the State the initial responsibility to investigate and prosecute, even for systematic violations. The

---

8; Optional Protocol to the Convention on the Rights of Child on a Communications Procedure, A/HRC/RES/17/18 (2011), Article 13; Optional Protocol to the Convention on the Rights of Persons with Disabilities, A/RES/61/106 (2006), Article 6; Optional Protocol to the Convention on Economic, Social and Cultural Rights, A/RES/63/117 (2009), Article 11; Siatitsa (n. 32), p. 611 n. 31; UN OHCHR, "Human Rights Bodies – Complaints Procedures," "Inquiries," available at: www.ohchr.org/EN/HRBodies/TBPetitions/Pages/HRTBPetitions.aspx; CEDAW Report on Mexico produced by the CEDAW Under Article 8 of the Optional Protocol to the Convention, and Reply From the Government of Mexico, 27 January 2005 (CEDAW/C/2005/OP.8/MEXICO), para. 261; Committee Against Torture, Summary Account of the Results of the Proceedings Concerning the Inquiry on Turkey, A/48/44/Add.1, p. 9, para. 38; Report on Nepal Under Article 20, A/67/44, Annex XIII, p. 299, para. 97.

76 ECmmHR, *The Greek Case*, Yearbook of the European Court of Human Rights (1972), pp. 24–25; ECHR, *Ireland v UK* (n. 19), pp. 391–392, 395–396; Medina Quiroga (n. 69), p. 853; Shelton, D., *Remedies in International Human Rights Law*, Oxford University Press (3rd ed.) (2015), p. 94.

77 Jessberger, F., "International vs National Prosecution of International Crimes," in Cassesse, A., *The Oxford Companion of International Criminal Justice*, Oxford University Press (2009), pp. 212–213. See also Schabas, W., "State Policy As an Element of International Crimes," *Journal of Criminal Law and Criminology* Vol. 98 No. 3 (2008), p. 974.

Rome Statute complementarity clause would be redundant if domestic systems were expected to always fail with regard to all systematic violations. As under IHRL, it is not systematic violations in themselves which necessarily preclude the State's ability to carry out an effective investigation. Rather, it is the subsequent repetitive failure to effectively investigate and prosecute which will demonstrate a State's inability or unwillingness to redress violations, and therefore the unavailability of domestic systems of redress (systematic impunity).

A measure of last resort: international mechanisms

The international legal system has therefore had to contend with domestic systems of redress being ineffective, and various international mechanisms of redress have been set up to deal with such situations. The first *ad hoc* international criminal tribunals in the 1990s were set up in response to systematic impunity, because the involvement of Heads of State and the entire domestic governmental institutions in the perpetration of the violations meant that justice could not be envisaged at a domestic level, and that only a supra-national entity could independently and impartiality criminally investigate and try such cases.[78] As well as international criminal courts or tribunals, other international accountability mechanisms include non-criminal investigations or oversight through UN bodies, whose mandates will usually be set *ad hoc* to every situation.[79] Regional mechanisms can also serve as oversight bodies and all have bodies which may carry out inquiries into specific situations or monitor ongoing cases. The international body which would perhaps be most appropriate for investigating systematic violations of IHL (from an initially non-criminal perspective) is the "dormant" International Humanitarian Fact-Finding Commission,[80] although this body requires consent of the parties to the conflict.

The advantages of international investigatory mechanisms lie mostly in their capacity for particular independence, and, depending upon the available resources, may bring together very developed expertise in investigating violations of IHL. They are a crucial tool of accountability into the actions of

78 Roht-Arriaza (n. 32), p. 81

79 Different forms of inquiries can be created by the UN Security Council, the General Assembly, Human Rights Council, OHCHR, or the UN Secretary General. See mapping of the different forms of inquiry in Debuf, E., "Evaluating Mechanisms for Investigating Attacks on Healthcare," International Peace Institute (December 2017), p. 5; Blank, L. "Investigations into Military Operations: What Impact on Transitional Justice?" *Israel Law Review* Vol. 47 No. 1 (2014), p. 86.

80 Kalshoven, F., "The International Humanitarian Fact-Finding Commission: A Sleeping Beauty?" *Humanitäres Völkerrecht: Informationsschriften* (2002). The IHFFC was used exceptionally in 2017 at the request of the OSCE in Ukraine. See Azzarello, C., & Niederhauser, M., "The Independent Humanitarian Fact-Finding Commission: Has the 'Sleeping Beauty' Awoken?" ICRC Law and Policy Blog (9 January 2018), available at: https://blogs.icrc.org/law-and-policy/2018/01/09/the-independent-humanitarian-fact-finding-commission-has-the-sleeping-beauty-awoken/.

States who do not take sufficient action regarding violations committed by their own forces or within their territory or jurisdiction. They can also provide a cross-cutting view of a domestic system which may not be possible on a smaller scale. It may be that the use of (or at the very least monitoring by) international bodies would also help to bridge some problems of both actual and perceived lack of independence and impartiality, and many individuals affected by IHL violations do call for international mechanisms to be used. The involvement of the international community may also matter insofar as the State's obligations to investigate arise under international, not domestic law. This may require that it is also perceived to be independent and impartial from an international perspective, regardless of against whom a violation is alleged to have been committed.

Nevertheless, such international procedures also come with many challenges and disadvantages. They are necessarily exceptional measures which take up a lot of time and resources, and are rarely to be considered the most effective investigations.[81] They can be seen as political rather than legal tools, and are not exempt from criticisms regarding lack of independence and impartiality, or indeed the perception of such, as individuals working in such procedures can be perceived as biased according to State political lines.[82] They are also very expensive and time-consuming, and can hold very little enforcement power beyond political naming and shaming. Investigators in such contexts can face substantial administrative, political, and practical obstacles in accessing information.[83] They can have mixed effects upon a State's attempts to transition to peace, from helping to provide answers in searching for the truth, to increasing entrenched differences in views according to conflict lines.[84] Criticisms of international criminal proceedings include their cost, their remoteness from the affected societies,[85] and that they do little to contribute towards long-term capacity-building of domestic judicial institutions.[86] They also arguably

81 See, e.g., Wong, S., "Investigating Civilian Casualties in Armed Conflict: Comparing U.S. Military Investigations with Alternatives Under International Humanitarian and Human Rights Law," *Naval Law Review* Vol. 64 (2015), pp. 138–150; Boutruche, T. "Credible Fact-Finding and Allegations of International Humanitarian Law Violations: Challenges in Theory and Practice," *Journal of Conflict and Security Law* Vol. 16 No. 1 (2011).

82 Meron, T., "Judicial Independence and Impartiality in International Criminal Tribunals," *American Journal of International Law* Vol. 99 No. 2 (2005), p. 362; Gordon, E., Burton, S. J., Falk, R., and Franck, T., "The Independence and Impartiality of International Judges," *Proceedings of the Annual Meeting (American Society of International Law)* Vol. 83 (1989).

83 See "Human Rights and Law of Armed Conflict: Investigations by UN Bodies, with Prof. Françoise Hampson and Prof. Charles Garraway," Essex Human Rights Centre Rights Cast (24 October 2019), available at: https://anchor.fm/rightscast/episodes/Human-Rights-and-Law-of-Armed-Conflict-Investigations-by-UN-Bodies-with-Prof--Francoise-Hampson-and-Prof--Charles-Garraway-e7tc25.

84 Blank (n. 79), p. 102.

85 Roht-Arriaza (n. 32), p. 81; Shelton (n. 76), pp. 126–127, 130.

86 Roht-Arriaza (n. 32), p. 103.

require at least some measure of governmental consent, as well as interest and support by the international community.[87] Further concerns include matters of fair trial for the suspects, including related to the independence and impartiality of investigators and judges in these tribunals.[88] Finally, the findings of international mechanisms (and some domestic mechanisms such as parliamentary inquiries) can take years to be published, which can create many substantial problems, not least that violations may be continuing during this time. Properly functioning domestic mechanisms which can effectively investigate the first time round are therefore crucial for the proper administration of justice. In the absence of effective domestic remedies, however, as can be the case for systematic violations, international investigative mechanisms may be the only redress option for victims of violations.

The matter of "unable"

A final note must be made on the matter of a State being "unable" to effectively investigate and prosecute violations. It is a concept which is provided for in the Rome Statute of the ICC but is also of interest to consider under IHRL and IHL. What happens in situations where the political will exists to investigate but States simply do not have the means to do so effectively?

International criminal law under the Rome Statute

Under the Rome Statute, a State being unable to genuinely investigate and prosecute systematic violations may lead the ICC to gain jurisdiction over a case, even though the State may in good faith be willing to carry out investigations if it could.[89] Little has been written on the criterion of inability in relation to investigations under the Rome Statute, although this link was made in the ICC admissibility decision of *Bemba* with relation to the investigation and prosecution already held in the Central African Republic. Three criteria are listed in Article 17(3) to assess a State's "inability": being unable to obtain the accused; being unable to obtain the necessary evidence and testimony; or being otherwise unable to carry out its proceedings. It was envisioned that such circumstances would most likely arise in armed conflict. An ICC informal expert paper on the principle of complementarity listed further possible criteria to take into account when considering the "inability test," including the "lack of necessary personnel, judges, investigators, prosecutor," the "lack of judicial infrastructure," as well as "amnesties, immunities rendering system [*sic*]

87 Roht-Arriaza (n. 32), p. 82.

88 Kreß, C., "Reflections on the Iudicare Limb of the Grave Breaches Regime," *Journal of International Criminal Justice* Vol. 7 (2009).

89 Rome Statute Article 17; El-Zeidy, M. M., *The Principle of Complementarity in International Criminal Law*, Nijhoff (2008), p. 193.

'unavailable.'"[90] With regard to the last criterion, however, it should be noted that due to the current evolving norms regarding combating impunity for the most serious crimes under international law, passing amnesties for crimes contained within the Rome Statute could well be construed as "unwillingness" to bring the perpetrators to justice.

It is clear that it is not the intent of the State that is being tested under the criterion of inability, as "a country devastated by conflict and facing a collapse of its system might be *willing* to conduct proceedings, and yet be *unable* to genuinely carry out proceedings."[91] Instead, it appears to rest on something more objective than the carrying out of the proceedings themselves. In the context of the collapse of a State, it is likely that lack of resources and capacity will create obstacles on the ability of investigators to, *inter alia*, gather evidence and testimonies, provide safety measures when necessary, or use appropriate investigative and analytical equipment such as forensic tools. However, such obstacles on their own are not sufficient to show that a state is unable to investigate, as "it was extremely important to many States [in the drafting process of the Rome Statute] that proceedings cannot be found 'non-genuine' simply because of a comparative lack of resources or because of a lack of full compliance with all human rights standards."[92] Rather, a judicial system may still be able to function in situations of armed conflict, for example due to the State "shifting resources or transferring the trial to other venues, to effect a genuine prosecution."[93] Therefore the conditions must be such that they render the State unable to achieve this desired "genuineness" in the proceedings, despite its best efforts. If the State can achieve a genuine investigation but chooses not to (for example, by not shifting resources), then it may fall under the unwilling criterion, although it is likely that a certain degree of "reasonableness" is to be applied in assessing these allocations of resources (see Chapter 6).

Although the situation of impunity and lack of domestic redress for victims may *de facto* be the same as in the case of unwillingness, there may be a case to be made that the case of inability would not necessarily lead to aggravated State responsibility, if the State in good faith would have tried to redress the violations. In order for such "inability" not to be interpreted as unwillingness, it is likely that the State in question would be expected to seek regional or international support in the investigation and prosecution of such crimes. Failure to do so could come across as an expression of unwillingness. The fact that some States have self-referred cases within their jurisdiction to the ICC,

90 International Criminal Court, "Informal Expert Paper: The Principle of Complementarity in Practice," ICC-OTP (2003) [ICC informal Expert Paper], Annex, p. 31.
91 ICC Informal Expert Paper (n. 90), para. 23.
92 ICC Informal Expert Paper (n. 90), para. 23.
93 Holmes, J. T., "Complementarity: National Courts versus the ICC" in Cassese, A. et al, *The Rome Statute of the ICC: A Commentary*, Vol. 1, Oxford University Press (2002), p. 677.

citing their own inability to investigate, could be demonstrative of one way of expressing such willingness.[94]

IHRL and IHL

There is no direct equivalent of being "unable" to investigate in IHRL or IHL international treaties, and it can be asked what it may mean under these bodies of law. For parties to the Rome Statute, the consequences of being "unable" are severe, as it is an admissibility element of the Rome Statute (the Court may seize jurisdiction of the case). Nevertheless, it may be possible to separate the State responsibility elements in such contexts: if a State has put all reasonable means into an investigation, it may have fulfilled its responsibilities under international law with regard to that investigation. The intervention of the ICC may be a separate action which does not relate to State responsibility.

A similar conception may be seen under IHRL and IHL. The State responsibility is to put in all reasonable means to carry out effective investigations. Arguably there may always be at least *some* means which can be put into an investigation, and as long as these are reasonable within the circumstances, a State would have fulfilled its international obligations. The concept of due diligence would also require a State to prepare in advance for contingency situations, such as armed conflict, to be able to carry out investigations in such difficult situations (see Chapter 6). Yet, the "means not results" test taken to its extreme may be contrary to the concept of effectiveness – if very few means are reasonably available to put into the investigation, the investigation may never be capable of achieving its purpose (e.g., of identifying a perpetrator). Even if this responsibility may not fall upon the individual State, the ability to achieve justice in such cases would be questionable. As in ICL, it is suggested a State may be expected to seek regional or international support in investigations when it is genuinely unable to investigate, in order to fully discharge its international obligations.

Systematic impunity within a domestic system involves the repetitive failure to investigate and more generally provide redress for violations of international law, usually due to a lack of good faith efforts by the State. This usually results in the unavailability of domestic redress mechanisms, and often leads to widespread and systematic violations. In such cases, the only option for redress for victims of violations may be to turn to international mechanisms, including international investigative mechanisms. Nevertheless, these international mechanisms are necessarily a measure of last resort, and their effectiveness can be limited. In the case in which a State is genuinely "unable" to effectively

94 The authorities of Uganda, the DRC, the Central African Republic, Mali, and Côte d'Ivoire have all requested the ICC's intervention in specific cases. "Statement by the ICC Prosecutor, Fatou Bensouda, on the referral of the situation since 1 August 2012 in the Central African Republic" (12 June 2014).

investigate, it is suggested that it should seek regional or international support in investigating serious violations of international law, in order to demonstrate its good faith in seeking to uphold its international legal obligations.

Conclusion

This chapter has served to clarify how and why a failure to investigate and patterns of violations might impact the effectiveness of investigations into violations of IHL. The purpose of such a clarification is in part to provide further insight into domestic differences as to the effectiveness of military investigations into violations of international law, and why regional human rights bodies may have differed so greatly in their view on the independence and impartiality of military justice systems. It may be argued that both the Inter-American and the African System of Human Rights were set up principally to deal with situations of gross and systematic violations, and are only more recently coming to deal with isolated violations, whereas the ECtHR was set up with precisely the inverse relationship (at least with relation to individual petitions).[95] The latter system has therefore had much less of a reason to find entire domestic systems (such as entire military justice systems) ineffective. It is suggested that beyond cultural or historical differences, or regime type, what draws ineffective investigative systems together is the presence of patterns of violations and systematic impunity which affect the very possibility of domestic remedies in a State.

Therefore, in trying to look at a domestic situation and whether or not domestic redress for violations of international law is likely to occur, one should look out for the possibility a pattern of violations and systematic impunity implicating the normal systems of judicial redress which could lead to ineffective investigations. It may be that only certain types of domestic mechanisms are ineffective, for example those involving a certain type of perpetrator, or a certain type of victim or type of violation. It will be necessary to identify the scope of the systematic problem in order to address what an effective investigation into such violations would look like.

The utility of this concept is limited; States will usually deny that their organs are implicated in the systematic impunity, and the possibility of holding States to account for patterns of violations at an international level is usually limited to the most serious "gross and systematic" cases. Even in such cases the enforcement capability of the international community is limited in a political status quo which prioritises State sovereignty. Nevertheless, the international legal system *de facto* provides many "second chances" to States to redress violations. Because IHRL and international criminal law are bodies based on subsidiarity and complementarity principles, they very much give

95 Reidy, Hampson, & Boyle (n. 44).

States the opportunities and incentives to go back and investigate a repetitive failure to investigate.

Policies to commit a pattern of violations are often secretive, yet they can manifest symptoms which are detectable from the outside, notably through repeated violations of a certain kind. Ideally, pointing to a pattern of violations should mean that victims would not have the burden to show the lack of independence and impartiality for each specific case in which such violations occur. Rather, a pattern of problems indicating the possible presence of systematic impunity may be sufficient to infer the possible implication of the justice system in the commission of the violations, and therefore the burden should be on the State to provide sufficient independence and impartiality in the investigation and subsequent judicial proceedings dealing with the violations. The perception of independence and impartiality becomes of particular importance in such cases. In practice, however, the concept is perhaps most useful for civil society and international bodies seeking to hold States accountable for the most serious of situations, by putting pressure on States to fulfil their domestic duties with a potential threat of international action. NGOs and civil society can play a crucial role in detecting the gross and systematic failure of States to uphold their international obligations.[96] Arguably, such actors may also help to make more transparent the obligations of States: if they are able to detect systematic violations (e.g. using open-source investigations), the State has less of an excuse to claim it did not know of the violations.

96 See, e.g., the work of Amnesty International's Citizen Evidence Lab (https://citizenevidence.org/); Bellingcat (www.bellingcat.com/); the Centre for Civilians in Conflict (https://civiliansinconflict.org); and Airwars (https://airwars.org/).

8 Conclusion

Introduction

In research for this book, it was not always easy to find out who in fact does carry out investigations into alleged misconduct by military personnel in different States. National documents on jurisdictional matters, as well as literature on military justice systems often refer to the nature of courts and judges, whereas the details on investigators are not always specified. This is not necessarily because the information is sensitive or classified, but perhaps rather because it has not been of great public concern until recently. The use of military investigators was a turning point of the 2021 European Court of Human Rights case of *Hanan v Germany*, in a State which supposedly has not had a military justice system since the Second World War. The German government's submission in the case was informative on the precise practical and legal considerations which led to the use of a hybrid military–civilian system in a conflict setting, which enabled the Court to scrutinise the legality of such a system. As is perhaps often the case, it is when things go wrong that external scrutiny is enhanced.

As investigations are increasingly receiving attention as an important part of the implementation of treaty provisions, as well as redress for violations, this book has explored whether and to what extent military investigations may contribute to efforts to secure accountability for violations of international humanitarian law (IHL). Military investigations are often criticised for lack of independence and impartiality due to their apparent institutional proximity to those under investigation. Part of the purpose of this research was not to contradict such criticisms, but rather to question many of their assumptions. For example, what is meant by a military investigation? Do investigations actually need to be independent and impartial? To what extent does being a military investigator affect the independence and impartiality of an investigation? I have suggested that there may be other questions which also need to be asked, such as how the context of armed conflict affects the administration of justice, and whether a pattern of violations may be affecting the likelihood of redress. To this end, this research has addressed what is unique to military systems, and what may not be so, when assessing the appropriate standards of

DOI: 10.4324/9781003360223-8

independence and impartiality of investigations into serious violations of IHL. It is hoped that the findings on precise standards applicable to the investigation stage contribute to the fair scrutiny of domestic military systems and to a better understanding of how they may contribute to or hinder accountability efforts for violations of international law.

Overview: independent and impartial military investigations

The role of military justice systems in investigating violations of IHL

As the current literature did not adequately address the scope and standards applicable to investigations into violations of IHL, one element which has been clarified through the research is the ways in which military investigations can be an effective tool for the implementation of IHL. Chapter 2 explored the evolution of military justice systems from commanders regulating internal discipline through to complex judicial systems with responsibility for implementing international law. It highlighted some trends and differences between common and civil law States, in particular in the scope of military jurisdiction, and on the different understandings of the concept of "discipline." Setting limits to the scope of military jurisdiction needs to be considered within the domestic and regional setting, and how it will affect the actual administration of justice and work to combat impunity.

The chapter also served in part to highlight the importance of distinguishing the "militaryness" of judicial institutions from their procedural flaws. Military justice systems are still relevant in at least some States for criminal investigations, and most States use military procedures for the suppression of some non-criminal violations of IHL. The different understandings of the concept of "fair trial" between human rights regional bodies has also affected the ways in which military justice has been scrutinised by these bodies. This difference has become important in the debate on the scope of military jurisdiction under international law, especially through the dissemination of the Draft Decaux Principles on the administration of justice through military tribunals. Military justice systems have rightfully had to align themselves with evolving understandings of justice, in particular as they have become institutions which may be used for the implementation of international law. Properly constituted military institutions can therefore have a role in the implementation of IHL through investigating possible or alleged violations. The rest of the book highlighted some of the ways in which the use of military institutions can serve or hinder the effectiveness of investigations into such violations.

The book has also clarified the framework of the duty to carry out an effective investigation into serious violations of international law, findings which apply beyond IHL and military investigations. Chapter 3 highlighted the importance of investigating both criminal and non-criminal violations of IHL. It explored the explicit and implicit obligations under IHL, international human rights law (IHRL), and international criminal law (ICL), inferred from the need to effectively repress criminal violations as well as the more general obligation to implement the provisions of these bodies of law. Furthermore, the obligation to provide an effective remedy and reparation for violations of international law leads to significant insight into how investigations can contribute to these remedies.

It also explored the concept of "serious" violations of IHL for the purpose of investigations, which has not been fully addressed in existing scholarship. Insofar as IHL is a body of law that deals primarily with State responsibility, it was considered relevant to explore the concept of serious violations beyond the traditional scope of war crimes and grave breaches. The chapter established that the duty to investigate "serious" violations of IHL may be understood as a duty to investigate violations which affect physical integrity and/or form a pattern of violations. Investigations into such violations therefore need to meet certain procedural requirements of effectiveness as procedural obligations under international law. The chapter also highlighted that the obligation of effectiveness means that all reasonable means must be put into the investigation with the view of it being capable of achieving its objective. This requirement means *inter alia* that the means must be adapted to the circumstances at hand and the nature of the violation.

Various chapters also considered the importance of the commander in investigating, and how this role has changed in the last few decades. First, commanders will always have a duty to report possible violations and trigger the appropriate mechanisms for assessment and investigation. In the case of criminal violations, this will most likely be under the "duty to refer," as elaborated in Chapter 5. As international law currently stands, it should not be the commander of an implicated unit who investigates war crimes. However, they may need to take reasonable steps to safeguard evidence and the scene of the incident. Furthermore, if the appropriate investigators and authorities are not able to immediately intervene, the commander may have certain responsibilities which differ from the norm, especially in situations of armed conflict. In all circumstances, a commander needs to maintain disciplinary control over their subordinates, and it is possible that disciplinary or administrative action may need to be taken alongside a criminal investigation. This will always be context-dependent, but commanders should be trained to know what they can and cannot do in such circumstances, and that it is in their interest to carry out their duties effectively.

The independence and impartiality of investigations in relation to their effectiveness

Having established in Chapter 3 that the obligation to investigate serious violations of IHL is one of effectiveness, subsequent chapters considered how the standards of independence and impartiality contribute to this overall requirement of effectiveness. It was necessary in Chapter 4 to deconstruct the concepts of independence and impartiality as applicable to investigations – as opposed to those applicable to judges, courts, and tribunals. Indeed, it is not obvious from the outset (even though it often seems to be assumed) whether and to what extent investigations into violations of international law actually do need to be independent and impartial. Furthermore, documents addressing the adequacy of military justice systems do not always separately consider the trial and the investigation stage.

As has been seen throughout the research, different standards apply to these different stages, therefore establishing the importance of considering the standards of independence and impartiality of investigations separately. By exploring the differences between the standards applicable to investigations in contrast to those applicable to judges, courts, and tribunals, Chapter 4 highlighted that the main difference may be understood as the need for overall versus absolute independence and impartiality. The independence and impartiality of investigations is different to that applicable to judges and courts because the former serve a distinct purpose. Whereas the impartiality of judges is necessary for the need to trust in the legitimacy of fair adjudication, what matters for investigations is rather that they are capable of achieving their purpose; namely, that they need to be effective. Independence and impartiality need to contribute to the effectiveness of investigations, alongside the other standards of thoroughness, promptness, and transparency. Whereas judges and courts need to separately meet the four requirements of objective and subjective impartiality, and personal and institutional independence under IHRL fair trial rights, the requirement for investigations is different. What matters is whether the investigation is overall sufficiently independent and impartial to be effective. Such overall independence and impartiality may be achieved in a broader variety of ways than those under fair trial rights.

Nevertheless, the standards applicable to judges and courts help inform those applicable to investigations, through the exploration of the concepts in case law and literature. For example, it is clear that safeguards of independence are means by which to achieve the ultimate desired goal of impartiality, although they have become a standard necessary in and of themselves. It is also clear that the concept of a perception of justice, provided in part through a perception of independence and impartiality, is necessary to a certain degree for the rule of law, and for the trust in State institutions by its population. The problems which arise with regards to this perception and trust in transnational and armed conflict situations, as well as with military institutions more generally, as explored in Chapters 5 and 6, are not unique to investigations.

Challenges to the independence and impartiality of military investigations

Having clarified that what is required for investigations is that they be overall sufficiently independent and impartial to contribute to the effectiveness of the investigation, it is possible to consider what this effectiveness might look like in challenging situations, especially in a military and armed conflict context. Crucially, effectiveness may be achieved in different ways, adapted to the circumstances at hand. Chapters 5, 6, and 7 examined some of the principal obstacles which may arise when conducting military investigations into serious violations of IHL.

Chapter 5 explored some of the elements specific to military institutions which can require particular consideration for achieving independence and impartiality. Hierarchical relationships in chains of command, especially those of subordination and discipline must necessarily be taken into account. Command responsibility and notions of implication in possible war crimes also justify the increased removal of commanders from criminal investigations. The chapter also addressed the matter of toxic loyalty within military institutions which may affect the administration of justice. Although this is not usually explicitly analysed, this concept may be understood to be the basis of many criticisms of military justice systems accused of "investigating themselves." The chapter problematised the use of toxic loyalty as a blanket dismissal of military justice systems, as it would be necessary in each circumstance to identify the scope of toxic loyalty and how it may affect the effectiveness of investigations. All of these elements are not necessarily obstacles prohibiting the use of military investigations, but they are factors that need to be taken into account and that require specific structures to safeguard the independence and impartiality of investigators in military settings.

Chapter 6 explored the practical and theoretical obstacles which can occur or be aggravated in situations of armed conflict. Such obstacles can affect independence and impartiality both directly in the choice of investigator available as well as more indirectly through issues of legitimacy often found in situations of conflict. Jurisdictional differences may apply in situations of armed conflict and extraterritorial operations, and ongoing hostilities and security concerns may affect who is legally and physically able to investigate. Commanders also have a crucial role in safeguarding initial investigative steps in situations of armed conflict.

Although the challenges associated with armed conflict are often considered on an *ad hoc* basis for specific investigations, this chapter served to provide a clear framework to show how these situations should be adequately prepared for. It built upon the findings of Chapter 3 to further explore how the concept of "reasonableness" may be interpreted in situations of armed conflict for investigations into violations of IHL. States have a responsibility to prepare for situations of armed conflict by ensuring that adequate measures and resources are put into place for independent and impartial investigators to be able to operate in such situations. States must prepare for such circumstances through structural safeguards and adequate training.

The chapter also explored the impact of armed conflict on the perception of independence and impartiality, as this can aggravate difficult theoretical issues related to legitimate governance. Such difficulties can arise within one State, for example between ethnic or religious groups who do not trust in the legitimacy of State institutions. But they may be particularly aggravated in transnational conflicts, where the legitimacy of one State making judicial decisions which impact on the population of another is put into question. Despite the difficulties in identifying and addressing these challenges, States still have an obligation to do what is reasonable to mitigate the perception of lack of independence and impartiality, taking into account as much as possible how appearances may affect the perception of justice.

Finally, Chapter 7 explored how the presence of systematic impunity may affect the independence and impartiality of investigations, and more generally domestic systems of redress for violations of IHL. The chapter sought to clarify some of the contrasting views on military justice systems, and why regional human rights bodies may have differed so greatly in their views on the independence and impartiality of military justice systems. It suggested that beyond cultural or historical differences, or regime type, what draws ineffective investigative systems together is the presence of systematic impunity which affects the very possibility of domestic remedies in a State.

The chapter explored the way in which a failure to investigate could lead to specific forms of responsibility, and how patterns of problems could affect the standards of independence and impartiality of an investigation. It considered the importance of cross-cutting examination in such contexts and considered how investigations can be used to redress pattern violations, either through the normal judicial systems or through exceptional or international mechanisms. It also explored the unique ways developed by international mechanisms to deal with systematic impunity, highlighting that the failure of domestic redress systems often requires international action for victims to be able to access effective redress mechanisms.

Safeguarding the independence and impartiality of military investigations

This book has demonstrated that military justice systems can carry out effective investigations into serious violations of IHL, as long as their independence and impartiality are safeguarded, and that the whole context is taken into account. It has also highlighted some of the ways in which the independence and impartiality of military investigations can be safeguarded. Ultimately, what matters is whether an investigation is, overall, sufficiently independent and impartial in light of the effectiveness of the investigation. This means that the entire set of circumstances needs to be assessed, including the promptness, thoroughness, and transparency of the investigation, as well as the nature of the allegation.

First, investigators as individuals need to be personally protected against undue influence and pressures. This means investigators should not be implicated themselves but should also be independent of individuals and structures whose responsibility may be engaged in the alleged violation. Given the notions of liability under command responsibility for war crimes, a superior may be considered "implicated" in a violation committed by their subordinates. Despite maintaining a crucial role in the initiation of appropriate investigation steps (such as reporting), in general commanders should not be tasked with directly investigating possible war crimes of their subordinates. Investigators also need to be sufficiently free from the hierarchy of those implicated in the violation, which means there should be no relationship of subordination to those carrying out the military operations involved in the alleged violation. There should also be practical independence from this hierarchy by considering possible relationships of influence other than formal hierarchy. Effectiveness also means that investigators need a level of expertise in the matters of investigation and need to be able to have the legal authority and the physical capability to investigate. Matters of jurisdiction and security concerns in armed conflicts may affect this.

Institutional safeguards are also necessary to ensure the independence and impartiality of investigations into serious violations of IHL. Although Chapter 4 established that the requirement of institutional independence is not the same as that applicable to judges, courts, and tribunals, it is necessary for the investigators (for example, military police or equivalent) to be institutionally protected from undue pressure in the performance of their investigative duties. While institutional affiliation is not always sufficient to undermine the overall independence and impartiality of an investigation, it can become an aggravating factor in cases which give rise to suspicions against the institution as a whole.

In the case of allegations which may be part of a broader pattern of problems, there is a need to carry out cross-cutting investigations which can adequately assess the root cause of the problems. This means that they will need to be able to investigate beyond a single individual incident and take into account the broader context and power structures which may be at play, in order to put an end to and guarantee non-repetition of possible violations arising from such patterns. Such cross-cutting investigative work may require further independence, as well as ongoing monitoring. In exceptional circumstances suggesting the existence of systematic impunity, further independence will be necessary in order to provide adequate redress and prevent impunity. Impartiality in such contexts can be problematic if violations are tied to entrenched beliefs within the institution or a broader affiliation such as nationality or religion. It will be necessary to identify the scope of systematicity and remove the investigation from implicated structures in order to carry out an effective investigation in such contexts.

Finally, as well as functional independence and impartiality, there is also a need for a perception of independence and impartiality to achieve meaningful justice with relation to investigations into violations of IHL. If it is security forces such as the military (and/or the police) who may be implicated in the violations, this ties into the trust in the State's monopoly of the use of force, which is crucial to maintaining the effective rule of law. In the context of a pattern of repeated violations, it may therefore be necessary to provide additional guarantees of independence and impartiality than are functionally necessary. There are difficulties in establishing a perception of independence and impartiality especially in conflict settings, yet increased independence can be a strong tool for accountability where the mistrust in military institutions may be widespread through society and even internationally.

Oversight mechanisms are important safeguards for both ordinary and exceptional justice procedures. Civilian bodies should have some form of oversight over military justice procedures, whether this be through appeals mechanisms, potential challenging of jurisdiction, complaints commissions, or other oversight mechanisms. Other domestic oversight mechanisms which can prove important for accountability include ombudsmen, complaints commissions, and *ad hoc* monitoring mechanisms. International oversight, whether judicial or non-judicial, can have a key role to play in accountability for violations of international law, even though such mechanisms must necessarily be seen as a measure of last resort.

Ultimately, a focus on combating impunity should drive domestic and international accountability efforts. The focus should be on the structural safeguards for independence and impartiality, as well as on consideration of the specific obstacles to the administration of justice in each context, including the possibility of systematic impunity. It is unlikely that the choice of investigator always needs to be a situation of "either/or" for military or civilian actors. As was seen in several parts of the book, many systems employ a mix of civilian and military actors in investigating offences committed by members of the armed forces. The role of military expertise in initial procedures needs to be highlighted, but so does the importance of civilian oversight throughout the administration of justice. In general, it will need to be asked what the most effective system is to combat impunity within a domestic system, given the structure of military institutions and the historical and political contexts. Exceptionally, there may be a need to consider whether specialised measures need to be implemented to combat impunity within a specific context, for example where there are allegations of systematic impunity. It will need to be asked whether the normal systems of justice, whether military, civilian, or mixed, are able to effectively access the scene, gather evidence, respect due process rights where relevant, and generally be free from inappropriate influences and pressures. Questions of how the system is checked and reviewed are also necessary in answering and safeguarding these procedures.

Going forward

This research has clarified the theoretical framework for the independence and impartiality of military investigations into serious violations of IHL. It has also raised various questions that could not fully be answered here, but it is hoped may spur further research.

One obvious area for further research is the independence and impartiality of military courts, a topic that was deliberately left out of the scope of the book. As mentioned in the Introduction, this is something that is far from settled from an international perspective and raises parallel, yet distinct, issues to the ones covered here. The findings on the ways in which military institutions and armed conflict may affect the standards of independence and impartiality may be informative in such research, as may the concept of systematic impunity in creating obstacles to effective redress. Nevertheless, as was made clear in Chapter 4, the independence and impartiality of judges, courts, and tribunals are to be measured differently to those applicable to investigations. Such research would require specific consideration of fair trial rights and would benefit from cross-cutting analysis of the ways in which domestic courts operate.

Chapters 5 and 6 also raised some issues that were not fully answered surrounding how perceptions of the military affect concepts of justice in conflict settings. These chapters explored issues concerning how public perceptions of military institutions can greatly affect the perception of their ability to carry out justice. Analysing the full theoretical framework and potential solutions to this problem would require further interdisciplinary research. It is suggested that answering such questions would be particularly important in situations of transitional justice, especially when seeking to promote lasting justice beyond armed conflict.

Chapter 7 began to explore the concepts of systematic impunity, but it is clear that these areas and their impact on accountability could do with further research. The need to monitor for patterns of problems in military operations is becoming clear for both operational and legal reasons. The need to set up adequate monitoring mechanisms to detect such patterns would require separate research, which was also left out of the scope of this book. Analysis of how patterns of violations affect redress mechanisms is also relevant beyond IHL, and further analysis of this concept, for example for violations of IHRL, would also be useful.

Finally, although the research is based on domestic as well as international legislation and practice, it is undoubtable that the practical implementation of its findings would require further research into specific domestic settings. Various chapters mentioned some general differences between civil and common law systems, while also acknowledging that such a divide oversimplifies, and by no means captures, every system globally. The aim of the book was to clarify the international standards applicable under IHL and international law more broadly. Further comparative research on how military law enforcement institutions are domestically structured and operate with relation to investigations would clarify application of the findings in practice.

Conclusion

Military justice systems are changing. At the time of writing, various States are undergoing serious review of their military justice systems, especially related to the scope of military jurisdiction over sexual offences, albeit usually focused upon offences committed against members of their own armed forces.[1] Although such situations are not part of the scope of this book, it is

1 USA: Lopez, C. T., "Executive Order Changes How Military Handles Sexual Assaults," DOD news (2 August 2023), available at: www.defense.gov/News/News-Stories/Article/Article/3479106/executive-order-changes-how-military-handles-sexual-assaults/; UK: "Victims of

worth pointing out that many of these situations could fall within the concept of systematic impunity (in these cases under IHRL), as explored in Chapter 7, through a repetitive failure to investigate related to cultural or structural problems within these military institutions. These reforms indicate that there is still much to be determined surrounding the role of military justice systems in accountability for violations of international law.

One question which has perhaps not directly been answered in this book is whether there is a *need* for military justice systems for the administration of justice in armed conflict. Although military institutions can contribute to effectiveness in investigating in important ways, it is conceivable, at least in theory, that the changing nature of warfare and technological advancements may make their military nature less essential. Insofar as there is a trend of "civilianisation" of many military judicial procedures, and perhaps increased scepticism of military institutions, it may be generally that military justice systems will become less commonly used. Nevertheless, the fact that even States that claim to have abolished military criminal justice systems still use military personnel for parts of investigation stages demonstrates that they are unlikely to be phased out altogether any time soon. Military justice systems should not be replaced if there is no effective alternative, and this is a further reason for existing systems to seek to be proper systems of justice. Furthermore, as has been remarked throughout the book, removing the military label of a proceeding would not suffice to warrant its legitimacy and effectiveness. Whatever the nature of an investigation, it would still be necessary to check whether it is overall sufficiently independent and impartial to be effective, whether it is subject to the rule of law and effectively able to combat impunity.

What has been argued across the book is that military institutional affiliation is not sufficient on its own to undermine the effectiveness of investigations, but that it is one factor which needs to be taken into account in assessing how overall independence and impartiality may be achieved when investigating possible violations of IHL. Properly structured military justice systems can, in many contexts, contribute to the proper administration of justice in armed conflict. Holding military institutions to account for violations of IHL may best be done not only by establishing what they cannot do, but by also laying out a clear framework of obligations of what they can and must do under international law.

Crimes Committed by Armed Forces Personnel to Have Say in Justice," Crow Prosecution Service (23 February 2023), available at: www.cps.gov.uk/cps/news/victims-crimes-committed-armed-forces-personnel-have-say-justice; South Korea: "Military Sexual Offenses to Be Tried in Civilian Courts under New Law" (24 August 2021), available at: https://en.yna.co.kr/view/AEN20210824009300315.

Index